YANGTZE SHOWDOWN

YANGTZE SHOWDOWN

CHINA AND THE ORDEAL OF HMS AMETHYST

BRIAN IZZARD

Seaforth
PUBLISHING

Copyright © Brian Izzard 2015

First published in Great Britain in 2015 by
Seaforth Publishing,
Pen & Sword Books Ltd,
47 Church Street,
Barnsley S70 2AS

www.seaforthpublishing.com

British Library Cataloguing in Publication Data
A catalogue record for this book is available from the British Library

ISBN 978 1 84832 224 0

Typeset and designed by M.A.T.S. Leigh-on-Sea, Essex
Printed and bound in Great Britain by CPI Group (UK) Ltd, Croydon, CR0 4YY

Contents

For Helen

Author's Note

For style and consistency the following names and spellings have been used: Chingkiang, Chu Teh (general), Formosa, Hankow, Hong Kong, Kwei Yung-ching (admiral), Mao Tse-tung, Nanking, Peking, Yangtze.

Some place names in Admiralty and Foreign Office reports and messages may not correspond to those in current use.

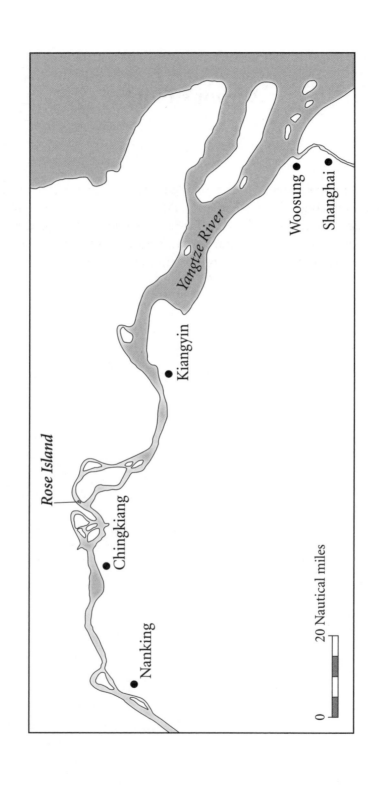

1

Under Fire

A COUPLE OF SHELLS WHISTLED overhead and a group of sailors on board the frigate HMS *Amethyst* came to the same conclusion: 'They couldn't hit a barn door.' *Amethyst* was heading up the mighty Yangtze River from Shanghai to the Nationalist capital of Nanking, where she was due to spend around a month as the guardship for the British embassy. The firing, medium artillery and small arms, was coming from a Communist battery on the north bank, the ship's starboard side. Large canvas Union Jacks were unfurled on both sides of *Amethyst*'s hull and the firing stopped after about 15 minutes. There were no hits. The ship was at action stations but did not return fire. The main topic of conversation resumed, the run ashore in Shanghai two days previously. Thomas Townsend, a 19-year-old able seaman from a village near Swansea, who was manning an Oerlikon anti-aircraft gun on the port side, said: 'We'd lowered the Union Jacks, they'd seen it, they knew who we were, they'll be no bother. Later on we discovered they could hit a barn door.'[1] The Union Jacks remained over the sides but it was no guarantee that Chinese soldiers who had spent their time fighting on land would recognise them as British, let alone a ship of the Royal Navy on a peaceful mission.

It was the morning of 20 April 1949 and a critical time during the civil war in China. Mao Tse-tung's Communist troops had swept south to strategic areas on the northern banks of the Yangtze and were set to cross the river, aiming to finally crush the forces of the ruling Nationalists. *Amethyst* was sailing between the two opposing armies. But it was a voyage she should not have taken. At the last moment she replaced an Australian frigate, HMAS *Shoalhaven*. The Australian government had decided the mission was too dangerous and refused to allow *Shoalhaven* to sail. The Australians were not the only ones with fears. The US Navy also refused a request from the American ambassador in Nanking to send a warship.

Forty minutes after the first attack there was a huge splash of water forward of *Amethyst*'s bow. Communist batteries near Rose Island, about 60 miles from Nanking, had opened up, this time with heavy artillery as well as machine guns. Full speed ahead was rung and the ship moved closer to the southern side of the river to increase the range. On the open bridge the captain, Lieutenant Commander Bernard Skinner, soon realised he was facing a much more serious attack. He shouted, 'Hoist battle ensigns', and gave the order to return fire.

Amethyst's main armament was six 4in guns in three twin turrets, two of them forward and one aft. Stewart Hett, a sub-lieutenant serving in his first ship after training, was at action stations to direct the fire of the main guns. 'The first few shots didn't hit the ship,' said Hett. 'Up in the director I was told to get on the target. In the director you have two people, one's the gunlayer and one's the trainer who both have binoculars looking at the shore. I'm sitting behind them and above them with a pair of binoculars which points in the same direction of the guns so I can see what they're looking at. We couldn't see where the fire was coming from. It had been foggy and it was still a bit hazy on shore. Eventually we got pointing in the right direction and it was at this stage that we got hit. Three shots hit us almost simultaneously.'[2]

The first hit, probably an armour-piercing shell, tore into the wheelhouse, fatally wounding a rating and badly injuring the coxswain, Chief Petty Officer Rosslyn Nicholls, who was steering the ship. Nicholls collapsed on the wheel and *Amethyst* veered to port. The bridge ordered 'hard a starboard'. Leading Seaman Leslie Frank, the only other crewman in the wheelhouse, who was dazed but unhurt, took over.

A shell hit the bridge, killing a sailor and wounding everyone else, Skinner mortally. Donald Redman, a 20-year-old navigator's yeoman from Bridgwater, Somerset, who had been standing next to the captain, said:

> The shell landed right in the centre. Lieutenant Berger [Peter Berger, the navigating officer] was also caught in the blast and he had most of his clothes blown from him and his underpants were in shreds. The Chinese pilot who was two feet behind me had the back of his head blown off. We were all spattered on the deck.
>
> Years later at a reunion in London Jimmy the One [Geoffrey Weston, the first lieutenant] came up to me and said, 'Hell, Redman,

I thought you were dead. I remember on that day coming up to the bridge, picking you off the skipper, looking at you and saying he's a goner and throwing you on the deck'. I said, 'Thank you very much, sir'. He promptly said, 'No problem', and trotted off to the bar for another brandy.

I was helped from the bridge by someone and taken below. I had large lumps of shrapnel sticking out of me and I was patched up by a shipmate because the sick berth attendant had just been killed. I was able to stand up but I was bleeding rather badly. I thought that if I don't get this stopped I'm going to bleed to death. There were lots of wounded. Someone said, 'What we need is a doctor down here'. It was one of the lower mess decks. I said, 'I'll go and find him'. I got on deck and the firing was still going on, ping pong, and the shrapnel was going around. I thought this is a silly thing to have volunteered for. I ran along the deck and found the doctor, who was obviously dead. So I automatically turned around to go where I'd come from and as I was passing the galley I was shot in the elbow. I went a little bit further and I was hit by another bit of shrapnel. The first thing I said when I got back to the mess deck was, 'The doctor's dead and if you don't mind I won't go out there again'. It drew a little smile from a couple of my mates.

I was then helped down on deck leaning against a bulkhead and they brought a shipmate towards me. He was in a poor state, his tummy had been ripped open. They propped him against me. Someone pulled his stomach together and with my good hand I held it. After about half an hour he died and they pulled him away from me.[3]

Another sailor desperate to find the doctor, Surgeon Lieutenant John Alderton, was Townsend, the Oerlikon gunner on the port side. 'From my position I never fired a shot,' he said.

I had nothing to shoot at. The only bank I could see was the Nationalist bank, and nobody was shooting at me from there. All the firing was coming from the starboard side. Before I knew it, I couldn't believe the carnage. I left my action station – there was nothing I could do, so I went to see if I could help anybody. I went round to the starboard side. The Oerlikon there was damaged from a shell burst. The fellow who was on the gun, his throat had been cut from one side to the other. I went down to the boat deck, there were people lying wounded and we tried to ease them as best we could.

One chap had a huge hole in his chest and I said I would find the doc. I went running down the boat deck, hit the ladder to drop down to the quarterdeck, landed in a crouch and as I did that a shell came in. The doc was on my right and he had a needle to give someone a dose of morphine. The sick bay attendant was at his side. On my left there was a fellow with acid burns on his face. A shell had come in, burst a battery and he had got splattered with it. As I say, as I hit the deck this shell came in – the doc was killed instantly, the sick bay attendant was killed instantly, the fellow who had the burns was killed, the ladder behind me went. Nothing touched me.

Amethyst could not train her two forward main turrets ('A' and 'B') on the Communist batteries because of the angle of the ship, and the aft 4in guns ('X' turret) were the only ones that could be used. But a shell had exploded in the low power room, making it impossible for Hett to direct the fire. 'The low power room provides all the electricity for the gunnery control circuits,' Hett explained. 'My attempts to get the guns to open fire failed because there was no electrical link between the director and the guns. When we pulled the trigger in the director nothing fired.' Hett ordered the guns to fire independently. 'As soon as I realised we couldn't do anything in the director I clambered out and got down to the bridge and could see it was a complete shambles. I decided the best thing I could do was go to the after gun and take charge and engage the enemy. I discovered that the after gun, which was the only one that could bear on the enemy, had been hit. The training rack had jammed so there was no means of moving the gun. We were in the position of not being able to fire any guns at anything.'

'X' turret had fired about thirty rounds before taking a direct hit, which killed one seaman and wounded three others. *Amethyst* was William Smith's first ship since joining the navy in 1947, and four days earlier he had celebrated his twenty-first birthday. The Scot made the surprising disclosure that 'X' turret had not been firing live ammunition. 'When *Amethyst* fired she used practice shells,' said Smith. 'Live ammunition had not been brought up from the magazines. The ready-use lockers were still filled with practice shells. So the first few shells that were fired off were practice and did no damage at all. By the time they got the real ammunition up the guns had been hit.'[4]

As a teenager Ronald Richards had survived the wartime bombing raids on Birmingham. When the bridge was hit, the twenty-year-old able seaman was wounded in the back by shrapnel. Richards was sent below and went aft where a shell exploded, smashing him against a bulkhead and breaking a shoulder blade. 'So I thought, sod this for a game of soldiers, I'm off towards the centre of the ship. That was a stupid thing to do because that was where all the ammunition was. And then another shell came in and I was wounded in the legs.'[5]

Charles Hawkins, an 18-year-old stoker, was off duty and having a shower when there was 'a thud on the side and I thought, what the hell?' Hawkins said: 'I ran out and saw everyone shouting and hollering. I didn't have any clothes on, so I grabbed a towel. The first thing I saw was two or three bodies lying around. Everybody was diving for cover. I remember a friend of mine, Harry Morgan, got hit. I pulled him off the deck. He wasn't dead at the time. I got him under shelter. Somebody else was screaming and crying, and I went to see if I could help. Of course, when I came back Harry was dead. There were bodies and blood everywhere.'[6]

In the wheelhouse Leading Seaman Frank was desperately trying to get orders from the bridge, unaware of the casualties and destruction. The wheelhouse explosion jammed the starboard telegraph and the starboard engine remained full ahead, with the port engine stopped. In the engine room Leonard Williams, who had survived the sinking of two ships during the Second World War and three and a half years as a Japanese prisoner of war, quickly realised there was a major problem with the starboard telegraph. The engine room artificer stopped that engine. But *Amethyst* was out of control and slowly ran aground on a mudbank near Rose Island in the middle of the river. The stern was almost facing the north bank. Only five minutes had passed between the time the Communists opened fire at 0930 and the ship's grounding.

After Lieutenant Commander Skinner's mortal wounding the executive officer, Lieutenant Weston, assumed command, but he had suffered a chest wound, a piece of shrapnel passing through a lung. He did, however, manage to go to the wireless office and arrange to send a 'flash' signal that *Amethyst* was under attack. The signal was not sent because of transmitter problems. Weston thought of taking the ship's motorboat, flying a white flag, to the north bank to 'parley with the Communists', only to find that the boat had been smashed.[7] It was feared that the Communists might try to board the ship. Bren guns and rifles were brought from below and armed sailors took up positions at key points on the boat deck.

Lieutenant Berger, the navigating officer, who was caught in the bridge explosion, regained consciousness. He, too, had a chest wound. At about 1015 he gave orders for the secret radar sets and Typex cipher machine to be broken up and the pieces to be thrown overboard.[8] This was no easy task, as Telegraphist Jack French discovered. He spent about half an hour trying to destroy the Typex machine with 'a massive spanner, the kind used for undoing bolts on cranes, and a hammer. Believe you me, trying to break steel is a lost cause, it just bounces back at you. You're liable to do more damage to your body than the equipment.'[9] Confidential books were also collected for burning. The boiler room was shut down to avoid the risk of fire.

At 1030 Weston told Berger to evacuate men, giving priority to the wounded, to the south side of Rose Island, with the aim of returning to the ship at nightfall and trying to refloat her. The first lieutenant would note later: 'It was an unpleasant decision to have to make, even partly to abandon one of HM ships which was not sinking but the situation was unusual. We were unable to inflict further damage upon the "enemy" even if there had been an orthodox enemy to engage.' The Communists were continuing to fire at the ship and the casualties were mounting. Some of the wounded had been taken to the quarterdeck, only to be hit again.

Amethyst was an easy target in the confines of the river for battle-hardened gunners on land. One of Mao's leading generals, Chu Teh [Zhu De], had long before set up a school of artillery in Yan'an to improve skills after failings against Nationalist positions. US ambassador John Stuart – thankful that his navy had refused to send an American warship – observed: 'Their marksmanship was excellent.'[10]

Part of a report that the Admiralty originally wanted to keep secret until the year 2025 – a staggering seventy-six years after the attack – revealed that *Amethyst* had tried to sail past an area on the north bank identified as San Chiang Ying, 'an assemblage point of craft for a main crossing of the Yangtze River. The batteries would, therefore, be very

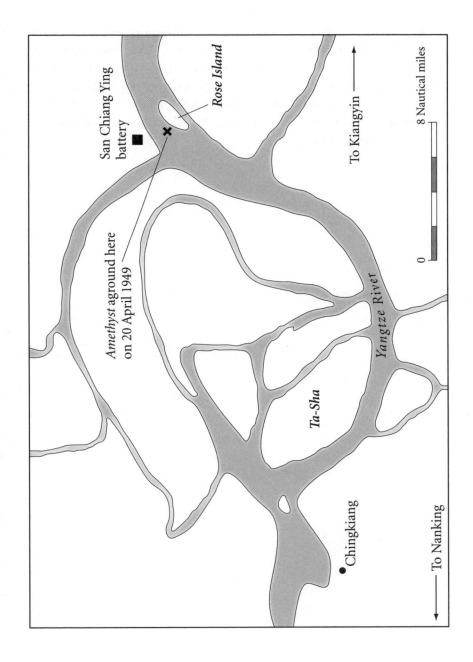

San Chiang Ying battery

Rose Island

Amethyst aground here on 20 April 1949

To Kiangyin

0   8 Nautical miles

Yangtze River

Ta-Sha

Chingkiang

To Nanking

7

much on the alert and extremely trigger happy.' The Communists were in no mood to show caution. Warships of the Nationalist navy had been 'extremely active' in bombarding Communist positions in the weeks leading up to *Amethyst*'s voyage.[11] That morning four Nationalist destroyers were reported in the area.[12] There were about forty junks, each capable of carrying between 500 and 1,000 soldiers, in a creek on the north bank opposite Rose Island. The attack on *Amethyst* cost twenty-three lives. But British sailors would soon be paying a higher price in blood.

2

The Fatal Decision

BY APRIL 1949 CHINA WAS a war-weary country. Civil war had broken out in 1927, going on to produce numerous complexities, military and political, and the loss of more than three million lives. The Communists grew from an insignificant guerrilla movement into a major army. Fortunes seesawed during the 1930s. The Nationalists, led by Chiang Kai-shek, had several chances to beat their enemy, but they were never able to land the fatal blow, largely because of poor strategy and the incompetence of some of their generals. In 1937 the Nationalists and the Communists found themselves facing a common enemy – invading Japanese soldiers who soon captured Shanghai and Nanking. The fight against Japan carried on during the Second World War, although the Nationalists and the Communists still were not averse to battling each other. In 1945, with the defeat of the Japanese, Chiang and Mao were involved in peace negotiations with the aim of rebuilding their country. But the truce collapsed in June 1946 and the civil war resumed with a vengeance. Mao's army had grown significantly, regulars and militias. His decision to use guerrilla tactics against the Japanese proved less costly in men and materials than Chiang's more orthodox campaign.

In December 1948 the British ambassador in Nanking, Sir Ralph Stevenson, knew that Chiang's government was on borrowed time. In a telegram to the Foreign Office in London, he warned: 'I do not believe situation of central government can be saved.' He had called on the Nationalist foreign minister, who put on a brave face, stressing that the whole government was determined to continue the struggle against the Communists. Stevenson added: 'Minister for foreign affairs was sure that His Majesty's government would agree that if Communists triumph in China it would be a disaster for cause of democracy throughout the world.' The minister wanted Britain and the United States to provide massive military aid.[1]

Two weeks later the ambassador noted: 'General atmosphere remains one of eternal doom but nobody any longer ventures to predict

9

date of final defeat and disappearance of existing discredited regime.'
Reporting on the latest developments, Stevenson said: 'There is little
change in Hsuchow area but eventual defeat of Chinese government
forces is now generally regarded as a foregone conclusion. Public
confidence has suffered further shock by the rapid withdrawal of
General Fu Tso-yi's forces from Kaimakam mining area followed by
Communist advance towards Tientsin and the virtual encirclement of
Peking. Fall of these two cities is regarded as imminent . . .' The
ambassador said Chiang was under considerable pressure from key
figures in his government to delegate his powers and step down.[2] The
Nationalist cause had been undermined by widespread corruption and
economic chaos, which resulted in high inflation. In contrast, Mao's
popular support was growing, particularly in the countryside, where
the poor were being promised a better life with land reforms.

But alarm bells had been ringing at the British embassy for some time.
The previous year, 1947, the ambassador had been given permission by
the Foreign Office to appeal directly to the Commander-in-Chief of the
Royal Navy's Far East Station for help in an emergency.[3] This represented a somersault by the Foreign Office, which had been keen to curb
the navy's influence in China, no doubt fearing it was an unhelpful
reminder of Britain's imperial past. Under the Treaty of Tientsin in 1858
British warships were given the right to patrol the Yangtze to protect
trade. It was the start of decades of so-called gunboat diplomacy in
which the United States also played a major part. The White Ensign,
however, ruled. The Second World War halted the gunboats but the
Royal Navy was keen to fly the flag again in 1945. In August of that
year the Admiralty had been alerted that the US western Pacific fleet
planned to send warships to the Yangtze, and by the following month
the Americans had 'a strong and well organised force' ready.[4]

The reluctance of the Foreign Office clearly irritated the Admiralty,
whose Director of Plans noted: 'The Foreign Office attitude, while it must
obviously be given due weight, does not appear to be realistic if at the
same time they are recommending the development of our commercial
interests in China.'[5] Indeed, British merchant ship owners wanted to
return to Chinese waters as soon as possible. As well as protecting trade,
gunboats had other advantages: they were the 'only reliable and effective
means of urgent and secret communications' between diplomats and the
outside world; they could be used to evacuate British subjects; they were

'a very considerable addition to our prestige' and a focal point of liaison between British interests and the Chinese authorities; and they could be used as an official means of transport.[6]

The Admiralty's Head of M Branch had suggested that the Chinese government could be given the responsibility of running gunboat patrols, which would deal with 'bandits and Communists', an interesting observation about the status of Mao's forces.[7] But the Director of Plans did not believe that Chinese gunboats would be suitable or competent. Five Royal Navy gunboats would be available in 1946, and in the meantime it was proposed to use sloops. The Foreign Office would be 'invited to obtain Chinese agreement to the re-establishment of Yangtze and West River patrols'. A formal request was necessary because under treaties signed in 1943 Britain and the US had relinquished rights to send their warships into Chinese waters.

When the Second World War ended the Royal Navy knew that it would have to cut its huge fleet. Britain was burdened with debt and years of austerity lay ahead. But the navy still believed that it had a world role to play. There was enormous prestige at stake, and it wanted to keep as many ships and bases as possible. A paper for naval chiefs stressed:

British interests are worldwide and the inherent mobility of the navy makes it still an effective and economical instrument for settling minor troubles or disputes. The mere existence of a strong navy is a considerable influence for peace and quiet, and the presence of HM ships at ports will often prevent unrest; the universal popularity of the bluejacket is also a national asset.

Trade follows the flag. This proved very true between 1919 and 1939 during which period it was found necessary, for economic reasons, to revive the South American squadron. If we wish to regain, let alone improve, our pre-war standard of living, our export trade will need re-establishing and greatly increasing. Without this we shall be unable to maintain armed forces commensurate with our territorial possessions and responsibilities. 'Showing the flag' by HM ships is one of the best ways of fostering British trade, and at the same time guarding British lives and property.[8]

The appraisal may not have reflected Foreign Office thinking, but in 1948 Sir Ralph Stevenson was certainly happy to have the support of the navy. As Mao's forces pushed forward and Nanking sensed the inevitable, the ambassador took up the navy's offer to station a guardship at the capital. The Yangtze flows past the west side of the city. Stevenson's previous posting was as ambassador to Yugoslavia, and he would be seen as having 'one of the best minds' in the Foreign Office. He had military experience, having served in the Rifle Brigade during the First World War.[9]

In November of that year the first warship arrived . . . *Amethyst*. The frigate brought food and was ready to take part in any evacuation. The voyage from Shanghai to Nanking, a distance of 177 miles, passed without incident. In December the destroyer HMS *Constance* replaced *Amethyst*, which evacuated six women and five children. Over the ensuing months several warships took turns in acting as the guardship – the frigate HMS *Alacrity*, the destroyer HMS *Concord*, the frigate HMS *Black Swan* and the destroyer HMS *Consort*. The Far East Station was short of ships and the Australians and Canadians agreed to play their part. Vice Admiral Alexander Madden, Second-in-Command, Far East Station, thought the risk of the Communists provoking a military incident was 'small and should be accepted'. The ships provided 'succour' to Commonwealth embassies. As well as bringing stores to the British embassy, they helped out the Australian, Canadian and Swiss embassies, and *Constance* left Nanking with the fleeing Czech ambassador and his family.[10] In reality, the ships were 'flying the flag', a morale booster for the foreigners who remained in Nanking – many had already left. In reality, one of the Royal Air Force's Sunderland flying boats based in Hong Kong could have brought the supplies and taken part in an evacuation. In December 1948 Stevenson's embassy staff totalled fifty, including twenty-two women, and there were forty-three British civilians elsewhere in Nanking. The Canadians had only six people at their embassy and the Australians had reduced their embassy staff to seven.

Australia's ambassador, Keith Officer, who had a reputation for caution, seemed particularly anxious not to put the lives of Australians at risk. In the November all female staff at the embassy and wives were evacuated in an emergency airlift. In January 1949 the Australian destroyer HMAS *Warramunga* was sent to Nanking to act as the guardship, replacing *Black Swan*. But shortly after *Warramunga*'s arrival it was decided that the ship should not stay because of the possibility of 'anti-foreign feeling'. The 'appearance of Australian sailors in the capital might cause incidents'.[11] The decision was almost certainly taken on the advice of Officer, who was in close contact with his country's Department of External Affairs.

There had not been any reported problems with previous visits by *Amethyst*, *Constance*, *Alacrity* or *Concord*. It was not, however, a popular destination. As one sailor from *Concord* put it: 'Nanking was boring. You weren't allowed into the city. We could only use a little bar in an egg-packing station and a football field. You were there for a month and it seemed like forever.'

In February 1949 peace talks were held between the Nationalists and the Communists following Chiang Kai-shek's resignation as president, but Mao's temporary truce was largely seen as a ploy to gain time to build up his forces on the northern banks of the Yangtze. The Communists were virtually demanding the complete surrender of the Nationalists. Officer sent an accurate assessment of the likely course of events to his Minister of State for External Affairs, Herbert Evatt: 'It now appears that, should peace negotiations fail, the Nationalists may intend to try and hold the Yangtze line, as they have 19 armies stretched between Kiukiang and Shanghai. Although this sounds a considerable force, most of the troops are ill equipped, badly fed and clothed, and with practically no morale left at all. I therefore do not think the Communists will have much difficulty in crossing the river.'[12]

The destroyer *Consort* was sent to Nanking as the guardship in March, replacing the Canadian destroyer HMCS *Crescent*, and she was due to be relieved on 12 April. Despite the fiasco over *Warramunga*, the Far East Station decided to use another Australian warship, the frigate HMAS *Shoalhaven*. But on 7 April Officer had urgent talks with the British ambassador. He asked for *Shoalhaven*'s departure from Shanghai to be delayed. The Communist ultimatum to the Nationalists had been rejected, and Mao's forces were expected to launch attacks across the Yangtze at any time. *Shoalhaven* could be in danger. Stevenson passed on Officer's misgivings to the Far East Station. The Australian ambassador's caution must have stemmed in part from his experiences during the First World War. He had served as an army captain during the disastrous Gallipoli campaign, which cost the lives of so many men from Australia and New Zealand. Officer, who went on to win the Military Cross, witnessed the horrors. The architect of the Gallipoli campaign had been the then First Lord of the Admiralty, Winston Churchill.

Vice Admiral Madden waited a week but the response was the same. The Australians made it clear that their ships could be used for 'mercy purposes only'. Two days later Madden decided to send *Amethyst* instead. The frigate arrived at Shanghai from Hong Kong on 16 April.[13] John Smith, senior researcher of the Naval Historical Society of Australia, explained: 'The Australian government – Prime Minister Ben Chifley – ordered that in view of the rapidly deteriorating situation *Shoalhaven* was not to complete the mission.'[14] Chifley was well aware that the approaching 25 April marked Anzac Day, when Australia and New Zealand honour their war dead, and he would not have wanted the possibility of his sailors becoming casualties at such a sensitive time. More than 27,000 Australians were killed in action during the Second World War, and there were painful memories of the First World War, especially Gallipoli. Chifley was also aware that his Labor Party would be facing a difficult election later in the year. *Shoalhaven*'s captain, Lieutenant Commander William Tapp, confirmed that 'government policy had effected *Shoalhaven*'s movements'. He noted: 'The morale of the ship's company was high during the period in Shanghai although the ship's role of waiting for events was rather trying.'[15]

The US Navy, of course, also refused to send a warship. American ambassador John Stuart had arranged with the commander of his country's western Pacific fleet, Vice Admiral Oscar Badger, for a vessel to be sent in an emergency. 'He assured me that whenever I asked for one it would be there in three days,' Stuart noted. 'I had accordingly sent a request ten days or more earlier [around 10 April] but there were delays and, fortunately for us, Admiral Badger finally stopped the sailing unless I overruled him.' Badger was not a timid commander. He had a distinguished career, winning the Medal of Honor. Stuart, a former missionary who was fiercely opposed to Communism, would later reflect: 'From the broader standpoint it was lucky after all that it was the British rather than American navy in view of the way we had been singled out for Communist vituperation.'[16]

Amethyst was a 1,350-ton frigate of the modified *Black Swan* class. Built in Govan, she had been commissioned in November 1943, the seventh Royal Navy vessel to bear the name, with a history going back to 1793. The ship was originally classed as a sloop, pennant number U16, which was later changed to F116. Her top speed was just under 20 knots. After commissioning, the ship served the remaining months of the Second World War in the Mediterranean and in home waters, mainly on convoy duties. On 20 February 1945 *Amethyst* destroyed *U 1276* with depth charges off the south coast of Ireland shortly after the German submarine sank the corvette HMS *Vervain*. Fifty-nine members of *Vervain*'s crew were killed and all forty-nine on board *U 1276* perished. After a refit at her home port of Devonport in May of that year *Amethyst* went to the Far East, where she remained, based in Hong Kong. From 1947 until the early part of 1949 she carried out patrols off Malaya, some of them as part of that country's Communist emergency.

Before sailing for Nanking on the morning of 19 April, 1949, *Amethyst* rendezvoused with *Shoalhaven* at Shanghai. The Australian frigate transferred the stores and oil she had been planning to take to Nanking. There was even time for the crews to play a football match. But some of *Amethyst*'s crew were puzzled that they were going instead of the Australians. Navigator's yeoman Donald Redman recalled: 'None of us was made aware of what we could expect. The only thing that we thought was funny – there was an Australian frigate that was due to do the run we were suddenly allotted to do. We were told that the Australian government thought it was inappropriate that a frigate should go up the Yangtze at this time. But we were told you're going up.'[17] *Amethyst* sailed after getting clearance from the Nationalist authorities, expecting to reach Nanking the following day, 20 April. The Communist truce was due to end that night. *Consort* would sail on the same day on her return trip. Vice Admiral Madden hoped that *Amethyst* and *Consort* would be safe at their respective destinations before the Communists launched their river crossings.

The main reason Madden gave for sending *Amethyst* at such a critical time during the civil war was a fear that *Consort* might not have enough fuel to return to Shanghai if she remained too long at Nanking. The Far East Station had a policy that a ship's stock of fuel should not be allowed to drop below 35 per cent. On 20 April *Consort* had an estimated 53 per cent remaining, which would have dropped to 43 per cent on arrival at Shanghai. It was also estimated that the last day the destroyer could have remained at the capital was 26 April. Her stock of dry provisions would have started to run out by 1 May.[18] But

Madden neglected to reveal that a large quantity of fuel was being stored at Nanking for emergencies – something that *Amethyst* would find extremely useful.

Madden was also contradicted on two important points by *Consort*'s captain, Commander Ian Robertson. On the question of being relieved on 20 April, Robertson reported: 'We could, in fact, have stayed some weeks more by eke-ing out our fuel.' Madden told the Admiralty that *Consort*'s time of departure from Nanking was not delayed but advanced on 20 April, from 0400 to 0330. In fact, Commander Robertson had not been told there was any urgency and planned to sail at 1200. He actually sailed at 1150 after learning that *Amethyst* was under attack, first dashing to a meeting at the British embassy to discuss the crisis with ambassador Stevenson and the naval attaché, Captain Vernon Donaldson. Earlier that morning Robertson had been out hunting snipe.

No attempt had been made to warn Communist forces of *Amethyst*'s sailing. Stevenson and the Governor of Hong Kong, Sir Alexander Grantham, had already made it clear that it would be 'inappropriate' to have diplomatic contacts with them. However, in January 1949 Captain Donaldson informed Vice Admiral Madden that he was 'endeavouring, by oblique methods which did not raise questions of diplomatic recognition, to inform the Communists that one of HM ships was being maintained at Nanking for humanitarian purposes only'. Madden reported: 'I therefore told assistant naval attaché Shanghai and senior British naval officer (afloat) Nanking to do likewise, using similar methods.'[19]

Could *Amethyst* have been recalled once she set sail? The First Lord of the Admiralty, Lord Hall, told Prime Minister Clement Attlee that an intelligence report revealing the Communists were likely to cross the Yangtze early on 21 April had been issued 'probably on the 19th'. He added: 'It has not been possible to establish at what precise time this report was received by all concerned but *Amethyst* was already well up the river and fairly close to her destination before effective action could have been taken to cancel her passage.'[20]

Attlee was not being told the truth. Donaldson, the naval attaché in Nanking, had sent the warning to Vice Admiral Madden in plenty of time to recall *Amethyst*. Two likely crossing points along the frigate's route were named, Kuaanl and Deer Island. The warning was referred to in a telegram from the Foreign Office to Stevenson on 20 April. The message was unsigned but may well have been sent by Foreign Secretary Ernest Bevin. It said: 'I am not clear why *Amethyst* had to pass through danger zone so close to the possible zero hour and shall be grateful for immediate information as to the precise circumstances in which *Amethyst* was proceeding to Nanking at this juncture.' The message was headed: 'This telegram is of particular secrecy and should be retained by the authorised recipient and not passed on.'[21] Stevenson replied that, like the admiral, he thought *Amethyst* could gamble on beating the deadline.[22]

The frigate's voyage could have been postponed before she sailed from Shanghai on 19 April, and there was a 24-hour window, from 0800 on 19 April to around 0800 on 20 April, when she could easily have been contacted and recalled. Donaldson's telegram, addressed to the Second-in-Command, Far East Station, was sent at 0655 on 19 April. There had been problems with communications from Nanking but the message would have been given priority. In a secret report dated 7 July 1949, Madden said he received the warning 'in the evening of 19 April', a bafflingly long delay. Even at that time, *Amethyst* was safely anchored at Kiangyin, well away from Communist forces, and in a position to return to Shanghai.[23] Lord Hall completely misled the prime minister when he said the frigate was 'fairly close to her destination' and it was too late to stop her.

The first part of *Amethyst*'s voyage proved uneventful. The frigate, with a crew of 171 plus a number of Chinese who worked as cooks, stewards or laundrymen, left Holt's Wharf, Shanghai, at the scheduled time, 0800, and headed 12 miles down the Whangpoo [Huangpu] River to Woosung, where the Whangpoo joins the Yangtze. An English pilot was disembarked off the Woosung forts. Then the frigate headed up the Yangtze with two Chinese pilots, anchoring at Kiangyin, 92 miles from Shanghai, in the late afternoon after getting permission from the Nationalist navy, which months earlier had warned that it could not guarantee the safety of Royal Navy ships using the Yangtze. At 0510 on 20 April, *Amethyst* continued her journey but stopped less than 90 minutes later because of fog. The voyage resumed at 0734. During the next hour it was decided to test the firing circuits of the main guns – perhaps not the wisest move – and this noise may have alerted Communist troops. The first attack came soon afterwards.

3

Machine-gunned in the Water

WHEN THE WOUNDED LIEUTENANT WESTON gave the order to evacuate *Amethyst* at about 1030 on 20 April, the Communists were still firing at the ship. In the confusion some men did not know the order had been given – those in the engine room, for instance – and there were ratings who 'were prepared to stay at all costs'. Weston had not intended to completely abandon the frigate. He was expecting some of the men who had not been wounded to find safety on the south bank of Rose Island and then return at nightfall so that attempts could be made to refloat the ship – and perhaps escape. The evacuation faced immediate problems. The ship's motorboat and one of the two whalers could not be used because they were too badly damaged. Oddly, it was the whaler on the starboard side, facing the Communist batteries, that had survived and not the port whaler. The starboard whaler was lowered and, along with Carley floats, towed round to the port side of the quarterdeck to take off some of the wounded. The wounded Lieutenant Berger was supervising the evacuation and Commissioned Gunner Eric Monaghan, who had survived the sinking of the battlecruiser HMS *Repulse* and the aircraft carrier HMS *Hermes* during the Second World War, took charge of the whaler, which was loaded with medical supplies and a small quantity of food. The whaler headed for the southern shore but came under heavy fire. One of the wounded, Ordinary Seaman Patrick Sinnott, was hit again and died.

When the whaler reached the shore, Berger gave an order that 'all able-bodied men who were able to' should swim to the bank, which was 50 yards away. Around sixty-five sailors jumped over the side, some with lifebelts. The Communists immediately targeted them with artillery and machine gun fire. Several men died, including Chief Petty Officer Stoker Mechanic Owen Aubrey, who may have drowned after being shot.[1]

Able Seaman Gordon Wright recalled:

When they said abandon ship I thought I might as well go as a lot of them had gone. A couple of the boats were all messed up because of the shrapnel. I put my head through a porthole and one of the stokers was going past the ship in the six-knot current. He was struggling and then I heard a machine gun. He put his hands up in the air and went under. So I thought this is the worst of two evils. I might just as well stay on board. They need able-bodied people so I'll stay. They were firing so much. One man in the boat was brought back dead [Sinnott] and we got him on board. But they all started to smell a lot. We had to cover them up. I was wearing a handkerchief round my face.[2]

About sixty men reached the south bank but by this time Berger had decided that the risks in carrying on with the evacuation were too great and he stopped it. He ordered a white flag – a sheet – to be hoisted but the firing continued and it was hauled down. It soon occurred to him that the sheet might be taken as a sign of surrender and a signal that the Communists could board the ship.

With machine guns raking the upper deck Weston crawled to the shelter of the radar office. Later he was helped to the wireless office 'where we set up our headquarters'. Soon after 1100 the artillery ceased firing. About half an hour later the whaler returned with Monaghan and three sailors who had volunteered to man it, including Jack French, who was told to get back on board the ship – he was now *Amethyst*'s sole telegraphist and he would play a key role in keeping communications open with the Far East Station.[3]

At this point *Amethyst* had a crew of around seventy men in reasonable shape, with seventeen dead and twenty-five wounded. The dead lay where they had been killed. Most of the wounded were moved to the after mess deck where they received limited first aid. The sick bay had taken a direct hit, which killed a boy sailor who was ill in bed. Helping the wounded was the manager of the NAAFI, John MacNamara, a civilian who had a first-aid action station. Later he filled a bucket with sweets and cigarettes and passed it round, without bothering to seek payment. The gesture was appreciated. But those lying wounded on the quarterdeck, where they had been waiting for evacuation, could not be moved without provoking small-arms fire and they were left there.

When the first sailors reached the south bank of Rose Island, which was controlled by the Nationalists, they faced another hazard – minefields. Fortunately, they were spotted by friendly soldiers and guided through the danger. But a friendly face had not greeted Donald Redman, the navigator's yeoman who had been wounded three times, the first time on the bridge. He was among a group of fifteen sailors who were confronted by a young Nationalist officer accompanied by eight soldiers with fixed bayonets. 'The officer probably thought we were mercenaries because he thrust this revolver in my face, which was painfully swollen, shouting and screaming,' said Redman. 'He beckoned towards a hut that was nearby. He pushed me inside and produced a pen.' Redman drew the outline of the ship with a Union Jack. 'With the wet brush I went plop, plop, plop to imitate the shell bursts and suddenly he said, "Ahh", and realised we were British. He produced a plate of rice biscuits. But what we needed was a doctor. I drew a cross like a red cross and he got the gist of it, that we needed a doctor and he started giving a few orders.' The group had to walk about a mile – Redman with only one shoe – to a spot where they received first aid.[4]

Other groups were also taken inland because they were attracting fire on Nationalist positions. Most of the sailors ended up at a village seven miles from the ship. But eight ratings, the last to get ashore, remained hidden in long grass on the south bank because Communist snipers had them pinned down. These men did not know about the minefields and several of them actually sat on mines, making the discovery when two soldiers appeared on the scene to lay more of them. Luckily, none of the mines worked. The two soldiers approached the ship and shouted to the remaining Chinese pilot. The pilot asked to go ashore to speak to the soldiers and he was given permission in the hope that he could arrange for a doctor to come aboard.

The whaler was manned, with Monaghan again in charge, and it left under the cover of the port side. The pilot was told he must return to the ship. Also in the whaler was the ship's Chinese tailor. Then it was noticed, as the whaler pulled away, that the pilot had taken his bag, and shouts to Monaghan made it clear he had to ensure the man's return. After landing, Monaghan and the two Chinese headed for the Nationalist headquarters, guided by the two soldiers. Then the pilot disappeared, never to be seen again. It was perhaps not surprising that he had no wish to return to the ship. Before dying, the other Chinese pilot, who had the back of his head blown away, tried to commit suicide by pushing his tongue down his throat and choking himself because he was in such pain. Monaghan arranged for an army doctor to come to the ship, and he also made telephone contact with a petty officer who had taken charge of the sailors at the village seven miles from the ship. Weston reported later: 'I had not intended them to go so far but had given them no specific orders.'

The colonel in command of the soldiers said the sailors could not be guided back through the minefields in darkness. Weston, hoping that *Amethyst* could be refloated that night, decided that the men should make their way to the mainland and then try to get to Shanghai by train. This message was conveyed through Monaghan, who returned to the ship with the eight ratings left stranded on the south bank, along with another disoriented sailor.[5]

That evening Hett asked for volunteers to collect the bodies, and MacNamara, the NAAFI manager, was one of the men who stepped forward. Because of the danger of snipers they could not use lights. MacNamara stumbled across a body in the darkness and one of his hands slid into a gaping wound. Shaken, he told Hett that 'we would do more harm than good', and the task was postponed until the morning.

During the night Able Seaman Thomas Townsend had the fright of his life. He was going to the upper deck to act as a lookout in case the Communists tried to board the ship. As he walked down a passageway to the quarterdeck the door at the other end opened and 'in stepped a fellow we had put out with the bodies'. Townsend said: 'He had a very bad head wound and we all thought he was dead. But he walked in and I remember looking at him and thinking I was seeing a ghost. We ran down to him and helped him to the mess deck, and made him as comfortable as we could. The memory of seeing him has stayed with me. I don't think you ever get over things like that.'[6]

Commander Richard Hare, an officer on the staff of the Commander-in-Chief, Far East Station, would soon find himself involved in an attempt to rescue *Amethyst* as one of the men on board the cruiser HMS *London*. Later he raised an awkward question: were some of the men on Rose Island deserters? Hare explained: 'I had the job of writing a report on the whole *Amethyst* affair. One aspect made this difficult because roughly half of *Amethyst*'s ship's company had left the ship and, goodness knows how, made their way overland to Shanghai. The question was, had they been told to, or had they deserted? It was no joke interviewing all these characters without the available evidence of those who remained on board. I concluded that some had permission and others had not, but drawing the line was impossible.'[7] Weston had expected the fit men to return to the ship. He hoped he still had enough crew to get out of danger and escape.

4

Consort's Dash

FOR COMMANDER IAN ROBERTSON IT had been a good start to the day. He returned to *Consort* in time for Colours at 0800 on 20 April having bagged six snipe. China may have been facing a critical time in its civil war, but it had been a busy month so far for the destroyer's captain dealing with the challenges of social engagements in Nanking. On 6 April US Army Day had been celebrated with a big party at the International Club. Three days later 100 guests were entertained at a cocktail party on board the ship, which was followed by a concert. On 11 April Robertson dined with the Egyptian ambassador and on 14 April there was lunch with a Burmese minister. On 16 April it was dinner with the French ambassador.[1]

At 0950 on 20 April, Robertson realised he would be facing a completely different kind of engagement. He learned of the attack on *Amethyst*, and before the day was out ten of his crew would be dead or fatally wounded, with many more casualties. The contrast could not have been greater. The naval attaché, Captain Donaldson, came on board at 1030, and the two officers then went to the British embassy to see the ambassador. There was some delay in getting there because of market-day crowds. Robertson was told that Vice Admiral Madden had decided *Consort*, the nearest ship, should go to *Amethyst*'s aid, though it was not clear where exactly the frigate had run aground. The last reported position, given in the confusion of shelling, put *Amethyst* on land, away from the Yangtze. Madden was aware that *Consort* would have to go through 'a reputed danger area' near Chingkiang but the 'risks must be accepted'.[2]

Robertson, awarded the Distinguished Service Cross and Bar during the Second World War, was back on board by 1125 and 25 minutes later *Consort* was heading down river. Seven hundred cases of empty beer bottles, which had been carefully lashed on deck, were thrown overboard, presumably to avoid the risk of flying glass in the event of attack and to help with speed. The empties, worth £160, a not

23

inconsiderable sum and the reserves of the canteen fund, were quickly fished out of the water by a 'swarm' of sampans astern of the destroyer. The 1,885-ton ship was soon making 20 knots, which would increase to a bow-waving 27 knots. *Concord* was racing towards *Amethyst*. When the destroyer left Nanking she was cleared for action. Her main armament – four 4.5in guns, 'A', 'B', 'X' and 'Y' – was lined up and checked, and shells placed in loading trays. There were also four 40mm Bofors and smaller-calibre anti-aircraft guns. Surprisingly, there were not enough sailors to man 'Y' gun because the ship was not carrying a full complement, but it was ready for action in case a gun crew needed to switch. Chinese stewards, 'unofficial' Chinese and mess boys were given the task of helping to supply ammunition. *Consort* was displaying two large Union Jacks on the sides of her hull, as *Amethyst* had done, and flying seven White Ensigns. As one officer observed: 'There could be no doubt as to our identity although the latter may have seemed somewhat provocative to the Chinese.'

The ship was reduced to defence stations until 1300 when actions stations resumed. There had been time for lunch but as soon as that finished the wardroom was turned into a sick bay. The dinning table became an operating table. That afternoon the wardroom floor would be 'inches in blood'. The main guns were left fore and aft to show 'peaceful intent', but the director controlling them had been ordered to sweep the north bank continuously for enemy positions so that there would be a quick response if the ship came under attack. As *Consort* passed Bethune Point there was a lot of automatic small arms fire. After several hits Robertson ordered one salvo to be fired, and there was a direct hit on a post with two machine guns. Firing from the north bank ceased.[3] The ship's main guns returned to fore and aft positions.

Stoker Thomas Flanagan's recollection: 'We were powering down. Our bow waves were sweeping up on the banks of the Yangtze. As we rounded a bend in the river there was a building on the bank full of troops and they were out of windows shooting at us. And they were running down the beaches shooting at us. The skipper brought the guns round and as we went past the building – whoosh – it just collapsed. We were out of range in no time and it went quiet again.'[4]

At 1340 *Amethyst* was sighted and she appeared to be flying two white flags. Unknown to *Consort*, two rocket-firing Nationalist planes had attacked the Communist batteries opposite Rose Island about an hour earlier. *Amethyst* signalled, 'If you are fired on I advise you to turn back.' Commander Robertson reported:

> I replied, 'Where are the enemy guns?' and slowed down to 15 knots from 27 knots. At this moment at least one field gun opened fire on *Consort* from a range of 2,800 yards. After two salvoes had near-missed, I opened fire with air bursts and later, when emplacements could be distinguished, with high explosives. After about four salvoes one gun emplacement was seen to suffer a direct hit, and fire was shifted to the next – a battery of three guns, which were effectively silenced, and then a four-gun battery was engaged at 1,200 yards. No hits were obtained mainly due to the large line spread.

According to one officer, when Robertson gave the order to return fire he used the words 'with knobs on'. The key officers on board *Amethyst*, Weston and Berger, seemed to have lost track of time and gave differing accounts of *Consort*'s appearance, no doubt because of their injuries. According to Berger, 'the mast' of *Consort* was sighted at 1500, more than one hour and twenty minutes after Robertson reported seeing the frigate. Weston thought the chances of refloating *Amethyst* under the devastating fire that was expected were remote and would only result in serious damage to *Consort*. He therefore told her to continue down river. At this stage Weston was still in his headquarters, the wireless office, continuing to direct operations, though he remained in considerable pain, vomiting frequently. Berger's activities were confined to the bridge and the wireless office because he had great difficulty walking.

Most of *Amethyst*'s crew were kept below because the ship was attracting machine-gun fire, but those who saw *Consort* were overjoyed. James Johnston, a 21-year-old able seaman, said: 'HMS *Consort* came steaming down river, her battle ensigns flying, and she let go with everything she had, which made us feel so grateful that we stood up and cheered.' *Consort* passed the frigate and signalled, 'Prepare to tow aft'. Able Seaman Raymond Calcott said: 'It was a glorious sight and it cheered us up no end. We thought that she was going to tow us off, and I was one of the volunteers who went to the stern to try and rig for towing.' Led by Gunner Monaghan, several sailors crawled out onto *Amethyst*'s quarterdeck and managed to get out a tow wire but were forced to retreat to safety because of heavy sniping. *Consort* carried on for about two miles, turned round and slowly headed up river. There was little damage and there were no casualties. The batteries opposite Rose Island had stopped firing after being 'well shaken up', and Robertson thought there was still a good chance of reaching *Amethyst*, which signalled that medical supplies were needed urgently. As *Consort* neared 'hell fire corner' she came under attack again but picked off four more emplacements with her main guns. The Bofors also 'beat up enemy concentrations'. But when the destroyer was one and a half miles away from *Amethyst* concealed 37mm anti-tank guns, as well as 105mm artillery, opened up. This time *Consort* took major hits. The wheelhouse was wrecked, killing the coxswain, wounding the others there, and putting the forward steering out of action. 'A' gun was knocked out.[5]

The tiller flat, the emergency steering position at the stern, was manned by sailors who were normally stationed at the torpedo tubes, and a phone call from the bridge alerted them to the switch. The tiller flat housed a steering engine, a small steering wheel and a magnetic compass. Sub Lieutenant William Robson, who was at this action station, recalled: 'We heard the battle going on above as we tried to silence the shore batteries. Presently came the order, "Switch to emergency steering". This meant disconnecting the steering engine from all its leads to the wheelhouse and working it by the small steering wheel in the tiller flat in accordance with orders received over the telephone. This was very soon done and seemed to be working smoothly.' Robson then decided to check on the bridge: 'I had heard stories of the war when the captain or his damage control officer had been killed or wounded and while everyone believed them to be in control they had been incapacitated and the necessary remedial measures had not been taken – with dire results.' He passed the wheelhouse, which was 'a shambles'. Reaching the bridge he found that the captain had been wounded in one leg by shrapnel but was sitting in his chair and 'obviously in complete control', though his uniform was in tatters.[6]

Robertson had sent the navigator, Lieutenant Jack Consadine, to check the wheelhouse and on his return the officer's tin hat went flying. When Consadine picked it up he found a bullet had gone straight through the front. At that moment the bridge was hit by two shells and a Chinese pilot was knocked out. A second pilot had to be dragged up from below and 'pinned in position by the navigator's dividers'. According to one sailor, the pilot was kept in place not by the navigator's dividers but by an officer pointing a revolver. 'B' and 'X' guns continued firing, knocking out three of the four guns of the battery being engaged. Then 'B' gun was hit and only 'X' gun was left. It silenced the fourth gun of the battery.

Consort stopped half a mile from *Amethyst*, turned and headed slowly down river again, firing all the time. 'We were still coming under accurate anti-tank fire from point-blank range,' Robertson reported. 'As my medical officer was overwhelmed with casualties I reluctantly decided to withdraw. At the rate we were being damaged the risk of being put completely out of action was considerable and it appeared wiser to go while we could and come back in force the next day. On reflection I consider that one of the reasons why enemy fire did not decrease was that a number of 37mm guns were rushed to the support of the original batteries and took up well-concealed positions.' *Consort* signalled to *Amethyst*, 'We'll be back in the morning'. The message was sent 'to cheer them up'. But there would be no return of *Consort*.

The survivors of 'A' and 'B' guns had gone to man 'Y' gun but 'X' gun had a stoppage and for 'a brief unhealthy few minutes' none of the main armament was in action. However, the Bofors kept firing and so did a Bren gun on the after bridge that was being aimed by an officer who had been stationed there in case either the captain or the navigator 'dropped'. When 'X' gun jammed, Petty Officer Henry Robinson got so excited in urging the party supplying ammunition to keep the Bofors in action that the top plate of his false teeth fell out. He promptly flung it at the supply party. Deciding that one half was no good, he flung the bottom set at those 'bloody Communists'.[7]

Stoker Thomas Flanagan found himself in a chain passing ammunition to the Bofors. It was dangerous work:

The Bofors were a quarter way along the ship from the boiler room hatches, and its open deck. The first bloke goes out carrying this box of ammunition and suddenly bullets were whistling all around him. So he had to speed up and throw the box of ammunition up on the gun deck and dive into a cubby hole. They knew he was there and they were machine-gunning and all sorts of calibre ammunition were popping around him. Then he had to leg it back. Next one goes and we got about four wounded. One of them fell on the deck and he had been hit in the middle. I went out and pulled him and he was coming apart in two pieces. I had to leave him and get someone to drag him in with me. That's hard to take. The forward part of the ship was taking a real thumping and several people were being wounded every minute. It was horrendous.

Flanagan went below to the forward gun hoist, which had been damaged.

A shell came in and landed between my feet, and blew my feet off. I was thrown ten feet backwards into the bulkhead. I was half sitting up. My right big toe was on my knee. I looked and my feet were shattered. A lad came over to me and said, how are you? I said okay. I said look at that – I had a new pair of socks on this morning. You're sick when you see these things and then he just vomited and went away. I was looking round and the place was on fire and there was a lad on the floor. He had been behind me and he was carrying a cordite charge. There was an explosion and the cordite exploded and set us both on fire. There was a fire extinguisher next to me and I got it and put out the fire out on his back. I thought I've got to get some help here and I was on my hands and knees and got to the bulkhead door, which was about eighteen inches off the floor. I couldn't get through it. I was shouting, we need some help in here, there's a fire, and this big petty officer came in and threw me over his shoulder.

Flanagan was taken to the wardroom – now the sick bay – but it was full and he was left on a landing. 'The petty officer said are you okay and I said yes, I wasn't in pain. I said straighten my foot out and he said you haven't got one. What was left of this left foot was folded underneath.' The petty officer was John Ackhurst, who became a fatal casualty shortly afterwards.

When Flanagan was taken into the wardroom Surgeon Lieutenant Mark Bentley told him he would have to remove what remained of his left foot.

I could feel him hacking away, cutting through the sinews. And then he threw my foot on the floor. He bandaged it up and then started cutting pieces off the other foot, and he did it with a straight razor. No morphine, all the morphine had gone. But I didn't feel anything. I can't say I was brave.

I was lying on the floor. I hadn't realised I was burned and my face was tightening up on me. There were blokes coming in all the time wounded. One of the lads, he had his hand off. He joined the navy with me and he was talking to me. He had been hit in the neck as well, and he was searching around for something to put his head on. He put this thing under him and said, 'That's bloody cold'. And it was my foot.

After a while they lifted me on to a bench. There were bloody shells hitting us all over the place and all I could think of was, if this goes down how am I going to swim. That was all that was on my mind. Time went on and slowly the firing stopped. I was drinking water and bringing it up again. Underneath me was a petty officer and he had been wounded. And I was drinking this water and bringing it up all over him, and I said to him, why don't you move. He said, I can't. And I said, I'm awfully sorry, but he said don't worry about it.[8]

Surgeon Lieutenant Bentley, whose most challenging task during the stay at Nanking had been organising the ship's concert, recalled: 'More and more casualties were brought in to me and I had to work for about twenty minutes with a torch before emergency lighting could be rigged. I concentrated principally on controlling bleeding at once in all casualties, removing surface shrapnel where possible, cleaning the wounds and applying field dressings. I also carried out amputations. At one stage the captain thought of attempting to land me on *Amethyst* but later changed his mind as we were unable to get close enough to her, and also our own rate of casualties was so high.'[9]

Ten minutes after breaking off the action *Consort*, hugging the south bank, came under fire from a battery of around eight 75mm guns. 'X' and 'Y' guns engaged the battery but the ship took more hits. The transmitting station and the wireless transmitting office were wrecked. It would prove to be the most devastating attack. Five men were killed and four mortally wounded. Fires broke out fore and aft but were quickly put out.

Bridge messenger Jess Greive had been sent to find the medical officer. 'As I made my way, I remember seeing the outer bulkhead repeatedly exploding inward with shell hits sending shrapnel flying through the air. As I went forward my legs turned to jelly and I honestly thought that every moment would be my last. I found myself in the port passage outside the transmitting station, which had taken a direct hit. It was a scene of twisted metal. I tried to pull out one casualty and saw that his arm was held to the metal by a single sinew. I tried cutting him free with my seaman's knife but it wasn't sharp enough.' George Andrews, an 18-year-old ordinary seaman, had a lucky escape. He was told to leave the transmitting station and go to the forward magazine to help out. Less than two minutes later the shell exploded.[10]

There was one last emergency. Because an order from the bridge had been misunderstood in the tiller flat the wheel was turned the wrong way and the ship headed at speed for the south bank, in danger of 'becoming part of the landscape'. The engine room reacted quickly to the order 'emergency full astern'. The ship hit the bank but glanced off because of the power of the engines and resumed her escape down river. *Consort* found the safety of Kiangyin in the late afternoon. The frigate *Black Swan* arrived soon afterwards and the cruiser *London*, with Vice Admiral Madden on board his flagship, anchored that evening. The medical officers of all three ships treated the wounded. With some irony, *Black Swan* had brought the medical officer from the Australian frigate *Shoalhaven*. The seriously wounded were transferred to *London*, which had an operating table. The badly-wounded Stoker Flanagan overhead a conversation: 'They said, what about him? No chance. I was looking to see who they were talking about and it was me. I thought, no chance, what are they talking about? Maybe that sparked something in me to say, I'm not going to die.'

Commander Robertson was called to a conference aboard the flagship and told to sail to Shanghai as soon as possible to get the less seriously wounded to hospital. Seven men were dead and thirty-four had been wounded, three of whom would die during the night. After taking on fuel and provisions from *London* and plugging some of her lower shell holes *Consort* sailed at 0400 the following day, 21 April. The destroyer arrived at Shanghai at 0930. US Navy personnel were waiting with ambulances and the wounded were taken to a local hospital before being transferred to the American hospital ship USS *Repose*, which was lying off Woosung.

The destroyer *Constance* went alongside *Consort* and Commander Peter Baker, *Constance*'s skipper, paid a visit. In a letter home, he wrote: 'They were in a nasty mess, simply riddled with shrapnel. Poor Robertson's cabin was a complete shambles, the only untouched thing being his wife's picture.'[11] *Consort* had received fifty-four hits from 105mm high-explosive shells, 75mm armour-piercing shells and 37mm anti-tank shells at close range.

5

The Navy's 'Charge of the Light Brigade'

SHORTLY BEFORE MIDNIGHT ON 20 APRIL an attempt was made to refloat *Amethyst*. The engine room had flashed up earlier, power was restored and repairs were made to the damaged starboard telegraph. Lieutenants Weston, Berger and Hett were on the bridge, and the engines and rudder were worked to free the ship – stuck bow first in the mud – for about an hour. The attempt was unsuccessful. Weston, who had hoped that *Consort* would return under cover of darkness, ordered the dumping of heavy fittings from the forecastle and the pumping of ten tons of fuel over the side. A second attempt was successful early on 21 April. *Amethyst* moved up river at eight knots but about an hour later, off Fu-te-wei, she attracted small-arms fire from the north bank. Berger noted: 'This was not accurate or particularly troublesome, but it indicated to us that although the ship was darkened our movements were visible to the Communists.' Navigation at night was made more difficult because 'half of the chart had been shot away and much of the remainder was obscured by blood'. *Amethyst* turned round and went down river for two miles before anchoring at a relatively safe spot some five miles from Rose Island.[1]

At about 0915 a sampan approached the ship, carrying two Nationalist soldiers who offered to help the wounded. Weston turned them down because he was expecting the cruiser *London* to come to *Amethyst*'s rescue. That morning the Nationalists made two further attempts to help, getting the same response.

Vice Admiral Madden had sailed from Hong Kong for Shanghai in *London* on 18 April. A 'full programme of entertainments', including a Saint George's Day ball, had been arranged for his visit. When *London* eventually arrived, on 21 April, she brought dead and wounded sailors. And Madden was in no mood to be entertained. Four of his ships had been shot up and the death toll would reach forty-nine, including two Chinese pilots.

The conference aboard *London* on the night of 20 April, when the flagship anchored at Kiangyin with *Black Swan* and the battered

Consort, had thrown up several possibilities for Madden. There was 'some small hope' that negotiation would secure *Amethyst*'s release. Despite the ambassador's earlier insistence that there could be no formal approaches to the Communists, Sir Ralph Stevenson asked the British consul in Peking to communicate with the 'high command' and try to get an assurance that British ships would not be fired on. At 0200 on 21 April, Madden received a message from the ambassador pointing out that it would take several days for any ceasefire order to reach the front line. The admiral decided that time was not on his side, and focused on another rescue attempt, despite the high price that *Consort* had paid. Twenty minutes after receiving the ambassador's message he learned that *Amethyst* had managed to refloat herself. He reported: 'Such was the need for assistance in the *Amethyst* that I considered an attempt must be made to reach her and escort her to safety. As a towing operation was no longer necessary, I was unwilling to expose HMS *Black Swan* to damage or casualties. I hoped that the morale effect of the *London*'s size and armament might reduce the opposition to sporadic or isolated resistance.'

Madden had considered using *Black Swan* in a night operation with the aim of embarking *Amethyst*'s wounded and then escorting her to safety. *Black Swan* would hug the south bank on the trip up river. But there was a problem – the Nationalists had imposed a curfew and might open fire on the ship. 'The consequences of detection and failure were unacceptable, since HMS *Black Swan* might be reduced to a plight similar to HMS *Amethyst*'s,' Madden noted. Another idea was to send ships' boats 35 miles along the channel between Tai-ping-chau and the mainland. This would have taken at least 12 hours and unknown hazards were likely. The proposal, with the limited objective of rescuing the wounded, was 'not worth while'. *Amethyst* could have been told to attempt negotiations with the local Communist commander, but the enemy had opened fire at the sign of any movement and disregarded the white flag. The admiral thought of using aircraft, apart from Sunderlands. But the nearest strike planes were in Malaya and it would have taken three or four days to get permission from the Nationalists to use an airfield. In addition, there was the question of getting enough intelligence through aerial photographs so that pilots could be fully briefed. And there was an overriding factor: 'I considered that the use of aircraft would be tantamount to an act of war.'

There was only one solution. *London* and *Black Swan* would go up river. 'I had no hesitation in deciding that this, the only possible urgent action must be undertaken as it was unthinkable that those in urgent distress in HMS *Amethyst* should be left without any assistance that could possibly be brought to them,' Madden reported. 'I was, naturally, fully aware that unless the opposition respected the outward signs of peaceful intention or, alternatively, their fire was inconsiderable, this operation in restricted waters at very close range could only result in heavy casualties and damage, and further attraction of fire to HMS *Amethyst*. I ordered its undertaking in the full knowledge that it might be necessary, in order to avoid further loss of life, to retire, and I informed the commanding officer of HMS *London* accordingly.'[2]

What happened on 21 April has been referred to by some survivors of the Yangtze Incident as the naval equivalent of the Charge of the Light Brigade.[3] The casualties were high but it was more like the Charge of the Heavy Brigade. *London* was a heavy cruiser of 9,850 tons, with a main armament of eight 8in guns and eight 4in guns, and a top speed of 32 knots. She certainly packed a lot of firepower. But if *Amethyst* and *Consort* were relatively easy targets for experienced gunners on land, then *London* was the proverbial barn door. The cruiser was a huge target in the Yangtze. Madden would gamble three times – *Amethyst*, *Consort* and *London* and *Black Swan* – and lose each time.

Off Woosung, *London* had embarked two Chinese pilots but the skipper, Captain Peter Cazalet, thought they might not be 'entirely reliable' if shooting broke out. In the pilot boat was William Sudbury, from Liverpool, who had experience of navigating the Yangtze. The fifty-year-old Sudbury had served in the Merchant Navy during the First World War and as a lieutenant in the Royal Australian Navy in the Second World War. Cazalet asked him to come aboard and he readily agreed, though there was no time to tell his family. His advice would prove 'invaluable'.[4]

Early on 21 April, *London* and *Black Swan* sailed 19 miles up river to Bate Point, where they anchored. They were about 30 miles from *Amethyst*. At 0930 Madden gave Cazalet the order to try to reach the frigate with the aim of escorting her back to Shanghai. *London*'s captain was under no illusions: 'It was perfectly clear both to the admiral and myself that the passage of the river against the opposition of determined and well-trained shore batteries was not a feasible operation – we considered that against light and sporadic opposition it was a reasonable proposition and hoped there would be no opposition at all. It was agreed that if fire was opened on the ship she would reply in self defence with all guns.'

Black Swan would play a supporting role, giving covering fire if necessary. Both ships were told to display large white flags – 'except when firing' – and a number of Union Jacks. The frigate sailed first and *London* began her journey at 1026. The cruiser was soon doing 25 knots. Ten minutes later she came under attack from batteries on the north bank in the vicinity of Liu-wei-chiang, which were firing 100mm and 75mm shells. Madden's hope that the sight of *London* would overawe Communist gunners disappeared in a gun flash. The cruiser took two direct hits. Both ships went to full speed and opened up, *London* with most of her armament.[5]

Acting Sub Lieutenant Christopher Parker-Jervis recalled: 'Our reactions were very clear – down white flag, train all guns abeam and open fire. We had to wait for them to open fire to provide a point of aim as there was very little to see. As the range was only 2,000 yards or so we were firing almost horizontally if not at depression, which meant that any errors in elevation, especially for the 8in guns, caused very large alterations in range in such a low-lying area.'[6]

The batteries stopped firing after four minutes, but at 1104 another battery, in the area of Kuo-chieng-chang, opened fire, hitting *London*'s bridge and hangar and boat decks. Cazalet, who had won the Distinguished Service Order and Distinguished Service Cross during the Second World War, reported: 'It was evident that damage and casualties were becoming heavy and I started to consider the advisability of withdrawal. I had in mind the fact that, even if it were possible for *London* to reach *Amethyst*'s position, the chances of a successful return with *Amethyst* at slow speed were almost negligible.'

Two minutes later the bridge was hit again, killing one of the Chinese pilots and wounding three officers, including Cazalet and the navigator. Damage to instruments and communications on the bridge was severe and the captain wondered if he still had control of the ship. It was unlikely that *London* could carry on at high speed and under heavy shelling using her emergency conning position. 'I was in no doubt that the time for withdrawal had arrived and ordered the wheel to hard starboard and the starboard engine to full astern,' Cazalet reported. With the river getting narrower, the cruiser made a dramatic turn, narrowly missing the north bank, and headed down river.

Commander Richard Hare, who accompanied Madden as an officer on the staff of the Commander-in-Chief, Far East Station, was called to the bridge. His specialisation early in his career was navigation and he took over as navigator with the help of Sudbury. The British pilot had been knocked unconscious but recovered. The remaining Chinese pilot fled the bridge and was somewhere in hiding.

'It was a crisis all right,' said Hare.

The captain had stopped the ship in mid-river and turned her before giving up. I had a wry thought that, while the ambitious G and T chaps were useless, it was the unambitious navigator who was required to get out of the mess. The bridge was swimming in blood and broken glass. Three bodies, including the Chinese pilot, had been pulled to one side. The captain and the ship's navigator were below, badly wounded.

Over 100 miles of the river to Shanghai lay ahead with five shore batteries to pass. The accelerator still worked. It was a navigator's dream situation. Luckily for me, crouching behind the bridge, was a British civilian. The Lord knows how he got there, but he had some knowledge of the river and once or twice emerged to say he thought we would be coming to a crossing. These were the dangers, of course, and it helped to be warned. So it was really too easy for me, and it was John Hodges [Commander and executive officer] who had the problems. Every shore battery caused casualties.[7]

Marine John Parker, who helped to man one of the 4in guns, said: 'When the ship turned round the other crews weren't closed up so we had to get quickly through from the starboard 4in guns to man the port ones. It was pretty tricky underfoot as, with the ship turning, all the shell cases were rolling across the deck. I remember at one stage we ran out of high explosive ammunition so we loaded starburst shells and fired them – the Chinese must have wondered what the heck was going on as this harmless fireworks display erupted over their heads.'[8]

Royal Marines Bandmaster Fred Harwood was helping with first aid and went to the sick bay, where he was told that men were below fighting a fire and there might be some wounded. 'Thick smoke was coming out of the hatch,' he recalled.

> I did not know what I would find down there but everyone seemed to be watching me so down I went. It was the lower steering position. What a mess. Men fighting the fire by secondary lighting, hardly able to see very much. One thing I did see was a young lad on the wheel conning the ship and listening to orders on the voice pipe, surrounded by men putting out the fire. He was brave. What I did not realise at the time was that the main control of the rudder had gone, and that all of us were in his hands. When you think that we were in a river which was getting narrower and all of us were relying on him. One young lad. It is very hard to describe that scene.[9]

Lieutenant Commander Tommy Catlow, who was supervising damage control teams, recalled: 'We were in a real mess. There had been many fires, including one in the paint locker. Paint burns well but it was floodable, so with some misgivings because I heard that our Chinese mess boys might be down there, I flooded it. I'm glad to say that the Chinese had gone somewhere else.'[10]

London came under withering fire again after turning round, worse than that experienced on the passage up river. Five batteries opened up, three of which had not fired when the ship went up river. The cruiser took more hits and casualties mounted. But at 1340 the firing from the north bank stopped.

Bandmaster Harwood was in the sick bay when he heard 'music to all our ears – the order, "Fall out from action stations". We could now at least try in a small way to make our injured more comfortable. We had ratings lining up outside the sick bay only to be told, "Go away. We will pipe you when we want you". Shrapnel did not count as wounded that day. One young lad in there had his buttock shot away. This we packed with gauze, and then it was plastered but we knew he could not live as gangrene had set in.' Later Harwood promised him 'my tot of neat rum when he came back on board and he gave me a lovely smile'. The rating said he knew he was going to die.[11]

Over three hours *London* had been under heavy fire for a total of 48 minutes. In return, she fired 155 8in shells and 449 4in shells, plus 2,625 other rounds. Her 4in gun crews and supply parties suffered 38 per cent casualties. Sixteen men, including the Chinese pilot, were killed or fatally injured. A total of fifty-four were wounded, fourteen of them seriously. *Black Swan*, which also turned back, received seven shell hits, wounding seven men, one of them seriously. Two of the shells hit the fuel tank but failed to ignite it. The ship could have blown up. Captain Cazalet paid tribute to his crew: 'The bearing and conduct of the ship's company, a large proportion of whom are very young and were experiencing action for the first time, was beyond praise.'

As *London* approached Shanghai later that day Bandmaster Harwood told his band to go on deck and play some rousing marches. One of the tunes chosen was *Post Horn Gallop* 'to let all the people know that although we were battered we were still winning'. The cruiser arrived at Holt's Wharf with her dead and wounded, peppered with shell holes and with fires still smouldering. The following morning a US Navy landing craft came alongside and took off the wounded for treatment aboard the hospital ship *Repose*.

Vice Admiral Madden's inquest verdict:

In the event the fire encountered was heavy, determined and effective, additional batteries to those previously located having been manned or alerted. It was soon clear that HMS *London* was suffering heavy damage and that many further casualties would inevitably occur before reaching HMS *Amethyst*; moreover both ships would suffer similarly on the down-river passage. I therefore authorised the commanding officer, HMS *London* to turn back and ordered HM ships *Black Swan* and *London* to proceed to Shanghai, where they arrived about 1845.

It was now clear that diplomatic action afforded the only reasonable means of extricating HMS *Amethyst* . . .[12]

One of the Foreign Office officials monitoring events on the Yangtze was none other than Guy Burgess, who would later be unmasked as a Soviet spy. He was unhappy that the British embassy in Nanking blamed the Communists for shelling *London* when an early report had suggested that the Nationalists were also guilty. Burgess warned that Britain could be accused of distorting the news and he wanted a more balanced approach. Perhaps it was an early sign of his true allegiance. The report blaming the Nationalists proved to be untrue.[13]

6

The RAF Flies In

ON THE MORNING OF 21 April, the remaining crew of *Amethyst* were waiting anxiously for *London*'s arrival. In the early hours Vice Admiral Madden had sent a signal saying that *London* would be heading up river to help the frigate and expected to arrive at about 1100. The crew were heartened by the news. *Amethyst* later raised steam and moved to the centre of the river to await the cruiser's arrival. When *London* failed to appear the frigate returned to her previous anchorage. The sound of heavy shelling in the distance prompted fears that the rescue attempt might be in trouble, and a message later confirmed that indeed it had been aborted. The morale of *Amethyst*'s crew was 'somewhat shaken . . . the seriousness of the situation was now brought home to them'.[1]

During the afternoon Weston told Gunner Monaghan to go the south bank and ask the Nationalists for medical supplies and a doctor. The Nationalists must have been puzzled. Monaghan had been on Rose Island the previous evening asking for help and when assistance was offered – three times – Weston rejected it.[2]

The surviving whaler had broken free during the ship's night passage and only Carley floats were left to make trips. The resourceful Monaghan managed to hire a sampan that was near the ship. 'I said, "Oh, I'm not going in a bloody Carley float when I've got a sampan – they're much safer". And so I waved him over. We had tons of Chinese money – Hett had gone down to the safe to get the *backsheesh*. You get nothing from them without the *backsheesh*. I got the money, waved it to him and he came over. I pointed to the shore.' Monaghan made contact with the Nationalists, and two Chinese doctors with medical supplies came on board during the afternoon, 'giving valuable assistance'. The Nationalists also agreed to provide sampans after dark to evacuate the remaining wounded, with the aim of getting them to the railway station at Chingkiang so that they could travel on for hospital treatment. Later that afternoon Monaghan made another sampan trip ashore to finalise arrangements for the evacuation. As he returned to the ship, 'lo and behold, a bloody Sunderland arrives from above'.[3]

The headquarters of the Royal Air Force in Hong Kong had been alerted to *Amethyst*'s plight shortly after the frigate ran aground on Rose Island, and 88 Squadron at Kai Tak was put on standby. All aircraft were made serviceable and their crews placed in readiness. At 2245 on 20 April, Kai Tak's commanding officer, Group Captain John Jefferson, was told that the navy had asked for a Sunderland flying boat to drop supplies to the sailors who were trying to make their way to Shanghai. If conditions were favourable the plane should then try to land alongside the frigate so that a navy doctor could go on board with medical supplies. Flight Lieutenant Ken Letford, a wartime bomber pilot who had won the Distinguished Service Order and Bar and the Distinguished Flying Cross, was chosen as the Sunderland's pilot. Two soldiers from the Royal Army Service Corps with experience of parachute drops were quickly recruited. And the RAF decided to send one of its doctors, Flight Lieutenant Michael Fearnley. Unusually, Kai Tak's commanding officer decided to make the trip as well. Early the next day, the Sunderland took off and headed for *Amethyst*, but on the way Letford received a priority signal from *London* ordering him not to approach the ship 'due to gunfire' and telling him to land at Shanghai. At that stage Vice Admiral Madden had decided that *London* and *Black Swan* would attempt a rescue – and perhaps it would not be necessary to involve the RAF.

The Sunderland arrived at Lunghwa airport and was met by the assistant air attaché in Shanghai, Squadron Leader Peter Howard-Williams, who had flown a Spitfire during the Battle of Britain. Howard-Williams, Jefferson and Letford then went to the office of the assistant naval attaché, Commander John Pringle, who stressed the need to get medical supplies and a doctor to *Amethyst*, which had run out of morphine. Later Madden made contact. He had changed his mind. Because of the failure of his rescue attempt he now wanted the Sunderland to try to reach the ship.[4]

One plan favoured by Howard-Williams was to land the plane in a creek near *Amethyst*, transfer the doctors and medical supplies, and take the seriously wounded back to Shanghai. The Sunderland would remain in the creek during the night and fly off at dawn. It would not be an easy task but Letford was willing to try. According to Howard-

Williams, Group Captain Jefferson, the senior officer, vetoed the idea. 'There was a risk involved but a justifiable and calculated risk, with so much at stake,' Howard-Williams reflected. 'I have always felt that we let down our friends in the navy on this occasion for want of a little more imagination and dash.' The plan given approval was to land the flying boat on the Yangtze near *Amethyst*. Oddly, Jefferson, in his report on the mission, said the intention was to land in the creek, but in the event no attempt was made to do this.[5]

The Sunderland took off from Shanghai and soon found the ship. The plane made one low approach. There was no hostile action. Letford landed on the Yangtze and taxied towards the frigate. The engines were stopped and the plane's anchor was dropped out. It was at this point that Gunner Monaghan in his hired sampan decided to make contact.

I said to the Chinese, 'That way – or else'. I had no money left and I got my revolver out. He took me alongside the Sunderland, the door was opened and Flight Lieutenant Fearnley was there. He jumped into the sampan and said you had better brief them so they can tell them in *London* what's happening. So I jumped aboard the Sunderland and then they opened fire. The Chinese sampan man took off immediately like a shot rabbit and left me aboard the Sunderland.' [Monaghan referred to a sampan man but according to one of the plane's crew, Gerry Moreby, the boat was being handled by 'terrified Chinese women'.][6]

Jefferson reported: 'As the artillery fire was accurate and heavy and as the aircraft was in full view of at least one battery, an immediate take-off was necessary if the aircraft was to avoid similar rough handling to that experienced by the naval vessels.'

Engines were started but the anchor could not be pulled up. 'It was stuck fast in the river bed,' said Gerard Devany, the plane's gunner.

I took one look round and if I had not been so scared it would have been funny. The co-pilot had attacked the split pin that holds the nut on the bolt, which in turn anchors the aircraft end of the anchor chain to the floor. He had chewed the head off with pliers. You really couldn't bugger it up any worse.

As I snatched the pliers out of the co-pilot's hands I saw the wireless operator frantically trying to hacksaw through the anchor chain. Fat chance, I thought. The noise of cannon fire was deafening and my hands were shaking. I looked up at Group Captain Jefferson, who was bending over me and looking at the messed-up split pin. May I tell you I was very, very impressed with what I saw. He looked at me, the noise was ear-splitting, but he was as cool and collected as it is possible to be.

I shouted at him at the top of my voice, 'I want a hammer and a screwdriver'. He in turn passed that on to the flight deck and down came a toolbox pronto. I had been an aircraft fitter before volunteering for aircrew. I had met the obstinate split pin situation many times. After straightening the tail end of the split pin, I tapped it through the bolt enough for the chewed up head end to stick out past the nut. This enabled me to get a grip on the split-pin head and with pliers I eased it out. The chain was free now and by letting it unwind through the winch it soon found its way to the river bottom. We were ready for take-off.[7]

The plane had a remarkable take-off. Because it was flying down wind and the tide was a factor, it took nearly three miles to get airborne. The return to Shanghai was uneventful, and that evening Jefferson, Howard-Williams and Letford went on board *London* to report to Vice Admiral Madden, who was 'most appreciative of what we had done'. Jefferson noted: 'I gathered that the transfer of the medical officer and medical supplies to *Amethyst* had raised everyone's spirits as *Amethyst* had almost given up at that stage.'

Fearnley managed to reach *Amethyst* in the zig-zagging sampan with a satchel of medical supplies, including much-needed morphine. But he experienced the same difficulty as Monaghan in persuading the Chinese to follow directions. They were panicking because of the gunfire. At one point Fearnley stood up and there was a struggle, with the sampan in danger of capsizing. Monaghan had dropped his gun in the sampan and the doctor grabbed it. Fearnley gestured towards the ship and they eventually reached her. Later he discovered the gun was not loaded. As he boarded *Amethyst* six artillery rounds were fired at the ship but they did not result in any casualties or damage. The frigate moved a short distance to another anchorage. The doctor did 'great work' on the remaining wounded, most of whom were landed by sampan that night with the help of Nationalist soldiers. The wounded, including the captain, Skinner, and Berger, were taken to Chingkiang railway station where they boarded the last train to Shanghai.[8]

Weston reported: 'The captain had been very seriously injured but though I saw him on the evening he left, I did not realise he was dying. Although he was in great pain and at one period without morphia, he continued to concern himself during his periods of consciousness with the fate of his ship. Lieutenant Berger had done valuable work on the upper deck and the bridge during the first 24 hours after the beginning of the action. Subsequently he succumbed to his wounds and could not stand.'

When the Sunderland arrived back in Shanghai, Gunner Monaghan was taken to see Vice Admiral Madden on board *London*. 'I had had no sleep for 36 hours and I was a bit bloody shattered,' said Monaghan. 'Admiral Madden gave me a large pink gin and said, "I want the story and you're the only one who can give it to me". So I told him. The admiral said, "We're having a conference now. You're going into my cabin and sleeping in my bed. You'll most probably be flying back tomorrow. We'll brief you at breakfast". I lay on his bed and I was out like a light.'[9]

In the early hours of 22 April, Fearnley gave Weston more morphine and Benzedrine tablets to help him carry out duties. A signal from Madden told the first lieutenant to move *Amethyst* and she went 10 miles up river, attracting sporadic machine-gun fire from the north bank – and the Nationalist south bank.

Group Captain Jefferson and Letford spent the night at Shanghai's Palace Hotel and in the morning returned to the office of the assistant naval attaché, where they learned that Madden had asked for another Sunderland flight to take eight naval officers and ratings and a chaplain – for burial duties – to *Amethyst*. The Sunderland took off later with the same crew and Monaghan but without the two soldiers because there would not be a parachute drop. Letford found the ship's new position and made three runs. The south bank was 'a hive of activity with the Nationalist troops digging in energetically', but there were few signs of activity on the north bank. The plane landed near *Amethyst* and an inflatable dinghy was tossed out, only to be swept away by the current, estimated at five to seven knots. The Sunderland, which no longer had an anchor, also found itself sailing past the ship. At that moment artillery and small-arms fire erupted from the north bank.[10]

'I opened the door, ready to jump out and swim to the ship,' said Monaghan. 'However, some of the damage control crew pulled me back and said, "Don't be so bloody silly". I said, "Let me go". But the door closed and we flew off.'

Amethyst was shelled again and moved further up river. The Sunderland remained in the area for about 45 minutes doing reconnaissance at the request of one of the naval officers on board, and then headed for Shanghai. From the rear gun turret Gerard Devany spotted two Mosquito fighter planes about two miles away and reported it to Letford. The pilot told him to keep an eye on them. Both sides were using Mosquitoes.

'During the war we used to have a method of making ourselves a difficult target to the enemy fighter aircraft by doing what we called corkscrewing,' Devany explained.

This simply meant at a given signal from the rear gunner the pilot would do a pretty vicious roll and dive to port, then roll and climb to starboard and keep doing this as long as necessary. It was assumed that this manoeuvring would make it difficult for the fighter pilot to line his sights on us in order to fire his guns.

Bearing all this in mind I called the pilot and said, 'Be prepared to corkscrew'. At this point one of the Mosquitoes did the usual turn in on our tail at about 800 yards. At 600 yards I said, 'Corkscrew now'. The poor old Sunderland must have wondered what had hit her. They are not built for this undignified type of flying. While all this was going on, I gave a couple of three-second bursts on my machine guns in the general direction of the Mosquito.

We will never know whether the pilot was startled or just highly amused at the incredible behaviour of a flying boat suddenly spitting bullets out of her tail and leaping round the sky like a skittish moth round an electric light bulb. He certainly had second thoughts for he turned off in the direction of Nanking.[11]

The Sunderland was still flying low when shortly afterwards there was small-arms fire from the ground. The plane was hit in two places, one bullet passing through the co-pilot's sleeve. Letford climbed for cloud cover and the plane returned safely.

Monaghan was asked to report to Vice Admiral Madden again. He told him: 'I wanted to get back to the ship but that crowd prevented me.' Madden replied: 'I'm glad they did. If you had got in the Yangtze, the way that tide was flowing, you would have drowned in no time.'

The next day, 23 April, Madden again asked for the Sunderland to undertake a mission. This time he wanted reconnaissance of the Yangtze to see the position of Nationalist warships, with the idea that these vessels might help *Amethyst* to escape down river. The Sunderland took off with the same crew but without navy or army personnel and headed for Chiangyin, flying at about 800 feet because the cloud base was 1,000 feet. Communist forces had already crossed the Yangtze between Chiangyin and Nanking. Some five miles south east of Chiangyin heavy machine-gun fire was directed at the plane and the port petrol tank was hit. It was an unlucky shot, as Devany pointed out:

These tanks are covered with a bullet proof skin, but just round where the straps hold the tank fixed to the wing there is a small area about the size of a coin that is not bullet proof. The bullet had gone in there. Why didn't it blow up? Search me. Petrol was pouring into the wing close to the wireless operator's cabin. All electrical switches we could do without were turned off and the wireless operator was busy rushing back and forth with cooking pans full of petrol. I held back from asking, 'Where are you taking it?' By the look of his face I will swear that he was a born actor and the direction he was heading told it all. It was going down the toilet. Now to my mind when I think of it that was a terrible thing to do. As soon as the petrol hit the slip stream it would be highly volatile and one spark would do the rest.

Devany had experienced his own close shave in the rear gun turret. 'I was rotating my turret from side to side when suddenly it went dead,' he recalled. 'I used the hand winder to bring the turret round to the fore and aft position and climbed into the rear of the fuselage. Then I could see the reason for it. In the body of the aircraft and just behind the gun turret there is a control valve called the dead man's release.

The object of this is to get the gunner out of the turret if he is out of action.' The dead man's release had been 'shot to pieces' and all the oil operating the turret had flowed out onto the floor. Devany was thankful: 'When you think this valve was about ten inches away from my back when I was in the turret, I felt I should take a lottery ticket as this was my lucky day.'[12]

Because of the fuel problem and other damage the plane returned to Shanghai. Some 300 gallons were lost in less than an hour. A second Sunderland had arrived from Hong Kong and the first flying boat was sent back to Kai Tak. But Group Captain Jefferson, wondering if another mission might be requested by Madden, decided to keep the original crew 'who already had experience of this difficult undertaking'. But no further requests were made because 'efforts were being made to arrange a safe passage down stream'.

In his report on the missions, Jefferson said there had been crucial help from the British Overseas Aircraft Corporation and Jardine Matheson at Lungwha airport. He paid tribute to the Sunderland's crew and the two soldiers from the Royal Army Service Corps, and 'I was particularly impressed by the great skill and coolness displayed throughout by Flight Lieutenant Letford'. He ended his report by saying that 'at no time was fire opened from the Sunderland'. But Devany was clear that he had fired 'a couple of three-second bursts on my machine guns' at a menacing Mosquito fighter. He would be ordered to deny this action.

Air force involvement was not confined to the Sunderland's missions. On 23 April the senior officer at RAF headquarters in Hong Kong, Air Commodore Adolphus Davies, was in bullish mood and sent a 'top secret' message to Vice Admiral Madden, with copies to the First Sea Lord and the Foreign Office, saying that 'if *Amethyst* has to fight her way out I most strongly advocate the use of Beaufighters as I sincerely believe that after a few attacks gun crews would desert'. The offer was not taken up.

7

Not Kerans!

LIEUTENANT COMMANDER JOHN KERANS WAS the wrong man in the right place on the morning of 20 April. If the Admiralty had been in possession of a list of officers who could be sent to help *Amethyst*, Kerans might well have found himself at the bottom of it. In fact, another officer was chosen to replace the wounded Weston and he had been on board the flying boat when the Sunderland made its unsuccessful second flight. Kerans was not a man in favour. There had been run-ins with authority, and he was sent to the Far East Station without an appointment and 'for disposal', a rather unfortunate term that was used if an officer had committed 'a misdemeanour' in his previous post. The 33-year-old Kerans was a heavy drinker and had 'an incorrigible desire for women'. He ended up in Nanking as an assistant naval attaché. Captain Donaldson, the naval attaché, needed help because he was being inundated with signals traffic stemming from the growing crisis over the civil war. On 20 April, after only a few weeks in the city, Kerans was about to experience a remarkable change in his fortunes, beginning with a journey that would see him become a national hero.[1]

He was born at Birr, King's County (later County Offaly) Ireland on 30 June 1915. His father, Lieutenant Colonel Edward Kerans, served in the Worcestershire Regiment during the First World War, winning the Distinguished Service Order. The colonel had shown bravery early on – at the age of 13 he was awarded the Royal Humane Society's bronze medal for trying to save a man from drowning. He was wounded at Gallipoli but went on to fight on the Somme and in the Battle of Arras. His health never fully recovered after his war service. John Kerans was 11 and a boarder at a prep school in Gloucester when his father died in 1927, aged 47. Two years later he entered Britannia Royal Naval College, Dartmouth, as a cadet. He was good at some sports but did not shine academically, and was often caned for flouting the strict discipline. In 1933 he found himself in the Far East as a midshipman in the cruiser HMS *Cornwall*. After a spell in the

Mediterranean he returned to the Far East in a staff job doing intelligence work. When war broke out in 1939, he asked to be transferred to Atlantic convoy duties, later going to the Mediterranean in the cruiser HMS *Naiad*, where he saw a lot of action. In May 1941, during the evacuation of Crete, the cruiser HMS *Orion*, carrying many soldiers, was attacked by dive-bombers, with the loss of some 360 lives. *Orion* managed to reach Alexandria, where Lieutenant Kerans was put in charge of the working party clearing the bodies. He was left traumatised. The previous month his brother Mickey, a captain in the Worcesters, had died of wounds received during the battle of Keren in Eritrea. On 11 March 1942 *Naiad* was sunk by the German submarine *U 565* after an air attack. Seventy-seven crew died but Kerans was rescued unhurt, though exhausted.[2]

In August 1944 he was given his first command, the destroyer HMS *Blackmore*. Alan Tyler joined *Blackmore* as navigating officer when she was having a refit at Sheerness, but he was not impressed with the new captain: 'Kerans was a senior lieutenant who had probably spent most of the last five years at sea under considerable strain, and in his case the escape was drink, which he did not carry well. He sometimes returned aboard the worse for wear and had to be helped to bed, which was embarrassing for the duty officer and for morale. He was also not a great ship handler, nor an easy man to work with.' On a trip to Scapa Flow during trials the ship was caught in a boom, and on her return to Sheerness a cable became entangled in one of the propellers, requiring the services of divers.[3] After convoy duties *Blackmore* headed east but returned home when the war ended, at one point grounding. Kerans was admonished after a court on inquiry. There was a more pleasant experience in Plymouth on 7 January 1946, when he married Stephanie Campbell Shires, an officer in the Women's Royal Naval Service.

Kerans was given another command in January 1947, the frigate HMS *Widemouth Bay*, which was based in Hong Kong. In the March, the ship was transferred to the Mediterranean to reinforce the Palestine patrol. By May Kerans had a crew verging on mutiny. Discontented sailors claimed there had been petty restrictions and 'insensitive practices' over several months. One incident brought matters to a head. Crewmen had been told to paint the ship during stormy weather. The trouble was considered so serious that it led to a board of inquiry.

But worse was to come. One night when *Widemouth Bay* was berthed at Malta, some of the ship's company – probably officers among them – returned from a heavy drinking session ashore and urinated over the side of the ship before stripping off and jumping into the harbour. Kerans may have joined in, or perhaps been thrown overboard by those seeking revenge. Unfortunately for Kerans, the antics were witnessed by the admiral superintendent of the dockyard, who was having a cocktail party on his veranda. The board of inquiry recommended a court martial, and Kerans was found guilty of negligence and a charge relating to alcohol. The commanding officer and his first lieutenant were dismissed their ship. A leading stoker was also punished. Interestingly, after Kerans's departure there was 'a notable change in morale'.[4] The lieutenant commander ended up back in the Far East with a desk job doing intelligence work. He was even seconded to the police in Kuala Lumpur. The future did not look promising.

With Vice Admiral Madden's options running out, the naval attaché in Nanking decided to send his assistant to *Amethyst*. Captain Donaldson also told Kerans to try to find out what had happened to a group of *Amethyst*'s wounded, as there were conflicting reports about their whereabouts. At 1000 on 21 April, Kerans set off from Nanking in a Jeep borrowed from the Australian military attaché, with medical supplies and Chinese navy charts of the Yangtze. He had a Chinese driver and was accompanied by the assistant military attaché at the British embassy, Lieutenant Colonel Raymond Dewar-Durie, who had been commissioned into the Argyll and Sutherland Highlanders. The first destination was the Nationalist navy headquarters at Chingkiang, but they had only gone a couple of hundred yards when the Jeep broke down. The driver leapt out, tinkered with the engine and swore, and they carried on, only to break down several times. The road surface was poor and dusty, and they arrived at the naval headquarters in the early afternoon. They were greeted by Captain Mark Meh, the local navy commander, whose English was 'as impeccable as his uniform'. Meh said fifty-six men from *Amethyst* had left Wu Tsin, 40 miles to the south east, by train for Shanghai. Kerans asked for a boat so that he could go to the frigate but the captain said it was too dangerous – and, in any case, there were few serviceable craft left. During the conversation a young Chinese lieutenant turned up. He had been near *Amethyst* in a landing craft earlier but was fired on by Communists on the north bank. Kerans spoke to Captain Donaldson by phone and was told to return to Nanking 'as there was nothing else we could do'.

But shortly afterwards Donaldson changed his mind and phoned to give new orders. Kerans should travel overland and try to reach *Amethyst* with the medical supplies. A doctor from the US Navy, Lieutenant Commander James Packard, arrived at the naval headquarters in a saloon car with an assistant and agreed to go with Kerans and Dewar-Durie. Packard, who ran a clinic in Nanking and also acted as the assistant naval attaché at the American embassy, had been alerted to the plight of *Amethyst*'s wounded and came with plenty of medical supplies. The Nationalists provided two trucks to evacuate casualties. Captain Meh insisted on going as well and the convoy set off on a heavily pot-holed road, arriving at a village about 23 miles east of Chingkiang. The trucks could go no further but the local army commander arranged to send on stretcher-bearers. The Jeep and the car continued for two miles until the track petered out. Waiting there were six soldiers who had commandeered a large wheelbarrow and two coolies to push and pull it. The wheelbarrow was loaded with the medical supplies, and the group set off on foot in single file on a path between rice fields, heading for a creek where they were told *Amethyst* lay. The path twisted and they rounded the southern slopes of a ridge.

'As evening drew on our shadows lengthened before us and it got much colder,' Dewar-Durie recalled. 'Conversation in single file is always difficult and soon there were no sounds but the shuffle of our feet, the creaking of the wheelbarrow, and the grunts and heavy breathing of the two coolies. Soon it was quite dark and it was while looking down to see where next to put my feet that I cannoned into the man in front and we all concertinaed.' For Kerans the journey seemed 'never ending'. They arrived at the river bank and found a creek, which turned out to be the wrong one. After a further 'appalling' trek they reached the right creek. There they came across four badly wounded sailors on stretchers. An uninjured able seaman, Raymond Calcott, was in charge of the men, and there were also about forty soldiers. Calcott was able to give Kerans some news. He said twelve wounded men had been escorted away a short time earlier using another track. *Amethyst* was not far and an RAF doctor was on board after arriving in a Sunderland flying boat. The US Navy doctor treated the four wounded men and decided he would accompany them to an agreed assembly point, Ta Kang, the village where the two army lorries had been left.

It was arranged that Kerans, Dewar-Durie, Able Seaman Calcott and a Chinese doctor would go to *Amethyst*, and after a 40-minute wait they set off in a sampan at 0100 on 22 April. The ship, not showing any lights, was soon spotted thanks to a misty moon but to the dismay of Kerans she started moving slowly away. He tried to signal with a torch but the frigate carried on, and there was no hope of catching her. The sampan headed back to the bank. It was a nervous time as Dewar-Durie pointed out: 'As the sampan made its return trip I couldn't help thinking that we were in rather an unenviable position, floating around between two rival armies. What if the Nationalist sentries mistook us for the first wave of the Communist assault? Every minute I expected some nervous soldier to let fly, but nothing happened, not even a challenge.' Before *Amethyst* set off the remaining wounded were sent ashore in a sampan, with Weston refusing to go, despite the advice of the RAF doctor, because too few officers would be left. 'How this batch missed us will never be clear,' Kerans remarked. These wounded were taken to a nearby village, where they spent the night.

After some 'very welcome' cups of tea at a farmhouse Kerans and his group walked through the night to the assembly point, Ta Kang, arriving just before dawn. Dewar-Durie recalled: 'Here in the dim light was a sorry sight. Around the lorries lay wounded waiting for their turn for treatment or to be bedded down in the trucks. Packard was busy moving among them, injecting, bandaging or giving blood transfusions. We soon realised that the two lorries would not be enough and so a call was put through to the Fourth Army headquarters, which readily agreed to send more. In fact, it was quite amazing how much help was given, especially if one remembers that everything was done under the shadow of an impending attack by an implacable enemy.' Packard's description of his patients: 'They were shot to hell.' Two men died on the journey to Ta Kang, *Amethyst*'s captain, Skinner, and Able Seaman George Winter. Soldiers had carried the badly wounded on stretchers for about nine miles over appalling tracks in pitch darkness and dropping temperatures.[5]

Packard stressed the need for the wounded to get hospital treatment. Lying on straw, they were driven to Chingkiang in the lorries 'at a dead slow pace' because of the terrible road. Kerans and Dewar-Durie went ahead to alert the American mission hospital in Chingkiang, whose matron was Charlotte Dunlap. Not only did Miss Dunlap help the wounded but later 'at considerable risk to herself' she passed on accurate intelligence of the Communist batteries covering *Amethyst*.[6] The officers then went to the local railway station to arrange for an extra coach to be put on the next train to Shanghai. Railway officials were reluctant to help, but Kerans remembered he had a letter from the commander-in-chief of the Nationalist navy, Admiral Kwei Yung-ching, and that 'worked wonders'. An extra sleeping coach was attached to the train, and nurses from the hospital helped the wounded to board. The wounded included a group who arrived separately in another army lorry. The bodies of Skinner and Winter were also put on the train. Packard was in the middle of a transfusion when the train pulled away, and was last seen 'festooned with tubes and bandages' and heading for Shanghai.

Kerans and Dewar-Durie returned to the Nationalist naval head-quarters where the assistant naval attaché argued strongly to be taken to *Amethyst* in a landing craft. Eventually it was agreed. Kerans phoned Donaldson in Nanking to confirm the plan. It was arranged that Dewar-Durie would wait for the arrival of the wounded Weston and take him to the mission hospital. Kerans left in the landing craft in the early afternoon, with medical supplies and charts. Dewar-Durie noted: 'I saw him off and it was a lovely summer day and as I sat on a jetty watching the little boat chugging away round the promontory, and the teeming life on the cluster of chunks below me, war seemed very far away.'[7]

As the landing craft approached *Amethyst*, which was some seven miles down river of Chiangkiang, Kerans noticed that machine guns were being trained on his boat and he stood up and waved his charts. He was right to be anxious. Weston had given an order to open fire on any suspicious boats approaching the ship, although the first lieutenant would say later he could not remember giving it. At that point it was not clear if the Communists were on both banks of the river. Weston was surviving on Horse's Neck, a cocktail usually made from brandy and ginger ale, and Fearnley, the RAF doctor, told him he needed to have a piece of shrapnel removed from a lung or it might become infected, proving fatal. After consulting Fearnley, Kerans insisted that Weston go ashore for treatment and, reluctantly, the first lieutenant left in the landing craft, hoping to return to the ship in 'a few days'. He was met by Dewar-Durie, who took him to the mission hospital. That evening Weston went to the railway station in Chingkiang, where on the platform Miss Dunlap gave him a large injection of morphine before he boarded the last train to Nanking. No trains were running between Chingkiang and Shanghai because the line had been cut.[8]

Dewar-Durie was told to remain in Chingkiang in case it was decided to scuttle *Amethyst* and the sailors needed help to make their way to safety. During the evening he paid several visits to the Nationalist navy headquarters, which was still in touch with the British embassy in Nanking. On his last visit, around midnight, he found everyone had packed up ready to leave by boat. The Communists had crossed the Yangtze at several points and were advancing rapidly. Early the next morning, 23 April, he was asked to return to Nanking as the plan to scuttle the ship had been postponed. Near the station he saw soldiers with red armbands and urged his driver to 'go like the devil'. On the main road linking Nanking and Shanghai he found the Nationalists in full retreat: 'Lorries and yet more lorries, horse-drawn carts and old Japanese tanks all rumbled past, while endless groups of soldiers plodded by in their soft-soled shoes. The congestion was terrific and the dust appalling.' Many civilians were also fleeing Nanking. The panic was understandable. This was the city that had witnessed a major atrocity in December 1937, when invading Japanese soldiers swept in. An estimated 200,000 civilians were murdered, many after being tortured, in a six-week rampage. Most of the massacre sites were along the south bank of the Yangtze. Some 20,000 women and girls were reportedly raped. Dewar-Durie, who had spent fifty-one days evading Japanese troops after the occupation of Shanghai during the Second World War, managed to reach the British embassy. As he was driven through the gates he 'could not help feeling satisfied' that the army had helped out the navy.[9]

After Weston's departure from *Amethyst*, which 'undoubtedly' saved his life, Kerans, who had been appointed the ship's captain by Vice Admiral Madden, turned his attention to the seventeen dead on board and made arrangements for their burial, 'an urgent necessity'. There were simple services for members of the Church of England and the Roman Catholics. Kerans planned to sail to Nanking that evening, hoping that the failing light would hinder accurate firing from Communist batteries and aiming to get south of Deer Island, which was still in the hands of the Nationalists. But the situation deteriorated with 'alarming rapidity'. Intelligence reports suggested that *Amethyst* was trapped between two Communist crossing points and that movement either way would 'undoubtedly have caused further loss of life and the destruction of the ship'. Soon after 2000 Vice Admiral Madden told *Amethyst* to prepare to evacuate the ship and to scuttle her. Kerans quickly realised there was a major obstacle. There were no boats and insufficient lifebelts, and the men were too exhausted to make the short swim to land, where they would then face a long walk.

Kerans sent a message asking if he could beach the ship instead. The demolition charges had been destroyed when the depth-charge store was hit but detonators were available. The ship's company was divided into three groups, led by Hett, now a full lieutenant because of the shortage of officers, Lieutenant George Strain, the electrical officer, and Fearnley, the RAF doctor, who must have been bemused at finding himself in charge of sailors. Kerans planned to be the last to leave, along with the electrical artificers. Chocolate and a small quantity of food were issued, and the groups were told to wait ashore until Kerans's arrival. They would all make their way to Soochow and then Shanghai. Vice Admiral Madden approved the beaching plan if the order to abandon ship was given. Kerans noted: 'Throughout all this trying period the behaviour of all officers and ratings showed admirable fortitude. Every change in events was at once passed on to them and the tenseness of the situation was fully realised by all. In spite of this morale remained high.'

At 2200 six Chinese warships, fully darkened, sailed down river past *Amethyst* but were not fired on by the Communists. About two hours later Madden signalled that the order to abandon ship would probably not be given that night. Most of the ratings were able to get some rest. Kerans reported: 'All of us were now physically exhausted and the prospect of a lengthy trek to Shanghai in the wake of the retreating Nationalist forces to avoid capture seemed the only solution. The isolation and inability to effectively fight back was acutely felt.' [10]

8

A Diplomatic Challenge

AMBASSADOR STEVENSON HAD BELIEVED FOR some time that it would be wrong to have any diplomatic links with the Communists. Protocol needed to be followed. But after the attack on *Amethyst* he realised that some contact was necessary to try to ensure the ship's safety. On 20 April he sent a telegram to the British consul in Peking asking for an approach to the 'Communist High Command'. The consul, Martin Buxton, was told to stress that *Amethyst* was on a peaceful and humanitarian mission, and that immediate orders should be given to the local army commander not to fire on her should she manage to complete repairs and get under way. It was this approach that Vice Admiral Madden hoped would resolve the crisis, but it became apparent that a swift outcome was not in sight, prompting his decision to send *London* and *Black Swan* on their ill-fated rescue attempt.[1]

The consul wrote a letter to the army chief, General Chu Teh, and took it to Peking's Aliens Affairs Bureau – which refused to accept it, insisting that the bureau's authority was limited to the city and surrounding area. Later Buxton had a long conversation with an official named Chen, who 'accepted my arguments' but declined to take the letter and refused to reveal where Chu Teh could be contacted. Chen suggested that the consul should take his letter to the post office. It is not clear where the letter would have been directed. Buxton pointed out that the post office was hardly the right channel for a communication of such importance. However, he ended up posting it, sending a second letter on the night of 21 April.[2]

Stevenson, meanwhile, was in touch with the Foreign Office, pointing out he would not make a direct approach to the Communists unless instructed. He argued: 'My own view is that by doing so we might risk prematurely compromising our position with regard to recognition of the Chinese Communist administration without real hope of obtaining action desired. As a result of Communist authorities having obstinately ignored our previous communications, I fear it is now in any case too late even to ensure immunity of *Amethyst* from continued deliberate attacks, which must be known by now to the Communists' supreme command who could have taken active steps to prevent them.'[3]

Stevenson was not the only one unwilling to give recognition. The Communists told Buxton they did not recognise him as a British official, and the ambassador would soon discover that he too had no diplomatic status in their eyes. When Stevenson realised that Buxton's letters were unlikely to achieve a breakthrough, he agreed to send Edward Youde, a third secretary at the embassy, across the Yangtze with the aim of trying to talk to the local Communist command – responsible for the batteries that had opened fire on *Amethyst* and *Consort* – which was believed to be based at Yangchow, opposite Chingkiang. The 24-year-old Youde, who was fluent in Mandarin, had volunteered for what was obviously a dangerous task.

To his surprise Youde quickly obtained a pass to go through Nationalist lines from the army headquarters in Nanking. On the evening of 21 April, he set off, carrying his pass, 50 silver dollars, a haversack of clothes and a letter to the commander of the Nationalists' Thirty-Eighth Army. This force was holding the Pukow bridgehead across the Yangtze. Youde persuaded the navy to take him in a launch to the north bank, and from there he went to the headquarters of the Thirty-Eighth Army, which had not been told he was coming. He presented his letter to the general in command, who said straight away that it would be impossible to cross the lines because the armies were too close and locked in combat.

Youde, a future Governor of Hong Kong, noted: 'Not without difficulty I persuaded him to agree to review his decision the next morning at dawn in the light of events during the night, and he then turned me over to his adjutant who treated me extremely kindly, fed me and gave me a bed. The adjutant and a friend of his, the ordnance officer, spent a pleasant evening raising my morale with warnings that the Communists would completely refuse to listen to reason even if I got into contact with them, but that it was improbable that I would get that far on account of the plain-clothes bandits who preyed on all who were rash enough to be caught between the lines.'

By early morning the general had changed his mind, saying there was one possible crossing point. A soldier was told to take Youde to the army's outpost in the area. The diplomat was given two packets of biscuits. He and his guide reached the outpost, where they found six 'very sleepy' soldiers, after walking along the river bank for about an hour and a half in drizzle. The guide left, giving instructions on how to reach the next town and warning that Youde should not argue with the bandits he was sure to encounter.

Youde carried on for a couple of hours, enjoying a 'rather pleasant' walk. He met groups of peasants 'whose eyes popped out of their heads' on seeing a foreigner. None of them had seen any Communists and did not appear to be worried about bandits. 'So much for Nationalist intelligence,' Youde observed. On the outskirts of the town a shot was fired at him and he dived for cover. He took refuge in a brick kiln, along with some peasants, when 'a spirited exchange developed between a Nationalist gunner on an island in the river and my assailant'. With the kiln becoming an increasing target, Youde and his new companions dashed to the safety of a graveyard. There he learned that a magistrate he expected to contact had fled, and the Communists were occupying a large chemical factory nearby. But no one seemed keen to take him to the factory. The diplomat was clearly a target for both sides.

He was sitting in the graveyard thinking of his next move when a Communist patrol came over a nearby hill. With his hands up, he walked towards them. The soldiers dispersed into surrounding paddy fields 'and had me covered from all sides'. Fortunately there was no firing. Youde explained his mission to the patrol commander, who told two soldiers to take him to a nearby headquarters. On arrival, he was given a new escort, a 'jolly' man, and learned that he would be taken to another headquarters. Despite being loaded down with a rifle, a pistol, five hand grenades, a pack and a supply of rice, the jolly man, an irregular who was wearing civilian clothes and a hat that looked like a bowler without the rim, marched off at a blistering pace. After an hour they came across a small group of Nationalist officials who were being taken to the same headquarters. The pace slowed, and they were all treated well, allowed to rest and drink hot water and to buy food from peasants.

At about four in the afternoon they arrived at the headquarters, which was in a village, where Nationalist officials, police and prisoners of war had been assembled. Youde was taken to a farmhouse to see the commanding officer and once again explained his mission and stressed the urgency, only to be told that the matter would have to be dealt with by a higher authority. That evening he would be taken to a different headquarters, which was in radio contact with 'the superior organ'. Before leaving he was given rice and vegetables and required to debate various subjects with the commander and his subordinates – the attitude of the British government to the Atlantic Pact, the Chinese civil war, the United Nations, and Britain's food rationing programme and social security system. 'The argument was amicable but not conclusive,' Youde remarked. He left with a group of prisoners, who appeared to be destined for a training camp to correct their 'misleading education', and was grateful for frequent stops because he had been walking since dawn, with only one long break. Their destination was reached soon after nine but it was discovered that the unit he needed to contact had moved, and they walked on to another village, where accommodation was found in a farmhouse. Youde slept 'like a log' on the straw-covered floor.

The group were on the road again at five the next morning, 23 April, and reached their destination four hours later. To his 'intense disappointment' Youde discovered that the forward headquarters had moved off during the night and he faced another long walk. The soldiers with him had no wireless equipment and relied on runners for information. It was not long before a serious problem emerged – a Nationalist minefield. While waiting for engineers to clear the American-made anti-personnel mines, a 'field propaganda group' of men and girls turned up carrying books and musical instruments, and Youde found himself in a captive audience listening to 'liberation' songs. After half an hour the commander of the soldiers decided it would take too long to clear all the mines and ordered that they walk in single file, with him in the lead. They arrived at a town called Puchen, which was also heavily mined. It then dawned on Youde that he had walked in almost a complete circle. Puchen was four miles west of Pukow, the Nationalist bridgehead, his starting point on the north bank. However, the direct route would have been extremely dangerous because of Communist artillery barrages.[4]

Youde was allowed to see the commander of the forward head-quarters about an hour after arriving in Puchen. He was received politely, but there was more frustration: 'My request for an unmolested passage for the *Amethyst* was refused after much discussion and reference to a higher organ.' During the talks it was suggested that the ship could be given safe passage if she first helped with the Communist crossing of the Yangtze. When Youde said that was impossible, the commander replied in that case 'you will have to find the solution yourself'. It was argued that *Amethyst* had not received clearance from the People's Liberation Army (PLA) to enter the war zone. There was no reply when Youde pointed out that the Communist authorities in Peking were refusing to accept communications from the British consul. The commander stressed that the 'ship's fire' had caused heavy casualties. Youde countered with the right of self-defence. But most of the casualties probably resulted from the guns of *Consort* and *London*. These ships, like *Amethyst*, were attacked first.[5]

The commander refused to make any approach to his superiors in Peking, and stressed that he had dealt with Youde as an ordinary foreign national, not recognising him as a British diplomat. He declined to provide a pass to allow Youde to cross Communist lines and return to Nanking. 'He assured me, however, that I would be protected and assisted wherever I went by the People's Liberation Army since it was their policy to protect foreigners and his assurance proved to be well-founded.'

Youde now faced the problem of how to get back across the Yangtze, having learned that the Nationalist bridgehead at Pukow had been wiped out on the morning of his departure. One possibility, which did not appeal, was walking to Hankow, hundreds of miles up river. An alternative was to try to cross the river at Nuhu, 50 miles away, in the hope that he could get a train to Nanking. He reflected: 'The only thing that seemed certain was that the Nationalists had sunk everything that floated on the north bank and that unless a miracle happened there would be no possibility of crossing at Pukow for some time.'

The diplomat was given a meal at the headquarters and then 'bidden farewell and left to my own devices'. It was dark and he had no wish to wander around the mine-strewn streets. The owner of the only inn in the town had fled before the Communist occupation. Youde asked two soldiers for help and he ended up sleeping on a straw mat in a hut. In the morning he tried to pay for his accommodation but found that there was 'no market' for his silver dollars, and soldiers suggested he should send a small amount back when he got hold of some Communist currency. Where to go? Despite the attack on Pukow, he decided to see what was happening there. It was only four miles away and, with luck, he might avoid a much longer trek. But all along the route he was told no boats remained and it was impossible to cross the river. He remained optimistic: 'I had a premonition that a visit to Pukow would not be wasted. To my delight as I arrived on the river bank I saw approaching from the other side a steam vessel which had already begun to ferry troops across to Nanking. The Nationalists had deserted the city and the People's Liberation Army was entering unopposed. Again I had no difficulty in obtaining assistance and the officer in charge of embarkation, on hearing of my desire to report to my ambassador as soon as possible on important discussions with the Communists, allotted me a place on the next ferry.'[6]

Youde arrived back in Nanking that morning. 'Profoundly happy', he walked the short distance from the jetty to the embassy, where he briefed Stevenson. The ambassador concluded that the Communists were doing everything to 'disclaim culpability' for the unprovoked attack on a neutral vessel. The British consul in Peking would be told to continue to press the case for a safe passage. 'Our only chance of success seems to be persistence and discreet publicity,' Stevenson reported.[7]

The ambassador acknowledged Youde's 'gallant and most commendable efforts'. Youde had been lucky on two counts: he could easily have become a casualty of the civil war, and he was fortunate not to have been held as a spy. He had crossed from Nationalist lines into Communist territory and then made clear his intention to return to Nanking. Although he was not recognised as a British diplomat, he represented a government that still had dealings with the Nationalists and did not have any sympathy for the Communist cause. Britain was a close ally of the United States, which – like its ambassador, John Stuart – was fiercely anti-Communist.

Youde had been aware that he needed to be cautious:

I purposely avoided asking any more questions than were absolutely necessary in order not to arouse any suspicions of spying in the minds of the Communists. My only documents of identification had been issued by the National Government and were all signed by 'war criminals'. In view of the persistent refusal of the Communist authorities to accept any official document from British representatives I carried no documents issued by the embassy. In these circumstances and in view of the fact that I wished to return to what I thought was Nationalist territory, I attempted to give the impression of having no interest whatsoever in their fighting formations or troop dispositions.

But he had carefully observed the Communist troops he saw, coming to the conclusion that they were 'of a type which one would not expect to find anywhere in China under Nationalist rule'. Their discipline would have 'delighted the heart of any English officer'. They were able to move quickly through the countryside because they treated the peasantry with respect. Relations between officers and other ranks were good, and they all ate the same food and shared accommodation. Morale was 'outstanding'.

Youde had three clear advantages during his mission – his determination, his transparency and his ability to speak fluent Mandarin. But over the three days he made no progress. Lieutenant Commander Kerans was about to find out how difficult it would be to persuade the Communists to accept a solution – and he would have a great deal longer.

9

Trapped

KERANS HAD BEEN INFORMED OF Edward Youde's mission, and was pinning his hopes on the diplomat achieving the breakthrough that would allow *Amethyst* to make an early return to Shanghai. As morning broke on 23 April, it was clear that the Communists had successfully crossed the Yangtze. From the ship there was no sign of any Nationalist soldiers. They had retreated rapidly south. A large area of the south bank would soon be in Communist hands.

Shortly before 0800, Kerans received a signal from Vice Admiral Madden suggesting that *Amethyst* might attempt to sail down river at night. The navigation would be tricky but the magnetic compass and gyro were in reasonable condition, and the steering and main engines were working. Repairs were carried out, and sacks of flour were packed around the bridge, wheelhouse, W/T office and 'B' gun to give protection against splinters. 'I had presumed that the risk of grounding had to be taken and considered that every effort was necessary and acceptable in order to extricate the ship while there was a temporary lull,' Kerans noted.[1]

Madden was told by Ambassador Stevenson that if *Amethyst* attempted to sail to Nanking it would probably result in a further loss of life, and even if the warship reached her destination it was doubtful 'whether the position would be improved in the long run'.[2] So within a short time, a huge question mark had arisen over the wisdom of having a guardship at Nanking at the time of a major Communist offensive. If *Amethyst*, in her weakened condition, had reached the capital she might well have been seized by the Communists or been destroyed by reinforced batteries in any attempt to escape.

Shortly after noon Communist troops were spotted apparently setting up a battery on Ta-Sha Island, within range of *Amethyst,* to cover another crossing, and Kerans decided to move the ship a short distance down river, but artillery fire opened up, probably from Yung lung-chew Island, and she headed back at full speed, anchoring close to the south bank at a spot between the villages of Tan ta-chen and Chen-pi Chen-kou. The firing stopped and there were no hits.

Amethyst was trapped: 'It now appeared all too evident that in whatever direction we went we were bound to come under heavy fire and that the Communists had no intention of showing any restraint towards *Amethyst*.' The ship was in danger of becoming caught in a withering crossfire. Against that, it could only reply with one 4in gun and an Oerlikon, manned by inexperienced sailors. 'This could not have been effective for long,' Kerans bleakly observed. 'It appeared that the Communists could destroy us when they chose.'

Morale was good 'in spite of the hopelessness of our plight'. Kerans added: 'I realised, however, that it might snap at any moment and that breaking point had almost been reached. Considering the youthfulness of the majority, it is a tribute to British spirit in adversity that it had remained as high as it did after three days under fire with heavy casualties and damage.'

But the captain had decided that if *Amethyst* came under accurate fire again he would beach the ship, open all seacocks and set her on fire. The remaining crew would then make their way overland to Shanghai.[3] Madden accepted that this was the last resort:

It was clear that if *Amethyst* was again deliberately fired at without any provocation, the Communists were determined to sink or capture her and there was no alternative except to destroy her our-selves. At the same time, this would be tantamount to a Communist victory, and voluntary destruction by us might anticipate this Communist move and so mitigate the loss of prestige. It did, how-ever, seem very unlikely that the Communists would, in fact, deliberately attack the *Amethyst* observing that this would be a direct act of war from which little would be gained, and they were already heavily engaged against the Nationalists.[4]

One man feeling the strain but bearing up well was Jack French, the only telegraphist on board, who was sending and receiving all the messages. He would spend six days at his post without a proper break. The RAF doctor gave him Benzedrine to keep him awake. When he learned that they might have to abandon the ship, French came up with his own contingency plan: 'I got a Durex from the sick bay and I put my Hong Kong money inside and tied it round my neck. I thought I could use the money to get passage. Most of us thought that way.' Throughout *Amethyst*'s ordeal on the Yangtze, the telegraphist, a West Country lad who left school at 14, would be the key link with the outside world.[5]

During the afternoon of 23 April Communist troops made significant crossings of the river ahead and astern of the frigate. Kerans was glad he had moved the ship in view of the fact that the previous anchorage would have been on one of the approaches. *Amethyst* was not threatened, but at about 2200 nine Nationalist warships came into view on their way down river, probably from Nanking. The fourth vessel suddenly fired shots at Ta-Sha Island. That was the signal for 'everything' to open fire. Kerans feared that *Amethyst*, which was deliberately darkened, might be illuminated and mistaken for one of the Nationalist vessels. The engagement lasted about an hour. None of the ships was apparently hit but two large fires were seen in the vicinity of one of the Communist batteries. Kerans thought of following the ships but decided against it: 'The political aspect and lack of knowledge of Chinese naval intentions would have been an unwarranted risk and nor was *Amethyst* in a fit state to accept further damage by gunfire.'[6]

Early the next day, 24 April, the frigate took on a serious list to starboard. Water was pouring through a hole on the waterline in the wardroom and plates had been weakened. Topweight, including the ship's disabled motorboat, was jettisoned. Water was pumped out of the wardroom and the hole packed with cement. The ship was littered with splintered wood and other debris, and it was also decided to reduce the fire risks. Ready-use ammunition went overboard with the rubbish. Decks were scrubbed and 'we got rid of all the blood'. *Amethyst* regained an even keel.[7]

The ship had taken numerous hits and was peppered with holes, including a large one in her stern. At one stage Lieutenant Hett had asked shipwright William Smith to check the hole in the stern. 'I suggested going on a raft on a line and floating round the ship and taking a look at it,' said Smith. 'So they got a raft ready with a length of rope and I floated round to the stern. Just then they started firing from both banks. Of course the ones on the quarterdeck all ran away and left me floating there. When the firing stopped they came out again and pulled me back. Needless to say I won't tell you what I said about that.'[8]

On the morning of 24 April, Kerans learned that Youde's mission had failed. There was disappointment but 'genuine admiration for his valiant efforts'. The diplomat was known to many of the crew because of *Amethyst*'s visit to Nanking the previous year. Civilian junks had started using the river again and Kerans thought of taking the ship a few miles up river to Chingkiang and try to contact the Communist authorities there. Madden had suggested earlier that a cautious approach might be worth considering. 'I eventually came to the conclusion that any movement was an unacceptable risk,' Kerans reported. Madden then advised him to remain in position in case 'local action might prejudice negotiations in Nanking'.

10

War of Words

THE FIRST SEA LORD, Admiral of the Fleet Lord Fraser of North Cape, had a simple philosophy: leave it to the man on the spot. Unfortunately, the most senior man on the spot was not there; he was with Admiral Fraser in London. Admiral Sir Patrick Brind, Commander-in-Chief, Far East Station, had left his headquarters at the shore base HMS *Terror* in Singapore to attend Exercise Trident, a major policy seminar for service chiefs at the Royal Naval College, Greenwich. It just so happened that 20 April was the first day of the conference. Fraser had been woken at the Admiralty in the early hours with news of the *Amethyst* crisis. At a press conference before the start of the seminar he felt obliged to make some comments: 'Of course the first thing to do is to think, what are we going to do about this? Our principle, of course, is always the same – leave it to the man on the spot, except where you can give him assistance, so that all the Admiralty had to do was to inform the Foreign Office, who informed the prime minister and the minister of defence. Then we waited for the reports from the flag officer out there, and, sure enough, a little later on came his dispositions.' The admiral, who led the hunt that destroyed the Gernan battlecruiser *Scharnhorst* in 1943, admitted there was not much news. There were 'some casualties', *Consort* had been in action, and *London* and *Black Swan* were not far from Shanghai. There was a barbed reference to his audience of journalists: 'You always, I think, regard the Royal Navy as a thorn in your sides, so I thought I would try and do my best to give you the latest information. Sometimes you are a bit of a thorn in our sides.'[1] Fraser was right to wonder how thorny the issue might become. The attack was about to generate headlines around the world, and there would be questions – taken up by some of Britain's leading politicians – about the decision to send *Amethyst* up the Yangtze when the Communists were about to launch a major offensive across the river.

Admiral Brind had taken up his appointment less than four months earlier, and was not involved in the original decision to station a guardship at Nanking. However, before he left Singapore he was made aware of the move to replace *Consort* with *Amethyst*. He felt uncomfortable being in London when the Far East Station was facing such a challenging time. In a letter to his wife Edie, who was still in Singapore, he wrote: 'As you will realise I am very disturbed about the "doings" in the Yangtze – poor little *Amethyst* and the casualties in the other ships. I have been feeling very sad, for I knew beforehand that the move was to take place and was a little anxious that it might coincide with Communist activity.' The First Sea Lord had been 'splendid', leaving it to Vice Admiral Madden to sort out.[2]

On a visit to Cardiff, Lord Hall, First Lord of the Admiralty, paid tribute to the 'magnificent gallantry' of *Amethyst*'s crew, and observed: 'It is an incident which should never have taken place, but it does indeed indicate the inhuman feelings of those who were responsible for such a catastrophe.'[3]

In a leader comment, *The Daily Telegraph* said:

Public opinion has understandably been deeply perturbed and shocked by the recent series of unfortunate happenings on the Yangtze involving casualties and damage to British naval vessels. This concern is intensified by the confusion in which the whole incident is wrapped. At a time when Chinese Communist forces were known to be attempting to cross the Yangtze, HMS *Amethyst* was sent up river with supplies for Nanking from Shanghai. There was, and could be, no question of any aggressive intentions, but in the circumstances certain obvious risks were involved. If it is entirely clear that the attack on the *Amethyst* by Chinese Communist artillery was unprovoked and indefensible, it is also clear that the possibility of such an attack might, and indeed should, have been foreseen. By the same token, the various attempts which have been made to extricate the vessel from its dangerous predicament were likewise evidently hazardous.[4]

The *Daily Express* took a similar line:

It was known that the Communist armies were about to launch a grand assault across the river. It was expected within a matter of hours. To get supplies to the British embassy in Nanking became a necessity. And it was no less urgent to provide a means of evacuation. But was the best method adopted to secure these results? Was a sufficient foresight displayed?

No doubt some risks were involved whatever course was adopted. Air transport would have perils of its own, and Shanghai, the air base, might fall at any moment. Even so, an expedition up No Man's River, when any hour might be zero hour, can only be justified if it is proved that every other method of performing the task had been rejected for good reason.[5]

Both newspapers mentioned the necessity of getting supplies to the embassy. Journalists had been misled on this point. *Amethyst* was taking supplies but that was not the reason for her mission to Nanking, as a briefing paper for Foreign Secretary Ernest Bevin pointed out: 'I should make it clear that *Amethyst* was not proceeding to Nanking . . . for the purpose of taking stores to the embassy, but to relieve *Consort*. We have had a ship at Nanking in order to come to the assistance of British nationals in the event of a complete breakdown of law and order. This is not the first time in the turbulent history of China that ships have come under fire from warring Chinese armies, but that does not of course make the present occasion any less regrettable.' [6]

The *News Chronicle* criticised naval chiefs in the Far East as they 'seemed to run things pretty fine', and the *Daily Worker*, newspaper of the Communist Party of Great Britain, called for all British military forces to be withdrawn from China immediately. The press in the United States, in general, took the attacks on the ships as a warning of the kind of treatment that Western nations could expect from Communist China. A leader in *The New York Times*, headed 'Murder on the Yangtze', said: 'What this tragedy seems to show is that Chinese Communists are as reckless of human life as their Russian brethren.' The *Washington Post* commented that Britain had paid no heed to danger signals on the Yangtze and that 'diplomats and naval men still had their heads in the nineteenth century'.[7]

The Chinese Communist media gave its account of events on the Yangtze, which differed greatly from reports in Western newspapers. According to the New China News Agency, the PLA had defeated a joint naval attack by the Nationalists and the 'British imperialist navy'. On 20 April two warships sailing from the east suddenly opened fire on

PLA positions on the north bank. Fire was returned and both ships were sunk, one near Chingkiang. On the following day two more warships (*London* and *Black Swan?*) appeared from the east. Troops fired first to keep them away from river crossing points, and the vessels were hit and headed back. The agency reported: 'This victory over the enemy vessels enabled the PLA to cross the river on a large scale in the afternoon of the same day.'[8]

At home, anger at the attacks on the ships was growing, as Harry Pollitt, secretary of Britain's Communist Party, discovered. He unwisely tried to address an open-air meeting in the naval town of Dartmouth. Some 1,000 people gathered and there were furious exchanges. The father of Petty Officer John Akhurst, from Dartmouth, who was killed in *Consort*, stepped forward and handed Pollitt a rope with a noose and a note saying: 'Judas Iscariot was presented with one of these and used it. I invite you to do likewise – C F Akhurst, father of one of the boys your friends murdered on the Yangtze River on Wednesday, April 20.'

Someone shouted: 'Who paid for the shell that killed Mr Akhurst's son?' Pollitt replied: 'I am prepared to say on the authority of *The Times* and the *Daily Express* that the shells which Communists and Nationalists are firing were sent from the US. I will apologise if, on the authority of *The Times*, it should be proved that there are any Russian arms in China at all.'

There were boos, cries of 'Down with Russia', an egg smashed at his feet, and a red flag was grabbed, trampled on and burned. A man shouted: 'What would you do if you were in the *Amethyst*?' Pollitt said: 'I should do what our British boys are doing. I should be asking, "Why were we ordered up here without someone making sure it was known to the authorities on both sides of the river?"' There were a few more exchanges and then the crowd surged forward. As police appealed for calm, fighting broke out. Pollitt was escorted away and took refuge in the home of one of his supporters, which was surrounded by about 100 people. He managed to escape in the early hours.[9] Despite his reception at Dartmouth, the brash Pollitt turned up in Plymouth, *Amethyst*'s home city, two days later for another speaking engagement. Sailors and ex-navy men forced the doors of the hall where the meeting was being held, shouting, 'What about the *Amethyst*?' A steward was knocked down and chairs were thrown at the platform. The doors were wedged shut with a ladder as around 5,000 people gathered outside, shouting and booing. Police pushed Pollitt and another Communist official into a side room. They eventually escaped in a police car.[10]

A similar incident took place in Melbourne when angry sailors and former sevicemen confronted Communist leaders at a meeting near the Yarra River. In response to shouts about *Amethyst*, Communist official John Arrowsmith said: 'The British imperialists sent warships up the Yangtze and they were inadvertently fired at by both sides because they were right in the firing line.' He taunted hecklers by saying they 'needed a full rum issue to stand up to the Russian army'. The sailors rushed at the Communists' platform with cries of 'throw him in the river'. Police broke up the meeting, and Arrowsmith was punched on the head as he tried to leave in a car.[11]

With some irony, Australia's prime minister, Ben Chifley, whose government had prevented *Shoalhaven* from sailing up the Yangtze to Nanking, was in London for the 1949 Commonwealth conference. It would be many years before the *Shoalhaven* decision was revealed. Chifley made no public comment on *Amethyst*. He was seen walking in St James's Park, smoking his pipe and 'admiring the spring showing of flowers'.[12]

On 24 April the *Sunday Express* devoted much of its front page to the crisis, with the banner headline, WHO FAILED BRITAIN?. Below the headline was the sub-deck, Questions on the Yangtze disaster that need to be answered. The report was bylined Group Captain H S L Dundas DSO, DFC, air correspondent, and Alan Brockbank, naval correspondent, and asked two further questions. Who ordered the ships up the Yangtze between two armies in full battle, without air cover? Who is responsible for the lack of aircraft in China to give coverage had it been ordered? It was pointed out that such questions would normally be answered by the minister of defence, Albert Alexander, in the House of Commons – but he was due to go on holiday the following day. Alexander had arranged to sail from Southampton in the 'luxury pleasure ship *Venus*' for Oslo, where he would be attending May Day celebrations. The report suggested that it might be 'judicious' to abandon the trip. On the question of air cover, there was specualtion that one wing of bomb and rocket-carrying aircraft could have averted disaster, but the RAF's Mosquitos and Beaufighters were left 'sitting inactive 3,000 miles away in Singapore'. And the nearest aircraft carrier was 'half a world away' in the Mediterranean. On 25 April a leader in the *Daily Express* accused the ruling socialists of a blame game involving the Foreign Office, Alexander and Lord Hall. It had further questions. Who is to be punished? Who is to be cashiered, so that never again can his folly jeopardise the lives of our fighting men?

That day Admiral Brind wrote another letter to his wife Edie: 'What a lot I have left on Alex's [Madden's] shoulders, though it is hard to say whether I should have been able to help him much more from Singapore. But it does seem to be wrong to be at home when this is going on. Poor Alex and his chaps have been having a very hard time; we have got to find a way out for little *Amethyst* and the Shanghai problem is a real bad one – with 4,800 of our nationals there' [The British Government was concerned that Communists forces would soon seize Shanghai, threatening nationals and business interests]'. Brind went on: 'I have felt very much at a loose end here, although I think I have been able to help to some extent. The press is (a large part of it) very hostile, some against the navy, talking of blunders in high places, and some against the ministers. This latter I resent, for they cannot possibly be held responsible for professional matters like the *Amethyst* operation.' He had decided to cut short his visit to Britain and return to the Far East: 'It is natural that folk should wonder why the blazes I am here.'

On the morning of 26 April, Prime Minister Clement Attlee held a Cabinet meeting. Among those present were Foreign Secretary Bevin and Minister of Defence Alexander, who had, in fact, postponed his visit to Norway. Lord Hall, Admiral Fraser, Field Marshal Sir William Slim, Chief of the Imperial General Staff, and Marshal of the Royal Air Force Lord Tedder, Chief of the Air Staff, were also invited. The main purpose of the meeting was to discuss a statement that Attlee would make on the *Amethyst* crisis in the Commons that afternoon. Lord Hall planned to make a similar statement in the House of Lords.

There was some discussion on whether reference should be made to the fact that movements of British warships in China had been done with the full knowledge and consent of the Nationalist government. But it was noted: 'Since it was obvious that the authority of the National government had been greatly weakened, it might be said that this was a formal rather than a practical step to have taken; and attention was drawn to a statement issued by the Chinese embassy in London on the previous day that the National government had advised foreign powers in February last to withdraw warships from the Yangtze in view of the risk of incidents.' It was decided to delete references in the draft statement to the 'inhumanity' of the Communists' actions because of the risks that *Amethyst* and British communities in China were still facing.

11

The Politicians Fight it Out

THERE WERE ANGRY CLASHES IN the Commons on 26 April after Attlee made a lengthy statement on the Yangtze attacks. The Conservative leader, Winston Churchill, accused the Labour government of blaming senior officers in the Far East for its own failings. Gesturing towards Minister of Defence Alexander, Churchill said: 'Should you not have kept in close touch instead of leaving it to the men on the spot? Would it not have been right for you to know that this ship [*Amethyst*] was to proceed up the river, with the Communists entrenched on the north bank for weeks and that the armistice was expiring in a few hours? Surely the government should have known that. It ought to have been in the closest touch with its officers on the spot instead of throwing the whole burden on them and expecting to get off behind them for all its muddles.'

Attlee leaped from the front bench 'as if he had been sprung up', and said: 'I am not prepared to take that from Mr Churchill. Of course we keep in touch with the situation. There is no question of sheltering behind any commander.' Churchill was perhaps being mischievous. As Admiral Brind had pointed out to his wife, ministers were not responsible for routine operational matters. It is not clear if even Foreign Secretary Bevin and Admiral Fraser knew about *Amethyst*'s movements, and it is doubtful whether Alexander or Lord Hall were informed. But Attlee would have found it difficult to admit to a packed Commons that his government had been in the dark.

Churchill raised the question of air power, and asked why the navy did not have aircraft carriers off the coast of China 'capable of affording protection to our nationals in the only way understood by those who attack and murder and insult us – namely by the effective power of retaliation'. Attlee stressed that there was no question of air cover because it would have turned a peaceful mission into an act of war. On the timing of *Amethyst*'s trip, he pointed out that the frigate sailed from Shanghai on 19 April, expecting to arrive the following day, and the Communist ultimatum to the Nationalist government did not expire until the 21st. Churchill demanded that the government deal with the crisis in a 'robust spirit'.

The question of air power was pursued by other Members of Parliament. Conservative John Boyd-Carpenter noted that there had been two aircraft carriers on the Far East Station two years earlier. 'Where are they now?' he asked. Attlee stressed again that *Amethyst* was engaged on a peaceful mission and not a punitive war – and none of the questioners had suggested what use would be made of aircraft in those conditions. When Conservatives derided that remark, the prime minister said: 'I am quite well aware that aircraft are used in warfare but this is not a matter of warfare at all. The ships were engaged in bringing up supplies and it would have been quite unusual to provide a bomber force in such an operation.' The point about supplies was misleading, as a briefing paper for the foreign secretary had already noted. The main argument for having a guardship at Nanking was to evacuate nationals in an emergency, and *Amethyst* was sent specifically to relieve *Consort*.

The Conservative deputy leader, Anthony Eden, argued that if it was not provocative to send warships up the Yangtze, why would it have been any more of a provocation to give them air cover? When Attlee appeared unwilling to reply, opposition MPs shouted, 'Answer'. The prime minister seemed to contradict his earlier statement about not sheltering behind any commander, saying: 'I leave these matters to be decided by commanders on the spot. I am not trying to shelter myself. I take full responsibility. But now I am being asked to give details of how to conduct this operation of keeping a warship at Nanking.' Conservative MP Brigadier Antony Head was shouted down by Labour members when he observed: 'The inference is that no air support was available.' Attlee admitted that the RAF did not have any planes based in Shanghai.

In his initial statement, the prime minister said that Ambassador Stevenson and consular officials had remained at their posts in China because of Britain's considerable interests. Movements of warships had taken place with the consent of the Nationalist government. 'I want to make the point, therefore, that the *Amethyst* was proceeding on her lawful occasions and that there was no other properly constituted authority to whom the government were under any obligation to notify her movements.'

Attlee pointed to the urgency of relieving *Consort* because the destroyer was low on supplies. This was misleading. *Consort*'s captain revealed in his report on the ship's actions of 20 April that he could have remained a lot longer at Nanking where, in any case, there was a large reserve of fuel oil. The prime minister also made the odd claim that *Amethyst* needed to replace *Consort* because a frigate was more suitable than a destroyer.

Two key questions had arisen from the attacks on the British ships. Why did they suffer such extensive damage and casualties? Why were they not able to silence the opposing batteries and fight their way through? 'In answer to the first, I would only say that warships are not designed to operate in rivers against massed artillery and infantry sheltered by reeds,' said Attlee. 'The Communist forces appeared to have been concentrated in considerable strength and are reported as being lavishly equipped with howitzers, medium artillery and field guns. These facts also provide much of the answer to the second question – the flag officer's policy throughout was designed only to rescue the *Amethyst* and to avoid unnecessary casualties. There was no question of a punitive expedition, and our ships fired only to silence the forces firing against them.'

Although there might have been an initial misunderstanding, there was no excuse for mistaking the identity of *Amethyst*, and the prime minister rejected as 'fantastic and unfounded' Communist claims that British ships had been trying to oppose the crossing of the Yangtze. He criticised Communist leaders for failing to respond to 'our ambassador's message'. This was misleading. Ambassador Stevenson had refused to be involved directly, and two messages had come from the consul in Peking. The prime minister continued: 'Moreover, had the Communist authorities objected in the past to the movement of British ships on the Yangtze it was always open to them to raise these through our consular authorities in north China. It is the fact that for reasons best known to themselves the Communists have failed to notify any foreign authority present in areas which they have occupied of the channels through which contact can be maintained and that they have rejected all communications made to them. In these circumstances the government can only reserve its position.'

The prime minister expressed deepest sympathy with the relatives of the dead and wounded, and paid tribute to the conduct of *Amethyst*'s ship's company, which was 'beyond all praise', especially as so many sailors were young and had not experienced being under fire before. Five people were named for their courage and fortitude – Lieutenant Commander Bernard Skinner, Lieutenant Geoffrey Weston, Telegraphist Jack French, Flight Lieutenant Ken Letford, the Sunderland pilot, and diplomat Edward Youde. Attlee continued: 'I have heard too that in HMS *London* and HMS *Black Swan*, when there was a possibility of volunteers being flown to the *Amethyst*, there was almost acrimonious rivalry for selection, as they put it, "to go back for more".'

In the Lords, Lord Hall repeated the prime minister's statement and then faced questioning from Lord Swinton, the acting Conservative leader in the house. Had it really been necessary to relieve *Consort*? The destroyer could have been ordered to return to Shanghai, and arrangements made for planes to take part in any evacuation from Nanking. When did the Cabinet, the Admiralty and the minister of defence consider the matter? Lord Hall seemed to confirm that ministers had been caught out by events, replying: 'We have not the whole facts. Certain facts were brought to our notice today. But further investigation will have to take place.' Tellingly, there was no mention in Parliament that *Amethyst* had replaced *Shoalhaven* because the Australian government refused to send its ship. Nor was there any reference to a similar refusal by the US Navy.

That evening the Admiralty issued a statement in which Vice Admiral Madden saluted the crews of all the ships. In addition to the names mentioned in the Commons, there was praise for Lieutenant Peter Berger, Surgeon Lieutenant John Alderton, Gunner Eric Monaghan and Electrical Artificer Lionel Chare, who had refused to take any rest until he had rigged up emergency lighting in *Amethyst* and helped with the wounded. Two Royal Marines from *London* who turned down medical treatment for 24 hours until more urgent cases were dealt with were also commended – Bernard How had a hole right through his shoulder and Robert McCarthy had a piece of shrapnel the size of a cork embedded in his neck.[1]

On the day that Parliament tackled the issue, Communist troops were still pouring across the Yangtze. Large numbers of junks passed ahead and astern of *Amethyst*. Shortly before noon there was a significant development. The Communists apparently were ready to talk. Three soldiers and two civilians appeared on the south bank and began shouting at the ship, indicating that they wanted a boat to be sent. *Amethyst*'s remaining whaler had been patched up, but Lieutenant Commander Kerans did not want to risk it in the choppy waters. A Chinese steward, shouting back, tried to point this out, and eventually the party left. At about 1600 the soldiers returned without the civilians. As the weather conditions were now calm Kerans decided to send the whaler and he called for a volunteer crew of strong swimmers, who quickly came forward. Kerans did not want to risk one of his few officers, and it was decided to put a volunteer, Petty Officer William Freeman, in charge and wearing Lieutenant George Strain's uniform so that 'face' – so important in Chinese society – would not be lost. When the boat reached the shore, Freeman and steward But Sai Tin, acting as an interpreter, were taken to a nearby village. After an hour's wait an officer arrived. He was identified as 'Major Kung', commander of the main battery opposite Rose Island that had launched the devastating attack on *Amethyst*.

Talks began and the first point raised by Major Kung was the responsibility for opening fire. He insisted that *Amethyst* had fired first. Freeman, of course, denied this. Kung said the frigate was recognised as British and he had given orders to his battery to return fire only if attacked. He went on to state that the ship would not be harmed provided there was 'no trouble' and she did not move from her anchorage. He was not empowered to grant safe passage down river – permission would have to come from the new authorities in Nanking. The Sunderland flying boat was fired on because it did not have clearance from the PLA. When it was pointed out that the plane had been on a mercy mission, Kung said his men would have provided medical help.

British gunfire resulted in some 250 casualties among Communist forces and the local peasantry. The inlet at San Chiang Ying opposite Rose Island had been packed with junks and other craft, and the area was 'plastered' by *Consort* when she passed *Amethyst*. Kung asked about British casualties and the figures were given. Kerans reported: 'The interview throughout was reasonably cordial and it became evident in conversation that he was worried about outside reaction to the People's Liberation Army. He wound up the meeting by stating that the Chinese and British had always been friends. Major Kung spoke a little English towards the close of the interview, and offered to assist us with a sampan in future.' Kerans was left with the impression that his superiors had reprimanded Kung for his hasty actions. There was also confirmation that *Amethyst* was trapped and that any further help from the air was out of the question because it would only attract fire. The meeting was reported to Madden.

On the next day soon after noon a junk went alongside *Amethyst* and delivered a letter asking Kerans to go ashore for a meeting with Kung. The captain still did not want to leave his ship at such a difficult time and Lieutenant Hett went in his place, with an interpreter. Once again the talks began with the question of who was responsible for opening fire first, and this went on for some time, ending in deadlock. Kerans pointed out:

> No amount of persuasion could convince him that *Amethyst* did not open fire first. In actual fact *Amethyst* did not open fire until the ship had been hit and was aground. It seemed evident to Lieutenant Hett that the battery commander had been present all the time at San Chiang Ying and that it was not hasty errors on the part of his subordinates. The meeting continued and Major Kung assured us of our personal safety in this area once again and at the same time subtly recommending us to remain where we were. He made the rather limp statement that Chinese [Nationalist] naval units were still in the upper Yangtze and might attempt to break out – if we moved down river the batteries would be liable to mistake us for one of these units.

Kung reiterated that a promise of safe passage could only come from the authorities in Nanking, and he suggested the British ambassador should make an approach. There were eight Chinese on board the ship, and Kung said they were free to go ashore. He was willing to give assistance, which was understood to mean medical help. Hett passed on a request for a meeting with the army commander in Chingkiang. Kerans reported: 'There is no shadow of doubt that Major Kung could have been under no misapprehension regarding the identity of *Amethyst*. The number of direct hits on the starboard side, including the bridge, indicated that there was adequate time to identify the ship. He could not have genuinely thought that *Amethyst* fired first, and I came to the conclusion that he was adopting a policy of vacillation for his own ends.'[2]

12

The Navy Sails Away

THE FIRST SEA LORD CAREFULLY considered the questions that had been raised in Parliament. Although Prime Minister Attlee gave answers, Admiral Fraser wanted to make his own assessment. After consulting Admiral Brind he decided there were five key points. Why was a warship used to supply stores for the British embassy and community instead of transport aircraft? Why was *Amethyst* not given fighter cover? When it was decided to use *London* and *Black Swan*, why was air support not asked for? Should the Admiralty have kept a closer watch? Why were there no aircraft carriers available?

Fraser considered the background, which echoed the reasons for the navy wanting to resume patrols in China after the Second World War: 'For years the White Ensign has been well known and respected on the China coast and on the Yangtze. There are innumerable examples right up to recent times of the steadying effect on both Europeans and Chinese of the presence of a British warship. By going about their ordinary business calmly and with dignity the British navy has frequently contributed greatly to the maintenance of law and order. It is quite clear in China now that this reputation, established during the last century, still stands.'

Fraser noted that *Amethyst* had been carrying some stores for the embassy, but the main reason for her presence at Nanking was to reassure the British community and to provide communications for the ambassador. Transport aircraft could have been used to take supplies but there may have been complications using the city's airfield, which was in Nationalist hands. On the questions relating to air support, it was clear that the ships were taking part in peaceful missions and fighter escorts would have been seen as a provocation. In any case, the only suitable planes, Beaufighters, were in Singapore and would have needed to operate from a Nationalist air base 'thus participating in the civil war'. After the attack on *Amethyst* Vice Admiral Madden, rightly, was not concerned with reprisals. Fraser pointed out: 'The possibility of reprisals or other action to redress the insult to our flag was for later consideration.' And the use of air support for *London* and *Black Swan* would have been a clear act of war.

Perhaps the most important question – and one pressed by Churchill – concerned the Admiralty's awareness of decisions taken by the Far East Station. On this point Fraser was clear. The general policy of supporting the British community at a time of crisis was 'fully recognised in London'. The policy had been reviewed in the January, and it was decided that the advantages outweighed the dangers. The First Sea Lord was also clear that it was 'quite impracticable' to control from a distance the day-to-day movements of ships. 'This must be left to the local senior naval officer who, in consultation with the ambassador, can alone possess the necessary local knowledge of a fluctuating situation.' On the question of aircraft carriers, these were withdrawn from the station at the end of 1947 because of poor facilities for training and to save money. However, the same arguments applied to carrier aircraft as to RAF fighters. It was not Madden's intention to inflame a growing crisis.[1]

In Nanking, Ambassador Stevenson remained at his post. Nationalist leaders had abandoned the capital, along with their soldiers and police, before the Communist takeover. There was considerable gunfire over several nights but this came from naval craft on the Yangtze. Before the PLA marched into the city local Communists broke cover and made some attempt to keep order in the face of looting by civilians. The looters targeted empty government offices and homes of officials who had fled as well as British firms. They took everything from plumbing and electrical fittings to windows and doors. At the airport the wealthy piled into planes with as many possessions as they could take, only to discover that the pilots had defected or disappeared. Demolition charges left by the Nationalists caused some civilian casualties and explosives destroyed the entrance hall of the railway station, although the tracks were undamaged. All shipping on the south bank appeared to be out of action. On the evening of 24 April, a small group of Communist soldiers entered the British embassy compound intent on making a search. It was pointed out to them that they could not do this without the permission of the ambassador. Stevenson reported: 'They were quiet and good tempered but looked slightly sheepish. On my instructions they were told that I could not permit a search and it was suggested that they should go and seek orders from higher authority.' The soldiers left and did not return.[2]

The US ambassador, John Stuart, had a more unpleasant experience at his residence. He woke early on 25 April to find Communist soldiers in his bedroom. 'I shouted at them asking what they were doing, and they withdrew, one or two muttering angrily,' Stuart recalled.

I jumped out of bed to see what it was all about when the whole group, some ten or twelve, returned and the spokesman quite politely explained that they were only looking around for fun and meant no harm. The soldiers were nothing more than country boys impressed into service and carefully indoctrinated. They had come with an easy victory to the great capital and were out seeing the sights. When they arrived at my front gate the terrified gateman on night duty lost his head and instead of reporting to the house as was the rule yielded to the threats and admitted the intruders. Still less did these rustics know anything about diplomatic immunity.

The State Department told Stuart to make a strong protest but there were no diplomatic relations with the Communists and, as Stevenson had found, it was impossible to make contact with their leaders. However, the leadership did learn about the incident and the soldiers were held in custody for 'further education'.[3] Mao, in fact, gave instructions on how soldiers should behave towards foreigners in Nanking. All foreign institutions were to be protected but there would be no recognition of embassies or their diplomatic personnel. Foreigners would not be arrested even if they broke martial law regulations.[4]

In Shanghai, the dead from *Consort* and *London*, along with a sailor from *Amethyst* who succumbed to his wounds, had been buried at Hung Jao Cemetery on 23 April. With some irony, the firing party was provided by *Shoalhaven*, which had remained at Shanghai in a communications role. Early the following day, Lieutenant Commander Skinner and an able seaman from *London*, Geoffrey Warwick, were buried at sea by *Consort* as she made her way to Hong Kong. That day, a Sunday, also saw a memorial service at Shanghai Cathedral, which was attended by a large number of foreign residents and officers and men from all the ships there. One man noticeably missing from both services was Madden, who decided he should remain 'in absolutely continuous touch with operations at this time'. The Sunday marked Anzac Day – another irony – but because of the crisis no special arrangements had been made, although Australian and New Zealand citizens in Shanghai were invited on board *Shoalhaven* in return for the hospitality the ship's company had received.

It is not known how this goodwill gesture went down with Madden, who had lost dozens of British sailors, but on 26 April he ordered *Shoalhaven* to leave Shanghai and go to Kure, Japan. Madden said this move had been planned for some, but the frigate's captain, Lieutenant Commander William Tapp, was taken by surprise. At the time of sailing, he had no idea of his mission: 'It was thought the government's policy had effected *Shoalhaven*'s movements, but this was only partly confirmed by Radio Australia, whilst the ship was on passage, and then definitely by the Commander-in-Chief BCOF [British Commonwealth Occupation Force] on arrival at Kure.'[5] Madden may have decided that he could no longer count on Australian warships and the presence of *Shoalhaven* was an embarrassment. He almost certainly came under renewed pressure from the Australian government. A report in the *Sydney Morning Herald* on 28 April stated: 'It was learned in the highest authority today that the Australian government would not send any warships or troops to reinforce British and American forces in China unless requested to do so by the British government. The authority said that the British government was in charge of all Far Eastern stations.' The Canberra government had, however, asked Britain to protect all Australian nationals.

Despite the attack on four British warships and the rapid advance of Communist forces, Tapp had other concerns. He lamented that very little sport had been possible in Shanghai because April was the month for switching from hockey and football to cricket. And there had been more cases of venereal disease.[6] The crews of *Amethyst*, *Consort*, *London* and *Black Swan* would all qualify for the Naval General Service Medal with the clasp Yangtze 1949. Remarkably, some of the men who were in *Shoalhaven* and *Warramunga*, which had made a hasty departure from Nanking in the January, also applied for the medal. Their requests were turned down.[7]

Madden received a number of messages of sympathy. They included condolences from the acting president of China, Li Tsung-

jen, the commander of the US Navy's western Pacific fleet, Vice
Admiral Badger, Foreign Secretary Bevin, Ambassador Stevenson, the
Board of Admiralty and even the mayor of Widnes, Cheshire, which
had links with *Black Swan*. No messages apparently were sent by
Australia's Prime Minister Chifley, Minister for External Affairs
Herbert Evatt or the Chief of Navy Staff, Rear Admiral (later Vice
Admiral Sir) John Collins.[8] Chifley's attitude was probably summed
up by an answer he gave in the House of Representatives when asked
about the fate of *Amethyst*. He said: 'It is not our problem to enquire
what the Royal Navy does about its ships . . .'[9]

The swift advance of Communist forces was another headache for
Madden, who faced two important questions. Should there be a
general evacuation of British nationals from Shanghai? How long
could he keep his ships there? If the Communists seized the Woosung
forts near the mouth of the Yangtze, his vessels could end up being
trapped on the Whangpoo River at Shanghai. Madden consulted the
British consul, Robert Urquhart, Admiral Badger and the senior
French naval officer. It was decided not to order Operation Legionary,
the general evacuation plan. Instead, women and children were
advised to leave, and people doing essential jobs were urged to remain.
Operation Legionary involved sending in British troops. Madden
reported: 'It was now clearly inadvisable – even if possible – to land
British troops at Shanghai and, in view of the *Amethyst* incident, the
presence of the Royal Navy was likely to be an irritant to the People's
Liberation Army.'

It was announced that women and children could sail in a Dutch
ship, the *Boissevain*, on 28 April. A Royal Fleet Auxiliary, *Fort
Charlotte*, was also made available. In the event, only 160 of the 700
places in *Boissevain* were taken and just twelve people boarded *Fort
Charlotte*. Most preferred to remain in Shanghai. Foreign business
interests in the city were so great that there was a widespread reluctance
to abandon them. There was also a feeling that the Communist leaders
would not want them jeopardised either. Communist soldiers were well
disciplined and reports of their behaviour in Nanking – with only a
few excesses – would have filtered through to Shanghai. By that time
London and *Constance* had left along with Badger's flagship, the USS
Eldorado, an amphibious force command vessel, the USS *Chilton*, an
attack transport, and the French minesweeper *Commandant de*

Pimodan. *Black Swan* was the last warship to leave, having waited for the arrival of *Boissevain*.

London, with Madden on board, headed for Alacrity anchorage at the Side Saddle Islands, east of Shanghai, where she rendezvoused with the cruiser HMS *Belfast* on 28 April.[10] The admiral transferred to *Belfast* and decided to form Force 68. Ships would be stationed in the vicinity of Woosung and at Alacrity anchorage in case of a full evacuation of Shanghai and to help *Amethyst* if she emerged from the Yangtze.

The American hospital ship *Repose*, carrying most of the wounded British sailors, went to Hong Kong. According to the *Daily Express*, the sailors were ignored by British residents. Under the page one headline, Nobody meets the *Amethyst* men, Bernard Wicksteed wrote:

If I were a resident of Hong Kong, I would not be feeling very proud of myself today. On this day 77 wounded British sailors from the warships *Amethyst*, *London*, *Consort* and *Black Swan* – 44 of them stretcher cases – were landed by the US hospital ship *Repose*. And so far as I can see not one civilian in the colony has taken the slightest interest. From mid-morning till early afternoon ambulances have been taking the sailors from the dockside up the hill to the naval hospital on The Peak, where the wealthy have their homes.

Not a steamer in the harbour hooted a welcome to the boys returning to British territory from the Yangtze. Not one extra flag was run up. The only band was part of a Chinese funeral passing the dock gates. No bystanders, no cheering, no interest.

Wicksteed took a taxi to the hospital to check the reception there but found 'not a soul but the hospital staff'. He continued: 'Not one basket of fruit had been sent, not one book, magazine or newspaper, not even one cigarette from Britons living in Hong Kong to greet the boys.' The correspondent pointed out that the men's arrival had been publicised but it was a Sunday, 'apparently a day for bathing and tennis and not a day for thinking of wounded men thousands of miles from home'. But Wicksteed then revealed that the naval authorities had not wanted publicity and reporters were barred from the dockside because newspapers in Shanghai gave details of wounds suffered by the casualties. At the hospital he saw the senior surgeon who 'said he was glad someone showed interest'. Wicksteed was taken to a ward where there were five men who had two books donated by US sailors. One man described the scene in *Consort*'s wardroom where the doctor had his instruments laid out ready for an operation when a shell burst scattered them. The petty officer he was attending to on the table remarked casually: 'Hey doc, look at this – the shell has just blown my knee-cap off.'[11]

On the day the story appeared the Commodore Hong Kong sent an explanation to Lord Hall and Admiral Fraser: 'Article is not merely exaggerated but incorrect as residents have accommodated ratings from *Consort* while on leave and both individuals and firms have sent gifts to Royal Naval Hospital for wounded and big subscriptions have been received for dependants and relatives of those who have lost their lives.' The commodore decided he would not issue a denial but instead release a statement thanking those who had provided accommodation or sent gifts.[12]

The *Daily Express* was not the only publication to make uncomfortable reading for those in authority. *The Economist* magazine launched a broadside at the Foreign Office. It reminded its readers Attlee had told the Commons that *Amethyst*, *Consort*, *London* and *Black Swan* were not designed to operate in rivers against massed artillery. *The Economist* pointed out: 'As this limitation of sea power was perfectly well known to the naval authorities it would have been madness for them to send a frigate to Nanking if they had been sufficiently warned that the Communists were likely to attack it. It is not the profession of a naval officer to estimate a political situation; he must rely on civilian officials for advice about risks of being attacked.' The Foreign Office was accused of passing the buck to the Admiralty by stressing that the Nationalist government had warned months earlier it could not guarantee the safety of foreign ships on the Yangtze. Yet British officials had been spreading optimism about the Communists, refusing to 'entertain the idea that they might pass from anti-imperialism in words to saying it with anti-tank guns'.

The Economist was right in questioning the response of diplomats, especially Ambassador Stevenson. At that stage it was not common knowledge that the Australian ambassador, Officer, and a US admiral, Badger, had quickly recognised the dangers of sending warships up the Yangtze at such a critical time. Stevenson knew of their misgivings, so why did he not warn Madden? Or were Stevenson and Madden blinded to the past power of the British Empire and the White Ensign?

The Economist also questioned the point of having an ambassador in Nanking when the Communists had no diplomatic relations with Britain and were committing acts of war against it – 'the presence of His Majesty's envoy in the deserted capital is merely ridiculous and humiliating, an unnecessary gift of face for the murderers of British sailors and an invitation to blackmail'. The US government had recalled its ambassador for 'consultation', and the British ambassador should not have been kept in Nanking 'a day longer'.[13]

The Economist's criticism of diplomats certainly stung the British consul in Shanghai, Robert Urquhart, who fired off a letter to the Foreign Office's Far Eastern Department. Urquhart pointed out that in the February he had warned against warships using the Yangtze.

> I personally canvassed the desirability of establishing the principle that warships should be withdrawn on the near approach of the Reds . . . The main point I am now making is to establish how dangerously wrong even the best newspaper can be, and to invoke your help to correct the attempt to fix any responsibility for the tragedy on me as distinct from the general service responsibility, of which I take my share although my precautionary views were overruled both by the ambassador [Stevenson] and the admiral [it is not clear if Urquhart was referring to Brind or Madden].

The consul also pointed out that no civilians on shore, 'which includes me', had known of *Amethyst*'s sailing from Shanghai on 19 April until late on the eve of the disaster.[14]

A Foreign Office official, W B Hesmondhalgh, took up Urquhart's protest and approached two members of *The Economist*'s staff dealing with the Far East and tried to point out to them 'the error of their ways'. Hesmondhalgh admitted: 'I have had little success. They appeared to hold strong views on the subject . . . they showed no sign of departing from views highly critical of His Majesty's government's policy in China.' But the press generally had recognised the value of Urquhart's work in Shanghai and in view of that, Hesmondhalgh recommended that no specific action be taken. The significant point that Urquhart had warned Stevenson and 'the admiral' against using warships was not pursued.[15]

Lieutenant Commander William Tapp of the Royal Australian Navy had been due to take his frigate *Shoalhaven*, (below), to Nanking in April 1949 to act as guardship, but the Canberra government stopped the voyage. *Amethyst* was ordered to go instead.
Australian War Memorial

Ben Chifley, Australia's blunt prime minister.
With an election looming, he did not want his
sailors put in danger so close to Anzac Day.

Keith Officer, Australia's ambassador
in Nanking. The cautious Gallipoli veteran sent
warnings to his foreign minister.

A rare picture of *Amethyst* starting her voyage up the Yangtze in April 1949.
Imperial War Museum Collection

TOP LEFT: *Amethyst*'s captain, Lieutenant Commander Bernard Skinner, who was mortally wounded on the bridge.

TOP RIGHT: First Lieutenant Geoffrey Weston, who took over from Skinner despite being badly wounded.

LEFT: Leslie Frank, who was in the wheelhouse but unable to stop *Amethyst* running aground.

elegraphist Jack French played crucial role in keeping ommunications open.

Shell and machine gun damage to part of *Amethyst*'s superstructure.
Stewart Hett/Imperial War Museum Collection

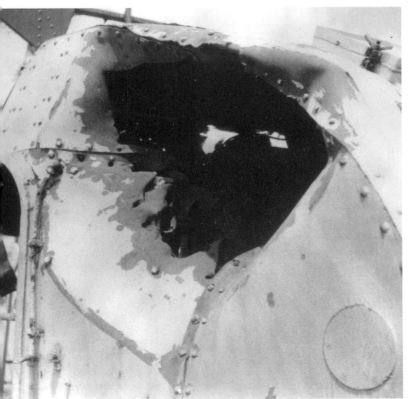

The gaping hole in the aft 'X' turret left by a direct hit.
Stewart Hett/Imperial War Museum Collection

The destroyer *Consort* went down the Yangtze at speeds of up to 27 knots in an attempt to rescue *Amethyst*. She suffered heavy casualties.

The cruiser *London* was an easy target in the confines of the Yangtze.

Lieutenant Commander John Kerans, an assistant naval attaché in Nanking and unlikely hero who had not endeared himself to his superiors, managed to reach *Amethyst* after a difficult journey and was given command.

Flight Lieutenant Michael Fearnley of the Royal Air Force landed in a Sunderland on the Yangtze near *Amethyst* and was able to give much-needed medical help. *Stewart Hett/Imperial War Museum Collection*

Commander-in-Chief Admiral Sir Patrick Brind.
The attack on *Amethyst* shocked him.
National Portrait Gallery

The second in command, Vice Admiral
Alexander Madden. He gave the order to sail.
National Portrait Gallery

The First Sea Lord, Admiral of the Fleet Lord
Fraser. He tried to stop *Amethyst*'s escape.
National Portrait Gallery

Ambassador in Nanking Sir Ralph Stevenson.
He ordered the *Concord* cover-up.
National Portrait Gallery

Sailors who escaped to safety from *Amethyst* after the attack on 20 April 1949, arriving in Shanghai.

Kerans with senior members of the crew during their captivity. The ship's dog, Peggy, was not interested in being snapped. Front row, left to right: Leonard Williams, Stewart Hett, John Kerans, George Strain, Michael Fearnley, William Freeman. Middle: Alfred White, Lionel Chare, Trevor Rees, John McCarthy, George Griffiths. Back: Hugh Blomley, Albert Garns, William Venton, Eric Holloway, Vernon Irwin, Ian McGlashen, John MacNamara, George Logan.
Stewart Hett/Imperial War Museum Collection

Primed for action. Shells for the ready-use lockers on board *Concord* – proof that the destroyer would have retaliated if the big guns of the Woosung forts had opened fire. The Ministry of Defence has always insisted that the ship was not in any danger.
Derek Hodgson of Concord

Amethyst alongside *Concord*, which transferred some personnel and supplies.
Derek Hodgson of Concord

Amethyst arriving in Hong Kong without the aid of tugs on 3 August 1949.
Imperial War Museum Collection

Kerans on the bridge making sure that his ship berths smoothly. A waiting Admiral Brind paid him the compliment, 'Manoeuvre well executed.'

Amethyst under repair in dry dock showing the large shell hole in her stern.
John Kerans/Imperial War Museum Collection

A shipshape *Amethyst* homeward bound, leaving Hong Kong after repairs on 9 September 1949 on the first leg of her voyage back to Britain.
Imperial War Museum Collection

Amethyst arriving home in Devonport on 1 November 1949 astern of the battleship *Vanguard*.

Among those on the quayside to welcome her home were *Amethyst* sailors who had returned to Britain earlier after being wounded.

Kerans reunited with his wife Stephanie, who brought along their three-year-old daughter Charmian.

oy sailor Sydney Horton receiving a warm welcome from family and friends.

Amethyst's battle-scarred ensign seems to symbolise the courage and fortitude of the ship's company. *Imperial War Museum Collection*

Marching along Fleet Street, London, on 16 November 1949. Leading the sailors are, left to right, Commander Robertson of *Consort*, the newly promoted Commodore Cazalet of *London* and Lieutenant Commander Kerans. The building on the left is the headquarters of the Press Association and Reuters, which reported extensively on the *Amethyst* story.

Amethyst's first lieutenant, Geoffrey Weston, was forced to leave the navy because of his shrapnel wound. He ended up joining the army and rising to the rank of brigadier. *Weston family*

The end. *Amethyst* at a Devonport breaker's yard in 1957.
Getty Images/Hulton Archive

Mao and his generals could not believe how easy it had been to rout the sizeable Nationalist forces south of the Yangtze, especially those in Nanking. Nationalist positions over a wide area fell quickly. Deng Xiaoping, a political commissar of the Second Field Army and a future leader of China, noted: 'We did not encounter fierce resistance anywhere. We made a wide, frontal crossing from scores of places, meeting with no substantial resistance in most places . . . Beginning on the night of April 20, nearly all the 300,000 men crossed the river in a twenty-four hour period, plunging the enemy troops into chaos. With just one thought on their minds – breaking out of the encirclement – they fled southward helter-skelter.'[16]

The Nationalist general who had the task of defending Nanking, Tang Enbo, took his retreating force to Shanghai, where he set up defensive positions around the port. Tang, nicknamed Iron Man, had 200,000 defenders. The month of May would see some fighting for control of the city but before it was out the Communists would emerge the victors. However, the success of the Communist armies and the growing confidence of Mao and his generals were about to make it more difficult to get *Amethyst*'s release.

13
A Chinese Puzzle

A NEW FACE APPEARED IN the late afternoon of 2 May. Captain Tai Kuo-liang, the local garrison commander, came alongside *Amethyst* in a sampan, accompanied by two soldiers. He was invited on board and Kerans spoke to him in his cabin. Also present were Hett and the Chinese steward acting as an interpreter. There appeared to be good news. Captain Tai had a message from General Liu Po-cheng in Nanking that agreement for the ship's safe passage would be given in 'a short time'. Tai declined to give more details, saying the general was very busy. Again, Kerans was told that *Amethyst* would be safe provided she made no attempt to move. He was asked to give an assurance in writing, stating the ship's position, and he agreed. Kerans asked for news about two wounded ratings who had been taken to the mission hospital at Changchow. Stoker Mechanic Samuel Bannister and Keith Martin, a boy seaman, were 'inadvertently' left behind on stretchers near Changchow after the main group evacuated *Amethyst* on 20 April. Both had shrapnel wounds and were known to be in Communist hands, and Kerans was keen that they should return to the ship if their condition allowed. One positive point during the meeting was that Tai did not bring up the question of who had fired first. 'I felt that at long last we were really getting somewhere,' Kerans reported.

The following day a junk with two traders offering eggs and potatoes arrived and the ship exchanged rice and flour for the produce. It added a touch of normality. Less normal was the fact that the Communists had set up another battery about half a mile away up river on the south bank. Any craft not flying a red flag was fired on – and so were some of the vessels displaying that symbol. With Madden's approval, Kerans was trying to make contact with the area commander in Chingkiang, Yuan Chung-hsien, who seemed to be another 'busy' general.

On 8 May Captain Tai made a second appearance, this time with an invitation for the Chinese on board to attend a party being held by General Yuan the following day. Kerans was surprised that the general could spare time for *Amethyst*'s stewards and laundrymen, and he was also aware that they could be interrogated and used for propaganda. He told Tai he could not spare them but the officer replied that a refusal to accept the invitation would result in the men being forced to leave *Amethyst*. Kerans did not wish to jeopardise an early agreement for safe passage and agreed that six of the eight Chinese could go. He then pressed the issue of when he would receive permission to leave. Tai was evasive but said he expected a messenger to return from Nanking shortly. The next day Tai turned up in a launch to take the six Chinese to the general's party – 'a dumber and more unenthusiastic collection it would be hard to find'. The group had lunch and then went to a Chinese temple on Chiaoshan Island, where there was a service for *Amethyst*'s dead Chinese. In the early evening the new battery on the south bank opened fire with machine guns at a steamer heading up river, even though the vessel was flying a red flag and carrying Communist troops. Most of the bullets came 'unpleasantly close' to *Amethyst*. A few minutes later Captain Tai returned with the Chinese and Kerans protested about the attack. Kerans wondered if flying a red flag might be one of the conditions of an agreement and he asked Madden for advice. The admiral decided that a red flag could be flown in addition to the White Ensign.

On 13 May Hett went ashore to check with Tai if there was any news but 'the usual replies of another telegram to Nanking and communication difficulties were made'. The day saw further bartering for eggs and potatoes. The delaying tactics of the Communists had become a major concern for Kerans, who feared that his ship might be trapped for a long time. As approaches to Nanking were proving fruitless, he wondered about asking the local command for permission to move down river to the limit of the Chingkiang operational area, perhaps to Kiangyin. Time would be saved and there was always the possibility of slipping away from Kiangyin under cover of darkness. Kerans suggested this possibility to Madden, who advised that it would be unwise to lose his local contacts as an agreement from Nanking was 'still clearly a possibility'.[1]

Captain Tai appeared alongside in a sampan on 17 May and suggested that an agreement might not come until the fall of Shanghai. Kerans wondered how much information Tai was passing on to his superiors. His letters were still not being answered. Getting ashore was a problem as it depended on the weather and 'the whim of a small sampan'. There was another problem – he did not trust the man he was using as an interpreter, But Sai Tin. Hett, who had taken the steward ashore, formed the same opinion. Most of the time But appeared to be carrying on his own conversation with Tai, and 'Chiang Kai-shek' and 'KMT' (Kuomintang of China, Chiang's political party) were frequently heard. Kerans was also suspicious because the steward said he wished to return to his native Wei-hai-wei, a port in north-east China, even though his family were in Hong Kong. Kerans noted: 'He undoubtedly had the remaining Chinese on board firmly under his control. He mended his ideas later and by the end of our time in the Yangtze was firmly convinced that Communism was the wrong horse to back.' There were also doubts about Captain Tai. Was he a committed Communist? Tai, a former student in Shanghai, was young for his rank and perhaps overconfident. Later on Kerans would come up with a plan to try to get him to defect 'and help me with certain matters'. But the plan was dropped after Kerans discovered that security agents were watching Tai closely.[2]

On 18 May Hett went ashore in an attempt to arrange an interview with the area commander. He was unsuccessful, but that afternoon saw a development. Two young army captains arrived aboard *Amethyst* with a written demand to enter into talks for a settlement. So, after nearly a month trapped on the Yangtze, only now were serious discussions on the table. Kerans had made no progress towards freedom. The interview took place in English and was 'somewhat frigid'. The area commander, General Yuan Chung-hsein, had appointed Colonel Kang Mao-chao as his representative for negotiations. The Commander-in-Chief, Far East Station, was required to appoint a representative – Kerans or another officer. The talks would centre on responsibility for 'invading' territory of the PLA by British warships. Kerans expressed the commander-in-chief's view that the ships were engaged in peaceful activity and that it was a matter for Nanking to settle at the highest diplomatic level. Back came the reply that the Communists did not have diplomatic relations and it would have to be settled at a local level. Kerans reported: 'They went on to state that safe conduct could be given by their headquarters but that it would not be discussed until a meeting had been convened and my credentials as a representative to negotiate were acceptable. The meeting was closed after it was pointed out that any projected movement of *Amethyst* would draw fire from their batteries.'[3]

It was clear that negotiations would be lengthy. Another concern was the ship's dwindling stock of fuel. On 20 May there were 170 tons, and it was decided to save fuel by shutting down all power at night. Admiral Brind, the commander-in-chief, who had returned to the Far East from London, recognised the fuel problem and thought *Amethyst* might run out by the end of the month. He proposed a rather dramatic solution to break the deadlock. If the Admiralty had no objection, he would fly to *Amethyst*, hoist his flag and attend talks with the Communists. He told Ambassador Stevenson: 'This offers far the best chance to release *Amethyst* and possibility of British warships being impounded is serious enough to justify risks involved.'

If the negotiations failed he would warn that he planned to sail *Amethyst* down river. Brind was optimistic: 'It is most unlikely that Communists would fire in the circumstances, particularly if we take every possible step by broadcasting and other means to tell Communist government.' Not taking action risked losing the ship to the Communists and the remaining crew becoming prisoners. 'I recognise it may be said we cannot afford another *Amethyst* incident in any circumstances and that to move her in face of every warning and without support is courting this. The best answer is, of course, success but apart from this the Communists have no right whatsoever to detain ship or to fire. Both sides of river are in their hands to Woosung and no battle area is involved.' Brind estimated that the risk was small and the chances of success good, and it was time to call the bluff of the Communists.[4]

Brind's plan rang alarm bells at the Admiralty immediately. The First Sea Lord, Admiral Fraser, warned there was a real risk of failure. In view of what had happened already, there was little chance of rescuing *Amethyst* with a surprise gesture. Failure would have three serious drawbacks: relations with the Communists would be further embittered, with far-reaching effects, particularly in Shanghai and Hong Kong; the British government would be justifiably criticised at home; and there would be a further loss of prestige. Ministers favoured the current efforts to get negotiations going.[5]

Brind dropped his plan to fly to *Amethyst*. On 20 May Ambassador Stevenson told the admiral he was concerned at the Communist demand for an admission of responsibility, which he saw as an attempt at blackmail. 'The Communists are, of course, encouraged to adopt this intransigent attitude because they hold the ship and crew as virtual hostages,' the ambassador noted.

I feel that nevertheless we ought to resist as far as possible this unilateral attempt to force an admission of responsibility for the incident upon us. In doing so, we inevitably run the risk of the ship being held up indefinitely. I fear, however, that this risk cannot be avoided in the circumstances. It is useless to adopt logical argument in reply to the communication addressed to Lieutenant Commander Kerans, who is in my opinion carrying on with admirable spirit and persistence. Local Communist headquarters are not likely to listen to reason in their present state of mind as disclosed by these latest developments.

Kerans needed to tell the Communists that he was not in a position to discuss controversial issues, which must be referred to his superiors. He could only deal with arrangements for the safe passage of *Amethyst* down river without the risk of further misunderstanding. In the meantime, the PLA should accept full responsibility for the safety of the ship and her crew.

Stevenson was obviously worried about Brind's proposal to force the issue and hoist his flag in *Amethyst* – and probably unaware that it had been vetoed by Admiral Fraser – because shortly afterwards he sent another message, stressing the need for patience: 'I fear we have no practical choice but to reconcile ourselves to a long drawn out and frustrating wait. Nevertheless despite hardships and nervousness unavoidable to the gallant crew of the ship, there is unfortunately no safe alternative to peaceful methods. I am convinced that we cannot afford the risk of another clash with Communists.' The Communists would have strong grounds for using force against any ships and aircraft that entered Chinese territory without permission as they now controlled key parts of the Yangtze. However, Stevenson was not opposed to Kerans suggesting that the commander-in-chief was willing 'in the interests of reasonable relations' to go to Nanking or *Amethyst* to discuss the issues with a PLA officer of similar rank.

On 24 May Kerans went to General Yuan's headquarters in

Chingkiang, delivering the message that he was unable to discuss controversial issues. A meeting followed and Kerans, without an interpreter, felt 'extremely lonely' facing a 'battery of Communism', which included Colonel Kang and press and propaganda representatives. The general made it clear that negotiations were not taking place in Nanking, and he refused to discuss *Amethyst*'s safe passage until the Royal Navy accepted responsibility for the Yangtze Incident. A political officer handed over a translated memorandum for Brind, accusing *Amethyst* and the other ships of invading China's inland waters and positions of the PLA. *Amethyst* was also accused of firing first, and it was claimed that the British ships were involved with Nationalist forces. As well as accepting responsibility, Britain would have to pay compensation for the loss of life and property.

Kerans stressed that *Amethyst*'s passage to Nanking was given full clearance by the 'competent authorities' and that it had been impossible to contact the Communists. Kang pointed out that his party's central executive committee decided in February 1947 that it would not recognise any diplomatic arrangements made by the Nationalists. Kerans replied that Britain had not recognised the Communists' stand. He then brought up the fact that his ship's fuel and provisions were running low and that 'we could not remain here for ever'. With power shut down at night, the crew were suffering in rising temperatures. Kang said his army bore no ill will towards the sailors and as a gesture he would arrange for the wounded Bannister and Martin to return to *Amethyst*. Kerans reported: 'This was the only success achieved out of this lengthy meeting and I wound up stating that detention of *Amethyst*, as a military necessity had long since ceased and we were neutral in the Chinese civil war, would only have embarrassing international consequences.' Kang made no reply.

Kerans came away from the talks with some hope although he sensed the issue might take time to resolve. It was the first serious meeting and he saw it as a face-saving exercise for the benefit of the local population. The next day Bannister and Martin were taken out to the ship. It was 'a great morale uplift for everyone on board'. They had recovered from their shrapnel wounds and were in fair condition. The men had ended up at a PLA camp at Tachiang, where one or both of Kang's interpreters interrogated them. Attempts were made to force them to admit that *Amethyst* opened fire first, and to their 'everlasting credit' they refused. Their return received a lot of local press publicity. Kerans spoke to Madden in a radio transmission, suggesting that similar publicity on 'our side' might be helpful for subsequent meetings.[6]

By this time Admiral Brind was flying his flag in *London* at Alacrity anchorage and had taken command of Force 68, the ships keeping watch at the mouth of the Yangtze. Madden returned to Hong Kong in *Belfast*. Brind sent a lengthy signal to Kerans, a memorandum that he wanted to be given to General Yuan. It set out all the points made previously, stressing the need for *Amethyst*'s safe passage. In a letter to his wife Edie, the admiral wrote: 'Now I am doing my utmost to put pressure on for getting *Amethyst* out. We have a particularly truculent opponent to deal with on the Yangtze and so far he has only beaten the big drum and has not attempted to talk sense! Whilst keeping him going I am now trying to get in touch with a higher general who, I believe, lives in Peking. So I am hoping to get an invitation to the great city!!'[7] The general was Chu Teh.

Kerans now had the bonus of an interpreter he could trust. The embassy in Nanking had been able to send one of its employees, Sam Leo, to help him. On 31 May Kerans was called unexpectedly to a meeting with Colonel Kang at a village opposite the ship. Kang expressed doubts about the sincerity of Brind's messages and accused the British of evasive tactics to avoid discussion on the question of responsibility. He was told this was incorrect and that the commander-in-chief would welcome negotiations at the 'correct level'. Kerans reported: 'I tried hard to shift the venue to Nanking, Shanghai or Peking but without success. I then queried Kang's authorisation through the area commander to discuss such high-level political matters. He quickly reiterated that the general was fully empowered by General Chu Teh in Peking to settle the incident, and that the PLA would not consider dealing with the incident other than in the area where it occurred. This would be in accordance with Communist doctrines where those at the top do not expose themselves.'

Once again, points raised previously were discussed without progress being made. Kang was asked what evidence he had to support his claim that *Amethyst* fired first. He stressed that he was in command of the battery at San Chiang Ying and witnessed the incident. He had ordered his troops to fire if attacked and there was no doubt the ship fired first.

Kerans told the colonel it was an extremely weak answer and Kang dropped the subject – never to raise it again. Kang was asked to give clearance for a Sunderland flying boat to bring a senior officer so that high-level negotiations could start, but he said General Yuan would have to consider the request after an application in writing. When Kerans mentioned the difficult conditions his crew were experiencing, Kang blamed the policy adopted by their senior officers. He took exception to a warning in Brind's signal that a continuing refusal to allow *Amethyst* to sail would cause 'most unfortunate complications between the PLA and the British people'. Kerans noted: 'It did appear that they were showing concern over outside reaction and the propaganda line to follow . . . I did feel that the time was now opportune for worldwide broadcast of the true facts of the case pointing out Communist vacillation and intransigence during negotiations. It was also clear that the political machinery of the PLA was the deciding factor and that it was hard to break in order to make a normal approach possible. It was also obvious that Kang and his interpreters were dealing in political matters above their heads.' After the meeting it dawned on Kerans that Colonel Kang and 'Major Kung', whom Hett had dealt with earlier, were the same person.[8]

After nearly six weeks on the Yangtze conditions in *Amethyst* were continuing to deteriorate. Flies, mosquitoes and cockroaches were a problem, and the after part of the ship was uninhabitable because of rats. Disinfectant had run out and it was only by 'scrupulous cleanliness' that disease could be kept in check.

'Life on board generally was work,' said Ernest Munson, an ordinary seaman. 'We used to make our own enjoyment, games of uckers [a game similar to ludo], crib. It was hot, temperatures up in the hundreds, and when the ship was shut down most of the chaps stayed on the upper deck. There were silly games of catching fireflies. When the Chinese [Communists] crossed the river we had a macabre way of passing the time. When on watch we would count the bodies of the Chinese soldiers, how many would pass one side of the ship, how many would pass the other side. It used to relieve the boredom. They were bloated.'

On one occasion a live pig was spotted floating down the river and sailors tried to lasso it in the hope of getting some fresh meat. They failed and the pig floated on. 'Sometimes we slept below decks because of the weather,' said Munson. 'A rat would run past my camp bed every night on his usual run. The other chaps used to try to hit it with boots and things. I was tucked away in my camp bed trying to dodge the boots and the rat. We did catch some of the rats in different ways but we were getting fed up with them. I can remember this chap waking up one morning and finding a rat swinging about six inches from his face. Someone had put up a fuse-wire snare on the pipes above.'[9]

The best rat catcher was a cat called Simon. A previous member of *Amethyst*'s crew, 17-year-old George Hickinbottom, had found the black and white cat wandering in the naval dockyard on Stonecutters Island, Hong Kong, in November 1948 and smuggled him on board. The then captain, Lieutenant Commander Ian Griffiths, discovered he had an extra crew member. However, Griffiths liked cats and agreed he could stay because rats were always trying to get at the food supplies. It was not long before Simon took up quarters in the captain's cabin, where he sometimes brought his trophies. Griffiths once found a dead rat on his bunk. The captain only had to whistle and Simon would accompany him on his rounds. When Griffiths was given a new command, the cat remained on board *Amethyst*. Griffiths's successor, Lieutenant Commander Skinner, also liked cats and kept Simon. The cat was asleep in the captain's cabin when *Amethyst* was attacked on 20 April.[10]

Lieutenant Hett explained:

Simon was hit in the captain's cabin. He suffered shock and blast and goodness knows what. He just went to earth. We don't know quite where he went and, of course, at this stage we were very much more concerned with saving the ship rather than looking after animals [a dog called Peggy was also on board]. About a week afterwards Simon crept out from wherever he was and he then went around with the ship's company. Simon had a scar on his ear and his forehead and his whiskers were a bit singed because a shell had burst in the cabin. But he settled down and killed rats. I had my foot bitten by a rat when I was in my bunk one night. The rats came through the ventilation trunking.[11]

The badly injured Simon had been found by Petty Officer George Griffiths and was treated by Fearnley the RAF doctor. He was not expected to survive but he made a good recovery. Simon resumed his duties, catching rats everywhere – the stokers' mess deck, the petty officers' pantry and 'spud locker', the portside galley, the bridge, the forward mess deck, the after mess deck, and the chief petty officers' mess. His greatest success was a rat nicknamed Mao Tse-tung, a particularly vicious creature that kept eluding the crew's traps. Simon cornered the rat and killed it quickly, delighting the sailors and earning promotion to Able Seacat. But Simon did experience one setback – Kerans was not a cat lover and turfed him out of the captain's cabin. As well as dealing with vermin, the cat also proved a tonic for some of the younger sailors who had been traumatised by the attack. At one point Kerans went down with a virus and was confined to bed for a few days. Simon sneaked into the cabin, jumped on the bunk and purred away, winning over Kerans, who allowed him to stay. On another occasion the cat was able to cement the relationship by presenting the captain with a dead rat. When Simon was not looking, Kerans threw it overboard.[12]

14

The Threat to Hong Kong

THE PLIGHT OF *AMETHYST* WAS not the only China-related problem occupying the thoughts of the British government and military chiefs. There was continuing concern about the fate of the British community in Shanghai. There were around 4,000 British nationals and by 13 May Prime Minister Attlee was worried that so few had taken up the offer of evacuation. And the significant progress of Communist forces also cast a shadow over Hong Kong. Would Mao, emboldened by the success of the PLA, be tempted to invade the colony?

As Communist troops headed towards Shanghai, the city was still busy as a commercial centre, despite problems that included crippling inflation. One line of argument among wavering Nationalist supporters was that the Communists would need Shanghai to carry on trading. The bourgeoisie had been so keen to save their city that they sent delegations to Peking in the February and March to discuss plans for a Communist takeover. Even a leading gangster, Du Yuesheng, who had helped to massacre thousands of Communists some two decades earlier, offered his 'sincere' co-operation to avoid major fighting.[1]

Those seeking a peaceful solution were stunned at the end of April when the former Nationalist leader Chiang Kai-shek suddenly turned up in the city and announced that there would be a fight to the end. Chiang, still an influential figure, had already secured his bolthole, Formosa [now Taiwan], where he diverted much of China's wealth, gold and cash reserves, as well as art treasures. Prominent citizens – and gangster Du – fled the city as Chiang ordered a crackdown on 'defeatists'. Hundreds were arrested and suspected Communist supporters were executed, sometimes in the street. The local economy was badly hit and those who remained saw a rising tax burden. Many people were forced to dig ditches and build a wooden stockade as part of the city's defences. But on 8 May Chiang, who had arrived in a cruiser, sailed away, destination Formosa, with more than a suspicion that the real purpose of his visit was to extract as much wealth as possible for his island fortress under the guise of helping the war effort.[2]

The main Communist army approached Shanghai from the north and fought a battle with a force trying to flee. Despite Chiang's departure, the crackdown on Nationalist opponents increased, with frequent executions. Western journalists were also threatened. Britain's consul, Robert Urquhart, and other foreign diplomats were instructed to appeal to Nationalist generals to 'spare the city from the consequences which would follow from its continued defence'. Attlee was concerned that a large number of British nationals would end up as hostages in Communist hands, and thought renewed efforts should be made to persuade them to leave. But he was told it would take 96 hours for merchant ships to reach Shanghai and 14 days to evacuate the entire British community. One reassurance was that Communist treatment of British communities in the captured cities of Peking, Tientsin and Nanking had been reasonably good.[3]

Urquhart did not share Attlee's concern about hostages, and he had sent a different message to British residents. 'Most of the fears which have been conjured up are founded on rumour and pure imagination,' he told them.

> We will stand by Shanghai if we possibly can. It will take the extreme of human folly, of military disaster, to dislodge us. Shanghai is home to us as a community, not merely a trading post, and we are not going to up and leave our community at the first signs of an approaching storm. Does anyone suggest that if there is a change of government here, the new one will be so unreasonable that they will make civilised life and normal trading impossible? I have great confidence that the government of China will not fall into the hands of any but responsible men, who will have the interests of their country at heart.[4]

On 24 May, four days after Communist troops surrounded Shanghai's two airports, the Nationalists, bizarrely, staged a victory parade. That night advance units of the PLA entered the city, finding little resistance. City Hall and the central police station were soon occupied.

Wing Commander Peter Howard-Williams, the assistant air attaché, who had helped to organise the Sunderland flights to *Amethyst* the previous month, was in Shanghai during the Communist advance. 'One morning I heard shooting and lay under the bed as bullets hit the outside walls of my flat,' he recalled.

> After a while I crawled out from under the bed and all seemed quiet. I went out into the street and found that I was now in Communist territory. I rang the consulate and found that my office was still in Nationalist territory. They asked me if I had any information as to where the fighting was, so in the afternoon a very frightened Chen [a servant] and an equally frightened assistant air attaché, ventured forth in my car. It turned out to be quite exciting when we found ourselves in no man's land and had a lot of problems getting back to the flat.
>
> It was noticeable that most of the senior Nationalist officers had been too busy arranging for their private possessions, even pianos and tables, to be flown to Formosa, to think of their men. After burning an enormous amount of their equipment a large part of the army embarked at Woosung in landing craft and sailed to Formosa, just before the arrival of the Communist army. The behaviour of the Communist soldiers was better than the Nationalists and they immediately created a good impression with many of the inhabitants. As soon as they had set up a headquarters I visited it with a request to drive a van to *Amethyst* with three sacks of mail. After several further attempts the request was refused. The real purpose of the request was to take some radio valves, which I intended to hide in the mail bags.[5]

There were anxious moments for Urquhart when Nationalist soldiers made a stand opposite his consulate on the Bund. But the Communists quickly consolidated their hold on the city and only a few areas witnessed significant clashes, including part of the waterfront. As soon as the fighting stopped, the Communists withdrew their frontline forces and propaganda units took over.

Howard-Williams, who had sent his wife and daughter to the safety of Hong Kong before the fighting, added: 'Life under the Communists was very different. There were no ships and the great port of Shanghai was at a standstill. No mail or papers were received from outside and we were forbidden to leave the city. The only letter I received was one from my bank about my overdraft, and to this day I do not know how it got through.'

Foreign residents were not targeted, and the only Western casualty appears to have been US Vice Consul William Olive, who may have been the architect of his own fate. Olive apparently drove his car at a parade, intent on knocking down marchers and ignoring police instructions. He was arrested. At a police station he allegedly attacked officers and in turn was badly beaten up. Olive subsequently returned to America, along with Ambassador Stuart.[6] Fighting between the Nationalists and the Communists continued in north west and south China but by the end of the summer the civil war was effectively over, with Mao the victor and more opposed to Western powers than ever.

On Hong Kong, the British government had been well aware in April that it needed to take decisive action to protect the colony. The Commissioner General for South East Asia, Malcolm MacDonald, warned:

Further victories in China in general and our naval reverse on the Yangtze in particular have gravely weakened our prestige recently. I fear that the effect of the *Amethyst* incident in particular is bad in Hong Kong as it is bound to be throughout South East Asia. It is universally regarded by the Chinese here [in Hong Kong] as a sign of our impotence to resist Chinese Communists, and as an indication that we shall not have the strength to defend Hong Kong if Communists wish to press for rendition or capture of the colony. Memory of 1941 is only too fresh in their minds and the Yangtze incident is painfully reminiscent of the loss of the *Prince of Wales* and the *Repulse* locally. This melancholy event has disturbed the unofficial European leaders almost as badly as the Chinese.

MacDonald stressed the urgency of dealing with a further loss of confidence in the colony, and suggested that a statement committing Britain to the defence of Hong Kong should be made in the House of Commons.[7]

It should be recalled that the battleship HMS *Prince of Wales* and the battlecruiser HMS *Repulse*, lacking air cover and involved in a dubious reconnaissance mission after failing to intercept the Japanese invasion fleet, were sunk by torpedo planes off the east coast of Malaya on 10 December 1941. Two days earlier Japanese troops had launched an assault on Hong Kong, which was defended by British, Canadian and Indian forces. The Japanese stormed through the New Territories and Kowloon, reaching Hong Kong Island. The defenders were heavily outnumbered and surrender came on 25 December 1941, known locally as Black Christmas.

Until April 1949 British military planners had thought that an attack on Hong Kong by the Chinese Communists was a remote possibility. The colony was valuable as 'a liaison centre and clearing house' for the Chinese Communist Party, and as a base for the co-ordination of Communist activities generally throughout South East Asia. However, the ease with which Communist forces crossed the Yangtze altered the picture significantly. The Communists had three army groups in the Yangtze area totalling around one million men. In addition, there were 400,000 troops in north China and 80,000 in the south east. The military planners identified four possible approaches to Hong Kong from central China: by sea; the coast road from Shanghai or Hangchow; the railway between Nankow and Canton; and the inland road from Hangchow. The Communists lacked shipping and the easiest route appeared to be the railway between Hankow and Canton. A briefing document noted: 'In assessing the value of the Communists' armies as a fighting force it must be remembered that it has never met resolute resistance from the Nationalist armies and cannot be judged by European standards. Nevertheless, its standard of training and fighting efficiency is rated very high by neutral observers. In addition the Communist leaders have shown a high degree of professional skill in the past in the tactical and strategic handling of their armies; most of them have been trained in Russian military academies.'[8] Hankow was nearly 800 miles from Hong Kong. It was estimated that it would take 20 days to move 200,000 troops from Hankow to Canton using the railway. The Communist navy and air force were considered insignificant.

On 25 April Minister of Defence Alexander and the heads of the navy, army and air force had met to discuss the threat. Admiral Brind, already in London, was asked to attend the meeting and he expressed the view that Communism in China would prove to be very different from Communism in eastern Europe. It might bring 'all sorts of evil' but it was not likely to lead to unanimity of outlook among the Chinese. In China the village was the unit, and it did not make much difference to any particular village what type of government was in control. He had heard that the Communists were at 'sixes and sevens amongst themselves'. Alexander said he feared Brind's view might prove optimistic.[9]

On 27 April Britain decided to send a brigade HQ and one infantry battalion to reinforce the Hong Kong garrison. However, two days later planners at the Ministry of Defence recommended a tougher response, stating that there was 'little likelihood of a direct Communist attack on Hong Kong if we show our determination to hold the colony'. The planners identified two threats, one from guerrillas, the other a direct attack. It was suggested that two infantry brigades, one armoured regiment, two artillery field regiments and one composite AA regiment should be sent initially. The navy would increase its patrols and the air force would contribute a fighter squadron and early-warning radar. If the threat increased, the reinforcements would be one army division, an aircraft carrier and frigates, and a fighter squadron and a light bomber squadron.

The planners pointed out that in March 1946 the British government had decided Hong Kong would not be defended if an attack came from a major power occupying China.

We consider that the effectiveness of the Chinese Communist government is not such that, even if the Communists control the whole of China, it could be classed as a major power. We therefore consider that Hong Kong could be held, unless we are engaged in a war with Russia. Hong Kong, like Berlin, may well become the stage for a trial of strength between Communism and the western powers. If the Chinese Communist government were able to force our withdrawal from the colony, the blow to our prestige throughout the world would be irreparable and there would be serious repercussions on the efforts now being made against Communism in the Far East.[10]

By 28 May the stakes were still being increased. Britain decided to send two further infantry brigades, a fighter squadron, and two carriers and four destroyers or frigates. Significantly, Commonwealth governments and the United States were being asked whether they would support publicly the policy of defending Hong Kong against Communist aggression.[11]

An intelligence assessment on 2 June concluded that the return of Hong Kong to China was an important piece of Communist policy but that 'they will do their best to achieve this without recourse to open attack'. The colony was too useful as a trading centre and a base for subversion. If the Communists decided on a direct attack, it was estimated they would not be able to launch one until late September. Such an assault would probably be delivered by one or two armies, each organised into three divisions of approximately 10,000 men, supported by up to 400 artillery pieces and 100 light tanks, and with three similar armies in reserve. The assessment added: 'The threats to Hong Kong by means short of full-scale attack may well continue for many months. We consider that the Communists would have no difficulty in maintaining a serious military threat over a long period.'[12]

15
Deadlock

THE MORALE OF *AMETHYST*'S CREW remained high despite the many problems. 'All on board were determined to hold out for the truth and were willing to accept the difficult circumstances with cheerful spirit and come what may,' Kerans recorded. On 3 June he was called abruptly to another meeting with Colonel Kang, who used 'every subtle device' to get the captain to assume overall responsibility for negotiations. Kerans refused, and Kang made it clear that he did not want to deal with a senior officer. The colonel referred to the 'invasion' of Chinese sovereignty and gave 'illogical' answers, but he did agree that the interpreter Sam Leo could go to Nanking to obtain Communist currency. Kerans would take this opportunity to send a letter to Ambassador Stevenson, stating that he had said nothing to embarrass the British government and he doubted if any other officer 'could better the arguments I had already used'. He also gave a date in July when the ship would not have enough fuel to sail down river.[1]

Admiral Brind was getting frustrated, telling his wife Edie in a letter written on board *London*: 'I wish to goodness I could get on with the *Amethyst* business. There seems to be an absolute deadlock at the moment and it is difficult sometimes to insist on doing what would have been best, for if it fails the government becomes "embarrassed".'

In London, the BBC was keen to broadcast a radio programme about life aboard *Amethyst*, and a correspondent approached the Far East Station. Brind liked the idea, believing it would boost the ship and the families involved, and he gave his approval. The correspondent collected material on conditions in the frigate and also obtained personal accounts from several members of the crew. But the Admiralty and the Foreign Office learned of the programme and forced the BBC to drop it.

The First Sea Lord, Admiral Fraser, told the corporation's director general, Sir William Haley: 'The Admiralty and the Foreign Office came to the conclusion that there were objections to this feature. It is government policy to avoid publicity in this country on the *Amethyst* case, in order not to prejudice the secret negotiations which are now being pursued for the release of the ship. We know that the Chinese Communist authorities are alert to publicity in this country.' Fraser pointed out that the Admiralty sent a regular letter to the families to keep them informed. He suggested that the information collected by the correspondent could be included in the next Admiralty letter.[2]

Haley replied: 'We were naturally sorry not to be able to carry out the broadcast, but I quite understand the situation.' He agreed that the Admiralty could use the material.[3] Brind was not happy about the censorship: 'We considered this carefully here and concluded the notes given to the BBC could do little harm and might well cheer up *Amethyst*.'[4] The Admiralty, however, had no objection to the *Amethyst* men making record requests for a Listeners' Choice programme. Some of the selections showed that the crew had not lost its sense of humour: *Cruising Down The River* (Ordinary Seaman Henry Harris); *You Get Used To It* (Able Seaman James McLean); and *Swanee River* (Lieutenant Hett). Flight Lieutenant Fearnley picked *A Life On The Ocean Wave*.

Foreign Secretary Ernest Bevin referred to the conflict in China during a speech to the Labour Party conference in Blackpool on 9 June, but he made no mention of *Amethyst* or the families waiting anxiously at home. His sympathies appeared to lie with the Chinese people: 'The civil war has gone on, the Chinese suffer, and if there is any part of the world that really deserves peace it is China after the horrors she has had to undergo for all these years.' He went on to stress the importance of trade.

That day Coxswain Frank recorded in his diary: 'King's birthday, but not for *Amethyst*, no flags, no holiday, no salute, in fact no nothings. It looks like being a nice day but after eight weeks in the Yangtze we have learnt to our cost that it can be very deceptive. We learnt by signal today that our mail has reached Shanghai and that the [assistant] air attaché Howard-Williams is going to try and bring it up for us by Jeep. Good luck to the air force, we already have one of their doctors staying with us, and how thankful we are that he is here.'

By 12 June Brind was having doubts about his approach to General Chu in Peking. Hong Kong was making discreet enquiries as to whether it was likely to be fruitful. The admiral decided that if he did not hear anything in a couple of days he would assume success in that direction was unlikely. Urquhart, the British consul in Shanghai, was also sounding out one of his contacts, who told him confidentially that a telegram recommending *Amethyst*'s release had been sent to Mao Tse-tung. But Communist leaders had taken exception to a crackdown on sympathisers in Hong Kong and Britain's well-publicised move to send reinforcements to the colony. Brind believed that if the approach to Chu failed, then Urquhart should put pressure on the Communists over the threat to trade. Brind told Ambassador Stevenson: 'Unless there are other delicate negotiations of which I am unaware I strongly favour going all out at Shanghai. There now seems to be no harm and much good in inferring that the early release of *Amethyst* is to say the least of it highly important to the progress of trade relations. In fact I should put on the screw here as hard as we possibly can for to continue friendly trade discussions whilst a British warship is forcibly detained is surely quite unacceptable.'[5] The admiral may have reflected on a comment made by Admiral Kwei Yung-ching, head of the Nationalist navy, the previous month. Kwei told Brind that the only person on the Communist side who had the authority to deal with foreign affairs was Chou En-lai, who would soon become premier. It would appear that no approach was ever made to Chou.

On 12 June Kerans had another meeting with Kang, who asked if there had been any message from the commander-in-chief. Kerans, briefed by Leo after the interpreter's return from the embassy, said negotiations at the highest level were being attempted in Nanking and Peking. Kang was unaware of these moves and said he was willing to give *Amethyst* safe passage if his superiors agreed. It appeared the colonel was 'hoping for a way out himself'. Further supplies of fresh vegetables were promised, and it was the 'last comparatively peaceful meeting' that Kerans would experience.

Two days later Kerans received a message from Brind, who expressed astonishment that Kang had doubted the sincerity of his earlier assurances. Unless Kang confirmed that he was mistaken there would be no point in trying to negotiate with him. 'I felt that if I passed on these words I might well find myself isolated,' Kerans noted.

A meeting on 15 June began with a long tirade by Kang. He insisted he was the only person who could discuss the political issues and that talks had to take place in Chingkiang. Fresh doubt was cast on the commander-in-chief's assurances. At this point Kerans decided he would let Kang know what Brind thought of him, verbally and in writing. 'He did not like this at all and appeared visibly shaken. I seized my opportunity and endeavoured to shift the scene of negotiations to Nanking or alternatively that Captain Donaldson should come down here.' After a long time Kang agreed that Donaldson, the naval attaché, could be involved, so long as he did not have any diplomatic status and appeared in uniform.

On returning from the meeting, Kerans received a message from Brind suggesting that the admiral might discontinue talks through Kang though that would not stop *Amethyst*'s captain dealing with him. The fuel position was a continuing concern. It was down to 94 tons. The weather was bad, with conditions hot and humid because of almost continuous rain, but the crew were still coping well.[6]

In a message to Stevenson, Brind criticised Kerans for getting caught up in long meetings. 'I hoped Kerans would have been able to take some initiative with a short interview just giving my message,' he complained, noting that relations with Kang, the 'original culprit', were strained. The admiral wanted Donaldson to be involved and to take a firmer line and 'not participate in protracted interviews punctuated by gross insults from Kang'. Donaldson should try to deal directly with General Yuan and sideline the colonel. Brind observed: 'As price for release Communists are trying to force us to admit something we know to be untrue. This is Nazi technique and not what we expect of Chinese.'[7]

At a brief meeting on 18 June Kang asked if the commander-in-chief had appointed a representative, and he was told it was being considered. Two days later Kerans went to General Yuan's headquarters. The general repeated points made at previous meetings and said the commander-in-chief needed to appoint Captain Donaldson as his representative. If the admiral acknowledged there had been 'intrusion' and 'infringement' of Chinese territorial waters, then it might be possible to consider a separate solution for *Amethyst*'s release while talks continued on the question of apologies and compensation. Kerans thought this went a long way towards forming a possible basis for an understanding. Yuan expressed regret for *Amethyst*'s isolation on the Yangtze.[8]

The British government – and Brind – faced another headache on 21 June. Nationalist aircraft bombed and machine-gunned the British merchant ship *Anchises* at the mouth of the Whangpoo River, leading to Shanghai. Four men were wounded and the ship ran aground. The Nationalists had decided to blockade ports in Communist hands. The frigate *Black Swan* was in the Yangtze and went up river to assist *Anchises*, a vessel of the Blue Funnel Line. But the frigate had orders not to enter the Whangpoo and she turned back. The First Lord of the Admiralty, Lord Hall, told the Cabinet: 'The result is the unsatisfactory situation in which a British ship may be attacked and put in urgent need of assistance, with a British warship close by and yet debarred from rendering such assistance.' Brind gave new orders allowing warships to fire on aircraft in self-defence and those attacking British or other neutral merchant ships. Hall said the Communist authorities in Shanghai would be asked to allow warships to give humanitarian assistance. The following morning *Anchises* was strafed again.[9]

By 22 June *Amethyst*'s fuel was down to 70 tons, and Kerans decided to shut off all power for 59-hour periods, even though the temperature was rising. Brind thought it was urgent to replenish *Amethyst*. The navy arranged for a merchant ship to take supplies from Hong Kong and was waiting for clearance to go up the Yangtze. But Kerans would learn 'what masters the Chinese are in vacillation'. At a meeting in Chingkiang General Yuan refused to give clearance, saying the merchant ship would be infringing Chinese territorial waters. Kerans pointed out that as the Yangtze was now open to shipping there would not be any violation. He asked if *Amethyst* could have some of the fuel stored in Nanking and was told he would have to make a written application. The general reiterated his desire for a peaceful solution, and suggested an exchange of notes in which Britain would acknowledge 'basic facts' that a British warship 'intruded indiscreetly' into the frontier area of the PLA. Kerans was struck that Yuan referred to only one warship. It appeared that the general thought further delays could only be harmful to Anglo-Chinese friendship and business relations. Kerans concluded that Yuan did not after all want Captain Donaldson involved in negotiations.[10]

In light of Yuan's proposal, Brind drew up a draft agreement, which he sent to the Admiralty for approval. There were two key points. *Amethyst* had been near a main Communist crossing point when 'a most unfortunate but not unnatural misunderstanding occurred which caused gunfire to be opened'. The other key point: 'The admiral and the general deplore this most tragic and unfortunate incident. The admiral personally regrets that it was not found possible to inform the PLA of the intended movement of HMS *Amethyst*, that his appreciation of the situation at the time led to the movement so nearly coinciding with active operations by the PLA and that the fire of his ships should have caused Chinese casualties, the general on his part regrets the misunderstanding which resulted in casualties and damage to HMS *Amethyst*.'[11]

In London, the Cabinet also considered Yuan's proposal, but it did not see Brind's draft agreement. Ministers recognised the hardships being suffered by the crew and thought 'every effort' should be made to take advantage of the Communists' change in attitude. However, the First Lord of the Admiralty had been advised that admitting *Amethyst* 'intruded indiscreetly' would probably prejudice the government's case if it decided to seek compensation. It was agreed that Lord Hall and the foreign secretary would think again about the response. So the crew would have to carry on enduring the hardships.[12]

There was some cheer for the men on 24 June when three bags of mail turned up after 'very persistent efforts' by Leo and one of the sailors at the post office in Chingkiang. The mail had been sent from Shanghai unsealed so that it could be checked easily, but Communist military and postal officials initially refused to hand over the bags on the grounds that everything should have been sealed. It was obvious, though, that the mail had been examined – and pilfered.

There appeared to be some progress on the negotiating front. Kerans told Brind that the general was prepared to give *Amethyst* safe conduct. The admiral sent a revised agreement, saying: 'I recognise that HMS *Amethyst* unfortunately entered the People's Liberation Army frontier zone without the knowledge and concurrence of the command of the PLA. I am sure that you will share my deep regret at the casualties on both sides.' Kerans was given discretion to change the wording but advised not to make any major changes without consultation. The admiral decided that he no longer needed to call on the services of Donaldson. Later he ordered the words 'knowledge and' to be deleted, and he did not want the use of 'indiscreetly' or 'imprudently'.[13]

Kerans believed the next meeting, dealing with the agreement, would be straightforward and quick, but he suffered a bad attack of fibrositis due to extreme dampness and when he tried to arrange talks he was informed that the general and Kang were away, and the first week of July would be devoted to victory celebrations. Brind told Donaldson: 'I think this is another trick on Kerans and feel he is nearing the end of his tether, that Communists know it and are playing with him.' The admiral thought Donaldson was needed.[14]

But Brind knew it was important to continue to support Kerans. 'It is increasingly clear that Kang is deliberately attacking you personally with typical technique of creating suspense to get you down,' the admiral warned. 'This delay after hopeful situation supports this. They may have read some of our plain language signals and think we are weakening our wording which we certainly are not. Do not worry too much about prejudicing your position. Communists certainly have anxieties too.'[15]

16

The Colonel's Big Mistake

IF KERANS'S TORMENTOR, COLONEL KANG, had been planning the complete humiliation of *Amethyst*, seeking her surrender, he made a major mistake. Kerans had asked General Yuan if he could have some of the navy's oil fuel being stored at Hogee Wharf, Nanking. The request was passed to Kang, who gave his approval on 30 June. 'This was welcome news indeed,' Kerans noted, though he was aware that getting approval and actually receiving the fuel were two different obstacles.

But late on 9 July a large junk towed by an underpowered launch was sighted near *Amethyst*. It was the fuel, 294 drums of it, amounting to 54 invaluable tons. The junk only came alongside the frigate after 'many altercations' with the local garrison, and a battle with the current, which kept taking it downstream. It was too dangerous to try to get the fuel on board in the darkness, and all hands faced the difficult task at dawn the next day. There had been heavy rain for many days but 10 July, fortunately, was clear.[1]

Able Seaman Thomas Townsend recalled:

The first question on everybody's mind was 'How the hell are we going to get it aboard?' Slowly the realisation came, it's going to be done with muscle. It was a hot day. Every barrel had to be hauled up by derrick and rolled along the deck and poured into the tanks by hand. It was incredible the way it was done. Everybody got stuck in. Everybody was covered in oil and sweat, and everybody was aching from head to toe. We started early in the morning and worked right through the day non-stop.

But there was never a time when we thought we'd have to give up. We knew that one day it was going to come right. When the food started running out and we went on rations there wasn't a complaint. Nobody moaned. We were prepared to stick it out even if we got down to the last crumb. We weren't going to turn round to these people and say, 'Please let us go'. I spent my nineteenth birthday up there.[2]

The operation to get the oil on board began at 0500 and was completed at 1600, with everyone 'working like hell'. Coxswain Leslie Frank was impressed: 'The impossible has been done, what an achievement, a feat that I should think is without parallel in the history of our glorious navy. What makes this all the more praiseworthy is the fact that not only have the ship's company had no exercise for 82 days but everything used in this operation had to be improvised.'[3]

All three of the fuel connections were on the port side and the ship developed a heavy list until steam could be raised and the fuel pumped over. The ship levelled off. 'The embarkation of this fuel was a great stimulant and came as a much needed tonic,' Kerans noted. *Amethyst* now had 116 tons of fuel. There was a setback that day, however. The last valve on the wireless transmitter went, which meant that power had to be used to send messages. Later Kerans would comment: 'The outstanding success perhaps of all our time in the river was the receipt of 54 tons of Admiralty oil fuel. I shall never know why the Communist authorities were so ready to accede to the entry of this invaluable oil fuel . . . This was the one mistake of Colonel Kang – for a long time he thought we burned coal!'[4]

The month of July had begun with some promise. The assistant naval attaché in Shanghai arranged to send an interpreter called Khoong with medicine, mosquito netting, Communist currency – and charts of the lower Yangtze. The persistent Khoong arrived in Chingkiang after a difficult rail journey and threats of arrest on two occasions. He handed over the supplies to Leo but the charts were confiscated because they were deemed secret and issued by the 'reactionary' Nationalist government, even though they had been bought in a shop in Shanghai and Khoong could produce the receipt. Kang no doubt thought that *Amethyst* could not get down the Yangtze without the charts, and Kerans, looking on the positive side, realised that the decision gave him some cover. As Coxswain Frank would point out: 'Little do they know that we can go down without them.'

With the fighting over in the areas surrounding the Yangtze, more and more ships were using the river, day and night. In the early hours of 2 July, the darkened *Amethyst* was almost rammed by two large merchant ships. The vessels moving at night were carrying military supplies for the Communists, and the frigate had not been showing any lights because of the danger of Nationalist air attacks. The following night another ship narrowly avoided hitting *Amethyst*. 'This is getting rather too much,' Frank recorded. 'Our nerves are not in a condition to stand many shocks like that these days.' Kerans decided the ship should display anchor and stern lights. He also asked the assistant naval attaché in Shanghai to warn shipping companies of *Amethyst*'s presence, although by this time she was almost 'a landmark'.

The interpreter Leo was trying to find out from the local garrison commander when talks would resume and learned that the wording of the agreement might be a lengthy process. Kerans sent a letter to Kang, saying the unnecessary delays were not understood, and were causing continued hardship to the crew. 'I always stressed the latter point whenever I could as it was always a sore point with the Communists,' Kerans reported. 'This was a depressing period and personally my spirits were low as I did not see what I could do next to hasten matters – and time was so vital. This was the longest wait [22 June to 5 July] between meetings and the period of activity was beginning to tell on us all.'

Without warning on 5 July Kerans was called to a meeting with Kang at the village opposite the ship. There was a 'distinct hardening' of attitude, with the Communists objecting to the wording of Admiral Brind's suggested agreement. They wanted a key paragraph to read: 'I recognise that HMS *Amethyst* and the other three British warships involved in the incident infringed into China's national river and the PLA frontier zone, without the permission of the PLA being a basic fault on the part of the British side.' Kang had originally wanted to use 'invasion' [invaded] instead of 'infringed' and 'fundamental guilt' instead of 'basic fault'. Kerans pointed out that the new wording was different from the agreement that General Yuan had in mind on 22 June. But he became optimistic when the question of safe conduct was brought up, with the offer of a pilot and a promise that all batteries would be warned. *Amethyst* might be able to sail in a week's time. 'This was, of course, all part of Kang's tactics to wear me down and build up false hopes,' Kerans noted. 'It was not apparent to me at the time.'

Kerans had been trying to get the diplomat Edward Youde involved in the talks. It was Youde, fluent in Mandarin, who had made the determined attempt to contact the Communist authorities soon after the attack on *Amethyst*. Kang blocked the diplomat's permit to leave Nanking but told Leo several days later that he was willing to have him involved in negotiations.

Kerans tried hard to persuade the colonel to return the charts brought from Shanghai but met only indifference. 'Regrettably I nearly lost my temper, I was so exasperated at this unreasonable attitude,' he admitted. 'I needed Youde's help badly, since Leo's advice and knowledge, good enough though it was, was insufficient when it came to technicalities over wording.' The agreement would be in Chinese and Kerans was worried in case 'infringed' became 'invaded' because the characters might be similar. He was unhappy about the wording anyway but decided it was the best he could do after an hour's discussion.[5]

Brind was informed of the outcome of the meeting and sent a message saying the proposed wording was 'quite unacceptable'. There was a sharply-worded telegram to Ambassador Stevenson from the Foreign Office, probably on the direction of the foreign secretary: 'I cannot accept any phraseology which involves our conceding that we were in the wrong. On whatever level it may be conducted the fact remains that this is the first important negotiation we are having with the Communists. If we show willingness to make concessions which jeopardise our whole position in the matter even before actual negotiations begin, the Communists will score such a triumph (which will no doubt be widely publicised) that we may never recover from this initial step.' Britain might end up taking the matter to the United Nations, but in the meantime, to secure *Amethyst*'s release, Brind had permission to admit that the frigate entered the frontier zone 'without the concurrence' of the PLA and it caused 'a misunderstanding'.[6]

A senior member of Brind's staff produced a lengthy assessment of *Amethyst* and her situation. Living conditions on board were 'fairly grim'. Meat would run out before the end of July and all basic foods by early August, although the ship was still getting supplies from local traders. Power was being shut down for long spells, with only emergency lighting and no ventilation. *Amethyst* remained badly damaged but she could still sail down the river, which was high. Surprisingly, the report made damning comments about Kerans and the ship's company.

On the crew, the assessment pointed out:

There is very little to show what the men are feeling like. The tunes they chose for the special broadcast showed they still had a sense of humour left on 23 June. She had not a reputation of a good ship before the incident and was very dirty. It has been suggested that the crew might be mutinous, especially as regards drastic action is concerned such as making a night escape. I doubt whether this is so; after all the ship is closed down for 54 hours at a time [Kerans originally decided on 59 hours] and the crew is thus denied every form of normal amenity. However, they may be submitting to this in order to avoid falling into the hands of the Communists and the possibility must be borne in mind.

On Kerans, the report said:

He led a roving life in the past, moving from job to job and tending to leave in a hurry. On one occasion he found himself in trouble for not controlling his men properly on Christmas Day. He is also reputed to be fond of the bottle but there is no need to exaggerate this. He has had experience of 'I' work and interrogation and is supposed to be good at negotiating. No great personality according to those who have met him.

Kerans lately has been showing signs in his signals of being under considerable strain. His emotions are obviously very near the surface and he flies from elation to depression very easily. His responsibility weighs heavily on him and this is not surprising as he must be aware that he is the focus of public attention. He is living in very poor conditions and he may well not be sure of the morale of his crew.

He may or may not have been worked on by his opponents but the effect on him seems to be the same whichever is true. There have been moments when he has been encouraged by statements or events to believe that the end was near – but these have all been shattered soon afterwards leaving him in what can only be described as a pitiful state.

The cumulative effect of all this . . . seems to have left him with nothing but the strongest desire to end it all at any cost with the greatest possible speed. The Communists to him represent something very powerful against which he regards himself as impotent – the only thing to do is to appease them. He no longer seems to believe in the efficacy of taking a firm line.

It was thought unlikely that the Communists wanted to seize *Amethyst*. Their probable aim was to 'humiliate the British', showing that they could defy foreigners and get away with it. The report recommended that Kerans should be relieved of his command if he did not take a tougher stand.[7]

Brind and his staff were not the only ones with doubts about Kerans and his tactics. 'By the beginning of July some of us were wondering whether we were ever going to get anywhere with negotiations,' said Lieutenant Hett.

> The only solution might be to break out. This is something I did not much discuss with Commander Kerans. Obviously he was the man doing the negotiations and he was the chap who would have to take a decision if we were going to break out. Lieutenant Strain and a few others did talk about this, and we began to start saying this to Commander Kerans but he didn't take these suggestions very sympathetically. He may well have agreed with what we were saying but he didn't give us any support. I suspect he didn't want the feeling going around the ship that sooner or later we were going to have to break out.[8]

Perhaps Brind and his staff had underestimated the resolve of Kerans and his crew. At about this time the captain announced that the ship would have to go on half rations. The men accepted it. According to Coxswain Frank, they were still backing him all the way: 'It looks as if the captain thinks that they [the Communists] are going to try to starve us in to giving in and using the wording they want. But then again Kang does not know the British sailor, and whatever the captain decides he can rest assured that we are all with him, and we shall not let him down.'[9]

On 10 July there was a significant disclosure. Vice Admiral Madden sent a signal to the commander-in-chief saying that Lieutenant Berger, who was seriously wounded in the attack on *Amethyst*, had told him the frigate tested her firing circuits shortly before the Communists opened fire. Berger was certain the main guns were trained fore and aft, but the weather was calm and still, and it was likely that the batteries heard the noise and saw the smoke. 'The possibility that in the keyed up state they mistook this for firing cannot be ruled out,' Madden reported. 'It is also possible that the battery commander's firm assertion in the early discussions that they did not fire first may have been founded on this.' The question of who fired first was no longer being pursued by the Communists in talks but, Madden pointed out, it might be raised again later on.

Earlier, Madden had officially recorded that he took 'sole and entire responsibility' for the decision to send *Amethyst* up the Yangtze. 'I judged that the need to fulfil the Nanking commitment justified the risk as I saw it; I did not foresee what turned out to be a determined and sustained attack on the ship. The subsequent loss of life in and damage to HM Ships, which I most deeply regret, was therefore due to my error in underestimating the risk involved.'[10]

Another meeting took place in Chingkiang on 11 July, and it was obvious to Kerans that Kang had been reading the plain-language signals between *Amethyst* and Brind. The admiral had sent a revised agreement, which Kerans thought went a long way to meet the Communist demands. Brind acknowledged that *Amethyst*'s entry into the frontier zone without the 'concurrence' of the PLA caused a misunderstanding. If the agreement was acceptable to the Communists, Kerans had permission to sign it. The meeting did not start well. For some 40 minutes Kerans was forced to listen to a tirade of abuse, including complaints about minor typing errors, which were deemed an insult to the PLA. Eventually he managed to steer the talks back to the point that General Yuan's proposal of 22 June differed significantly from Kang's demands on 5 July. Kerans asked to see the general but was told that he would first have to make an application in writing and, in any case, Kang was authorised to carry on the negotiations. All the previous arguments were reiterated before Kerans was able to present Brind's 'final' proposed agreement. There would be no concessions beyond keeping to the truth. The talks went on for three hours before Kang rejected the admiral's solution and insisted there could not be a separate guarantee of safe conduct, despite the general's earlier assurance. *Amethyst* would have to stay.

Clearance for a merchant ship to bring supplies from Hong Kong was again refused on the grounds that it would be an attempt to 'invade', despite the obvious fact that the Yangtze was open to shipping. Kang also refused to allow Youde to participate in negotiations. 'This was probably the worst meeting I endured, in which a virtual ultimatum had been delivered to accede to their demands and every effort was being made to ensure our isolation and increase the severity of living conditions on board,' Kerans reported. 'The fact that I was unable to see the general was clear that Kang was playing his own game . . . Deadlock was reached and when Kang realised I was not going to give in to his wishes the meeting broke up.'[11]

17
Thoughts of Escape

LIEUTENANT HETT'S HINTS THAT THE only avenue remaining was an escape attempt had not registered with Kerans, or so it appeared. However, the possibility of escape seems to have been on the captain's mind for some time. After the failure of the meeting on 11 July *Amethyst*'s dire position was once again put into sharp focus. Negotiations could get worse and stores, food and especially fuel, were continuing to dwindle. On the other hand, if Kerans broke off talks, there could be repercussions for the British communities in China. And a breakout might lead to loss of life. How acceptable would that be?

Kerans thought the best chance of escape would be before or after a typhoon, with heavy rainfall providing cover. The weather should silence the batteries but there would be enough visibility for the ship to see the banks, although without radar the risk was high. Since the earliest days, after destroying secret equipment and code books, *Amethyst* was hampered by the fact that she did not have a secure means of communication with the Far East Station. Kerans needed guidance and he sent a plain-language signal to Admiral Brind: 'Grateful your advice on my actions if menaced by a typhoon. Have informed general on several occasions of this possible danger in order to hasten matters.' There were some on the admiral's staff who saw no hidden meaning, but Brind realised it was an opportunity to give permission to escape and sent the reply: 'Typhoons are unlikely to reach you in serious strength and you are in good holding ground, the golden rule of making an offing and taking plenty of sea room applies particularly.'

Kerans concluded, however, that the admiral was not giving his permission, and admitted later he had made 'a grave error of judgement'. Hett 'and others' realised straight away that Brind wanted him to try to escape. The advice to get sea room was too strong a hint. A few days later Brind's second-in-command, Vice Admiral Madden, sent a signal that added to the confusion: 'Presumably her [*Amethyst*'s] anchor is now deeply embedded by silt and unlikely to drag. Best action therefore to veer as much cable as possible using second anchor either to control yaw or back up first anchor. I should be able to give *Amethyst* ample warning of approach of typhoon.' Kerans decided that this was confirmation that he should stay and try to negotiate his way out.[1]

It is perhaps not surprising that Kerans ended up being confused. For a long time Brind had resisted suggestions that there should be an escape attempt. Commander Peter Dickens became the admiral's staff officer operations in the May. When *Amethyst* was attacked he had been digging early potatoes on the family farm in Wiltshire. He remarked to his father, Admiral Sir Gerald Dickens: 'She'll have to make a run for it – there's no other way out.'

Brind's flag lieutenant, David Scott, recounted:

Peter never deviated from this view, and as soon as he felt himself settled in his new appointment he voiced his opinion to Admiral Brind. At that time the C-in-C still believed he would be able to bring the negotiations to a successful conclusion, and he gave Peter a decisively negative response, leaving no room for discussion. Peter nevertheless continued to take every opportunity to repeat his conviction, hoping that it would eventually take root in the mind of the C-in-C. The Chinese negotiators played into his hands. Exasperation and frustration caused by their attitude began to change the mind of the C-in-C. Finally, it was the receipt of a signal from Kerans asking for advice as to the action he should take if engulfed by an approaching typhoon which caused Admiral Brind to believe that an attempted break-out by *Amethyst*, even if it resulted in heavy casualties and the loss of the ship, was the best course of action for the Royal Navy and the country. He tried his thoughts out on his staff officer operations very late one evening while at sea in HMS *Alert*. Needless to say, Peter was delighted. For the C-in-C to determine on such a course of action was a most remarkable display of moral courage, for Whitehall policy was that further casualties were quite unacceptable.[2]

Despite the confusion, Kerans realised he might be left with no alternative but an attempt to escape. He feared that the Communists would soon demand *Amethyst's* unconditional surrender or complete acceptance of their terms. There was a heartening factor: 'One thing I knew was certain, and that was that no one on board would give in; Kang had, I felt sure, little conception of British spirit.' He was worried, however, about relatives in England who were obviously growing more anxious as each day passed, especially as the crew had not been able to send any letters home.

After dark on 13 July there was a surprise visit from Captain Tai, the local garrison commander, who brought a long despatch from General Yuan intended for Admiral Brind. This communication pointed out that Kerans was not fully authorised to negotiate, unlike Kang. The general expressed regret that the British had been using delaying tactics and urged a speedy settlement. Kerans found it significant that Yuan was involving himself again. The ship's power had been shut down for the night but steam was raised so that the message could be sent to the admiral.

Captain Tai's evening visit inevitably prompted rumours, and the next morning Kerans addressed the crew, who thought there might be important news. Kerans spoke for about 15 minutes but, of course, there was little to reveal. The Communists were still playing mind games. He spent most of the time reminding his men of the need for security. Although the crew were not allowed ashore, unguarded comments could be picked by the Chinese on board and passed to the traders who came alongside in sampans.[3]

That day saw a message of reassurance from Admiral Brind, which was pinned up on notice boards around the ship. In view of the fact that messages could not be sent in code, it is perhaps surprising that Brind decided to be so forthright, ignoring prying eyes and the sensitivities of the Chinese:

It is clear that the Communists have been holding you hostage to wring admissions from the British government which would not only be untrue and dishonourable but would harm the cause of free nations in the future. For the present therefore you are in the forefront of what is called the 'cold war' in which the cause of freedom is being attacked. I know it is a pretty hot war as far as you are concerned and your stand is widely recognised and greatly admired. No one can say how this will end, but of one thing I am quite sure, neither the British government, the *Amethyst*'s ship's company nor myself will ever submit to threats or perversions of the truth; nor shall we do anything to harm our country's honour.

The crew should know that they were in the thoughts of the government, the people at home and sailors throughout the fleet.[4] Kerans added his own note: 'Keep this notice clean so all can read.'

Brind replied quickly to Yuan's communication. He confirmed that Kerans was his representative, who could pass and receive messages and sign a safe-conduct agreement. This authorisation would be signed on the admiral's behalf by naval attaché Donaldson – so long as contact with Nanking could be made. Brind asked for the involvement of the diplomat Youde, who would help as an interpreter. In a message to Kerans, the admiral suggested he should keep contact with Kang to a minimum.

After a religious service on the morning of Sunday, 17 July, the ship's company posed for photographs. They were divided into groups: all the thin men, led by Kerans; all the 'fat' men, led by Fearnley the RAF doctor; all the 'glamour', led by Hett; all those wearing beards; everyone not in those groups; and all the Chinese. It is surprising that fat men were still on board, given the weeks of deprivation, the searing heat and the manual work. Perhaps they were just slightly overweight. The photo session illustrated the high morale, as Coxswain Frank noted: 'This caused a lot of merriment among the ship and I am perfectly sure that if Colonel Kang or the general had seen us he would have said, "We shall never make them give in". And believe me, he won't. Our ensign has been flying since the incident and although rather tattered and torn now and riddled with gunfire it is still flying and will remain so as long as *Amethyst* stays afloat.'[5] The men had something else to cheer them. A consignment of emergency stores from Shanghai arrived. They included medical supplies, disinfectant and rat traps, as well as cigarettes, sweets and books. All the boxes had been opened in Chingkiang. During the afternoon a plane flew over and dropped a couple of bombs on land, a reminder that the civil war was still going on.

Brind continued to agonise over *Amethyst*'s fate, coming to the conclusion that any further negotiations were unlikely to make progress and that the frigate would have to be rescued, or 'cut out', as he put it. A night operation was envisaged. The admiral came up with Plan A and Plan B, and the date he had in mind was 25 July. Plan A would see *Amethyst* under way by 0200. Two destroyers would be sent up the Yangtze the previous night, anchoring at a suitable location during daylight, and then dash to rendezvous with her, aiming to pass Kiangyin by 0500 at the latest on the return. Two other destroyers would pass Woosung at speed and wait below Kiangyin to give cover. Plan B involved sending all four destroyers up the Yangtze at the same time. Brind noted: 'Plan B is intended to have *Amethyst* under way with a strong escort before Communists realise, and be one jump ahead of them all day.' He added: 'The political implication of operation is fully appreciated particularly the seriousness of failure. Nevertheless it must be examined as an operation and its chances assessed.'

Brind's plans were outlined in a top-secret message to his second-in-command, Madden. The Admiralty was not consulted. Madden must have shuddered when he saw Plan A and Plan B. Only a short time earlier he had admitted to major errors of judgement in sending *Amethyst* up the Yangtze in the first place and ordering the subsequent rescue attempts by *Consort*, *London* and *Black Swan*, with great loss of life. Tactfully, he replied that he had 'carefully considered' the plans. Madden pointed out that there was a lack of intelligence about Communist batteries. There were navigational hazards, with buoys probably out of place, and river craft such as junks could be mistaken for them.

Madden told his superior:

Our opinion is that both Plans A and B would jeopardise surprise, and draw most unwelcome attention to *Amethyst* before anything could be done. The chances of ships not being spotted in daylight is extremely small. By night destroyers at speed or their wash will certainly be heard if not seen. After full consideration we reluctantly conclude that neither Plan A nor B offers more than a slender chance of success with a high degree of risk that we might have at least one other ship in a predicament similar to *Amethyst* and a near certainty of considerable casualties.

I regret, therefore, that I could not recommend to you the adoption of either plan as a practicable operation. Unless we have carrier-borne rocket-firing aircraft after reconnaissance, it is not justifiable to assume that conditions would differ greatly from those which obtained on 20th and 21st April.

Madden thought *Amethyst*'s best chance was to make a lone dash down river, though he rated success at only 50 per cent. If the escape attempt were unsuccessful, the Communists 'would probably not give the crew much quarter'. As a last resort a submarine might be able to reach *Amethyst* and take off the crew if there was a decision to destroy the ship.[6]

Monday, 18 July marked 90 days since the attack on *Amethyst*. Frank recorded: 'Still going strong. I wonder how much longer that Bastard is going to keep us?' The heat was becoming a major problem and the following night, with no wind, the messdecks were 'like an oven'. Rats remained a challenge, and 52 traps were set with 'nil result'. Frank acknowledged: 'I don't think you can beat the cat [Simon] for catching them.'

One challenge, however, had resulted in a solution. Brind's flag lieutenant, David Scott, gave much thought to the problem that *Amethyst* could not send secure signals to the Far East Station. While at sea with the admiral on board the frigate *Alert*, he came up with an entirely new code. 'The starting point of my thoughts was simply this – what has *Amethyst* got on board in the way of anything written or printed, of which we, the staff, could lay our hands on an identical duplicate, but which the Chinese could not?' Scott recalled. 'Books such as reference books or novels were dangerous, as there could be no assurance that they could not be recognised by the Chinese. Eventually, the idea of using *Amethyst*'s next-of-kin list, a duplicate of which was held at headquarters in Singapore, occurred to me. *Amethyst* did still hold the government telegraph code, which could certainly not be regarded as secure. However, it could be used for the initial instructions to *Amethyst* as to how to construct the cipher . . .' The new code involved using a surname, first name and city, town or village from the next-of-kin list, and then letters would be substituted for four-figure groups of numbers. Blocks of numbers could be sent and then decoded to reveal the message. With some 70 men on board, each with three words, the total for conversion to figures was more than 200. Years later Scott was annoyed to see a claim by author C E Lucas Phillips in the book *Escape of the Amethyst* that the code had been 'borrowed from the Germans'. Scott complained: 'I have no idea who propagated this myth, or the motivation in expounding it. To this day I have never been able to trace any such German code.'[7]

On 22 July Kerans, accompanied by Lieutenant Strain, went to a meeting in Chingkiang, which would turn out to be his last attempt to negotiate with the Communists. General Yuan once again stressed he was keen to come to an agreement. Then came the obstacles. He would not accept Captain Donaldson's signature as authorisation – it needed to be that of Admiral Brind. 'Nothing I said would convince them that this was an impossible request and that signalled authorisation was legitimate,' Kerans reported. The general suddenly widened the discussion to include *Consort*, *London* and *Black Swan*, as well as *Amethyst*. All four warships had entered the PLA's frontier area, and it was necessary to acknowledge 'fundamental guilt' and give an assurance over apologies and reparations. The general rejected the admiral's proposed agreement and the request to allow Youde to take part in talks. When Kerans complained that Kang's conduct had been unsatisfactory, he received a rebuke that this was 'libellous'. The general hurried away from the meeting, and Kerans was left to deal with his old adversary Kang. For two hours Kerans argued that Youde's presence was essential so that the wording of the agreement would be acceptable to both sides. He made it clear that the commander-in-chief would not go back on previous statements. Kang, surprisingly, was 'a good deal less vociferous than in the past'.

The meeting adjourned for lunch, a six-course meal with Shanghai beer, and Kerans was astonished to hear Kang speaking to Strain in 'perfect English'. The colonel had always insisted that he could not speak the language. Strain stressed the difficult conditions that the crew were continuing to endure, and Kerans wondered if Kang was starting to show concern about outside reaction, or perhaps 'feeling the ground' before presenting terms for surrender. Before the meeting closed Kerans asked for clearance so that a Chinese ship could bring 250 tons of oil fuel and provisions from Shanghai. Kang said he would consider the request, and *Amethyst*'s captain left 'reasonably hopeful'. He returned to the ship with four precious bottles of beer, which were raffled in each mess.

The next day Kerans was once again worrying about the level of fuel, which had dropped to 79 tons. There would have to be further economies. Signals could be read without power but it was necessary to raise steam to send replies. The intense heat was taking its toll on the sole telegraphist, French, who would be dripping in sweat. He was supposed to produce every message in triplicate, using carbon copies. These became so 'sticky' that he cut down to two copies, hoping that it would not be noticed. Frank had written in his diary: 'I am afraid that if the oil gets much lower we shall be shutting down again for 48 hours at a time, then it won't be uncomfortable any more, it will be just plain hell. Even to write this I have four sheets of blotting paper under my wrist and it is soaked through.' Interpreter Leo was sent ashore for 36 hours so that he could have a well-earned rest. He was asked to return with local money – and the views of the embassy on the latest talks.

18

Typhoon Gloria

ON 23 JULY KERANS BECAME aware of another problem, or perhaps it was a difficulty that would help to provide a solution to *Amethyst*'s plight. Typhoon Gloria had formed to the south of Formosa and was moving north towards the coast of China. It was likely to pass over the Yangtze to the west of Shanghai. Vice Admiral Madden warned Kerans that *Amethyst* would probably be in Gloria's path, with winds of 80 knots and heavy rain on the night of 24/25 July. Steam was kept at half an hour's notice throughout the night, but the weather remained relatively calm.

Kerans, of course, had failed to take the hint of escape when Admiral Brind suggested 'plenty of sea room' on 11 July in dealing with a typhoon. On 25 July Brind sent the following signal to *Amethyst*: 'I am very interested in how you fare. Typhoon Gloria has already been chasing some of us. I think you should be quite safe. My previous advice applies, and you may think it wise to warn Kang that it may be essential for you to move downstream because of weather. I shall, of course, support your judgement.' Kerans replied: 'If [anchor] cable parts will run for it. If wrecked and salvage impossible will blow up ship. Personnel to Shanghai.'

Amethyst's captain finally realised he had permission to escape using a typhoon as cover. But the admiral's signal arrived at noon, and the weather had deteriorated rapidly during the morning. 'By now I felt that I had left it too late as the wind was increasing and turning in the narrow part of the river would have been a lengthy operation,' Kerans reported. 'Visibility did not close down as far as the shore opposite was concerned until about 1400 and then only for a short while. I nearly decided to slip and run for it there and then . . .' Of course, if the anchor cable had parted there would have been no choice. The ship was actually riding out the typhoon quite well, though conditions in the middle of the river were extremely rough. *Amethyst* was light and Kerans feared that his battle-scarred frigate might not be structurally sound in strong winds and buffeting waves.[1] By 1900 the storm had eased and the crew were able to relax. Those on watch were treated to a few bizarre sights, including a dog sitting on top of a haystack floating downstream and a pig trying to swim as far away from the frigate as possible, presumably anxious not to provide a supply of fresh pork.

Kerans had time to reflect on Brind's messages, still annoyed that he had failed to act decisively: 'I was somewhat depressed at having been so slow to sense their true meaning and by now, since the typhoon had passed, an opportunity had been missed, and it must certainly have appeared so to those elsewhere.'

The next day everything was back to normal, according to Coxswain Frank, with 'the same old game of waiting, waiting and more waiting'. He wrote in his diary: 'Everyone is now enjoying a little relaxation after the tension of yesterday, and I should say no one deserves it more than the captain, who was on the go all the time from morning until evening, and if the cable had parted he would have had to make a quick decision regarding the ship and everyone on board. We are all very relieved that it was not necessary for him to do so.' A trader appeared with a welcome consignment of Shanghai beer, which was regarded as a 'historic' occasion for sailors not used to going so long without alcohol, though the price was an extortionate twelve shillings and sixpence a bottle against the usual one shilling and three pence. Frank was so moved that he peeled off the label and kept it as a souvenir, marking it with the date – and the price.[2]

On 27 July Brind sent a revised agreement to be passed to General Yuan. It was essentially the same as the previous proposal but it did mention all the warships, *Amethyst*, *Consort*, *London* and *Black Swan*, as the Communists had demanded. The vessels had caused a 'misunderstanding' by entering the PLA's frontier zone without agreement. There was no objection on the British side to any investigation that might be ordered by 'our superior authorities'.

If the general and Kerans could not agree on the terms, Brind suggested that the alternative was a personal meeting between himself and Yuan. The admiral said he was willing to come by destroyer and asked for clearance. If that was not acceptable, permission was sought for Youde to join *Amethyst* and an aircraft to be allowed to fly to Nanking with the admiral's letter of authorisation, so that Kerans could sign the agreement.

In Nanking, Ambassador Stevenson was pessimistic about making progress after Kerans's last meeting with Yuan. He told Brind: 'They seem to have to have returned to their original aim of forcing us to accept the responsibility for the whole incident as a condition for the release of *Amethyst*.' It was clear that the Communists wanted to avoid high-level negotiations. The ambassador agreed that the admiral should try to arrange a personal meeting with Yuan, though he doubted this would be acceptable given 'his present aggressive mood'. But it was worth pursuing if only to cause embarrassment.[3]

Stevenson reported his doubts to the Foreign Office and warned that the time was approaching when alternatives would have to be considered to break the stalemate. Britain might have to accept 'unquestionably ignominious terms' or resort to 'drastic expedients' such as scuttling the ship or allowing *Amethyst* to make a dash for it under cover of darkness. The sailors could not continue to endure physical hardship in the intense heat. 'We are, of course, under no delusions as to the risky nature of latter two courses and serious consequences of failure,' the ambassador noted. The only other potential weapon was publicity, which would be 'problematical in view of traditional Communist disregard of humanitarian and sentimental considerations'. Some publicity might be necessary anyway to prepare the British public for the possible shock in the event of a drastic attempt to resolve the crisis. Stevenson thought the time had come to 'modify gradually our policy of reticence' and counter the false claims of the Communists and reveal the true picture. This could be done subtly with parliamentary questions and answers. Communist leaders would quickly learn of these and they could hardly object to facts being presented through the democratic process.[4]

There was another warning of a typhoon on 29 July. It was travelling northwest from a point east of Formosa, and Kerans had high hopes that it would head for the Yangtze. This time he would be ready. But it curved towards south-east Japan. Using his interpreter Leo, Kerans made several attempts to contact Kang about the request for more oil and to find out the date of the next meeting. There was no response, and it was learned that the colonel had gone to Nanking.

Kerans tried to remain optimistic, sending a positive message to Brind:

I cannot speak too highly of the conduct, bearing and fortitude of my remaining ship's company. They have endured a long period of hardships under almost intolerable conditions, with cheerfulness and courage, which can have few equals in time of peace. Many of them are new arrivals on the station and nearly all extremely young. British spirit in adversity has once again shown itself to be unassailable. Please tell the fleet we shall keep the old flag flying, riddled though it may be by gunfire and come what may. Good luck to all.[5]

After some difficulty *Amethyst* managed to acquire a working knowledge of the code devised by Lieutenant Scott. There had been problems with decryption and repetitions were avoided on security grounds. By 30 July the fuel position was again a serious concern. There were 55 tons left but 16 tons would have to be deducted for 'loss of suction', leaving 39 tons. Power for communications and distillation would reduce that figure to 33 tons. Kerans thought it unlikely that the Communists would give clearance for a destroyer or a plane. Talks could drag on for many more weeks. 'Clearly I had to make my decision now or face operational immobility to leave the Yangtze,' he reflected.[6]

That day had started like many others for Frank: 'We never thought we were going to be stuck up here all this time, but there it is, we have been, and as far as we can see are just as likely to be here for another month or so. We are, of course, sincerely hoping that we shall not be.' Later that day the coxswain saw signs that there 'must be something brewing', with the captain demanding complete security on board.[7]

There was indeed something brewing. At 1500 on 30 July Kerans made his decision. *Amethyst* would attempt to escape. Using the new code, he sent a flash signal to Admiral Brind: 'Top secret. I am going to try to break out 2200 tonight.'

19

We're Going Tonight

THE SHORTAGE OF FUEL AND Colonel Kang's mind games were not the only factors that Kerans weighed up before deciding that he needed to try to escape. With further fuel economies, the crew would not have been able to endure the intense heat for much longer, despite the fact that they were still in reasonable shape physically. Telegraphist French, stuck in his cramped office for long spells, was suffering the most. He was starting to miss messages, and on some occasions he found it impossible to write down signals. The only way to give him some relief was to pump a bellows at him. The ship had run out of some basic items of food. Flour was almost exhausted and the sugar had gone bad. By late August the ship's company would have faced starvation. Supplies of fresh food from local traders had been severely disrupted because of flooding of the Yangtze's banks caused by Typhoon Gloria. Kerans hoped that the flooding would have forced the Communists to reposition their batteries further inland. And it was reasonable to assume that most of the artillery moved south during the PLA's advance. Kerans learned from the BBC that the merchant ship *Anchises*, which was attacked by Nationalist aircraft in June, had left Shanghai, so she could not be held hostage as a reprisal. The moon on 30 July was suitable for a breakout and it would not be favourable for another month. The moon would set at 2315 but Kerans was willing to go at 2200. *Amethyst*'s captain knew he had the backing of Admiral Brind – and, perhaps most important, he would have the element of surprise.[1]

The first person Kerans took into his confidence on board *Amethyst* on 30 July was George Strain, the electrical officer who days earlier had been promoted lieutenant commander. Then Leonard Williams, the senior man in the engine room, was informed. 'Four hours before the escape I was called for a personal conference with the captain,' said Williams. 'He told me he was going to make a run for it that night. I was told to keep secrecy. It was going to be an eight-hour dash at full speed and the engines needed to be in first-class order. It takes four hours to flash up the boilers so that's why he told me when he did. I had to make an excuse to the others in the engine room that Commander Kerans had told me to flash up because we were expecting a typhoon.'[2] At 1945 Kerans called seventeen chief petty officers, petty officers and key ratings to his cabin, and gave them a full briefing. The men were told to discreetly pass on the information to other members of the ship's company.

'I don't think there was one of us whose heart did not give an extra beat,' Coxswain Frank recorded. 'I know mine did, not with fear, but I think it must have been with excitement or quite possibly the feeling that at last we were going to give Kang a smack in the eye.'[3]

One of Kerans's concerns was the reaction of his eight Chinese. A shout to shore or an attempt to signal would put the entire escape plan in jeopardy. 'I was perfectly prepared if necessary to shoot my Chinese if all else failed,' he admitted. They were watched carefully and several of them were locked below. But in the event they did not cause any trouble. Another difficulty was the position of Sam Leo, the loyal interpreter who had volunteered to help the negotiations over *Amethyst*. Leo was an employee of the British embassy and his wife was in Nanking, with two sons fighting for the Nationalists. 'He alone of all on board besides myself was fully aware that Colonel Kang would keep his word and destroy the ship by all means possible if I attempted to break out,' Kerans reported. To give him a cover story the captain sent Leo ashore with a letter for Kang asking for permission to go to the mission hospital in Chingkiang to collect urgent medical supplies for a rating who was very ill. To add authenticity to the letter Fearnley the RAF doctor listed the medicine needed. Leo was told to remain in Chingkiang overnight so that he could make an approach to Kang in the morning about the request for more fuel, stressing the growing plight of the crew. 'I much regret having taken this course, but obviously I could not bring him into my confidence and his reactions might have jeopardised the whole operation,' Kerans reported. 'It was one man's life against the rest of us on board.' Sadly, Sam Leo would pay with his life.[4]

Kerans revealed that as early as May he had been thinking of escape. He wanted to change the silhouette of the ship, giving orders for the mast and upper deck to be stripped of as much equipment as possible.

'No officer or rating was ever aware of my real intentions. I gave as cover the necessity to reduce top weight and increasing stability by striking heavy weights below.' Another reason he gave for this work was to keep the men busy, and he admitted that many thought him 'somewhat eccentric'. Removing these items also lessened the risk of splinter wounds, which had been suffered by many sailors in the main attack on 20 April. Kerans noticed that a large number of former US tank landing craft were using the Yangtze commercially, and he hoped that *Amethyst* might be mistaken for one of these vessels. Shortly before 2200 on 30 July the forward section of the ship was camouflaged by rigging black canvas, which was also stretched from the back of the bridge to the funnel. Red and green lights demanded by the Communists for shipping were positioned, but they would be used as a last resort. Black paint was thrown over white parts of the superstructure. It was important to slip the anchor cable without making any noise, and Kerans had previously arranged for it to be soaked in grease and soap and covered with bedding, which no doubt was seen as another eccentric act. All the ensigns were lowered except one. At night the ship had been in darkness, apart from two small warning lights for shipping, and it was hoped that sentries on shore would not notice any difference.

There were only enough sailors to man one of the 4in guns and the port Oerlikon. Ammunition considered dangerous had been thrown over the side. The only navigation aid was the echo sounder, which Yangtze pilots did not regard as accurate because of the fast flow of the river.[5]

And if the escape attempt failed? Kerans had a plan and it involved the ultimate sacrifice:

My intentions were, if hit and sinking, to beach if possible, to save life, then to blow up the ship. I had 24 detonators kept ready for this eventuality but only two people knew of this, and they will not be named. These two would have gone down in the ship with me. A and B magazines and the Bofors magazines were full. I would have set alight to the oil fuel and made the last signal myself before destroying the W/T office. All seacocks would have been opened, and I considered the ship could have been fully destroyed. Ensigns would have been left flying.[6]

Admiral Brind did not initially tell the Admiralty or his second-in-command, Madden, about the secret code that had been devised by his flag lieutenant. He was uneasy about keeping this quiet and the fact that he had given Kerans permission to try to escape. On 29 July he sent a signal explaining the position, but it was marked 'priority', which in the curious world of naval signals did not mean that. A priority signal had a relatively low precedence and was not considered of immediate operational importance. The admiral was playing for time.[7]

The signal read: 'I have told *Amethyst* that I shall support him in any decision he makes to break out. I have made it clear that I am not pressing him to do so and that suggestion only applies if he considers conditions of weather and visibility suitable. There was some hope he might try during passage of recent typhoon. He is being carefully watched and navigation is difficult. Unless fuel and stores arrive within ten days it may be necessary to order him to destroy the ship.'[8]

Brind was aboard *Belfast* berthed in Hong Kong on 30 July when Kerans's signal warning that *Amethyst* would attempt to break out came in. That evening the admiral was hosting a dinner party and he was dressing for the occasion when he saw the message. It was garbled but there was enough of it to realise what Kerans planned: 'I am going to try to brea . . .' It took about 40 minutes to get a correct repeat of the signal and a few more minutes to decipher it. For security reasons Brind decided not to cancel the dinner, which began at 2015. After the loyal toast he proposed another, 'HMS *Amethyst* and all who sail in her.' It was important that guests did not leave the ship before 2200, the time *Amethyst* would sail, and after the meal they were directed to the quarterdeck for coffee and liquers. Bidding them farewell, Brind explained that 'an urgent operational matter had just arisen, which demanded his immediate attention . . . and that they would be able to read about his problems in the morning papers'. The dinning cabin was turned into an operations room. Vice Admiral Madden, based in Hong Kong, was invited on board *Belfast* with members of his staff. 'I shall always remember the shock and surprise which showed on the faces of Admiral Madden and his staff when they learned what was about to occur,' Lieutenant Scott wrote.[9] Another visitor was the colony's RAF chief. It was planned to send Sunderland flying boats to pick up *Amethyst*'s crew if they were forced to abandon ship.

Local traders, who often turned up late, almost ruined Kerans's escape plan. That evening a sampan carrying vegetables and eggs was spotted approaching the ship. Would they see the preparations and report them? But suspicions might be aroused if they were told to go away without making the delivery. Kerans was checking on everything and gave orders that the traders were not to get past the top of the gangway. Sailors were told to put camp beds out on the quarterdeck and pretend that they were ready to turn in as if it were a normal, monotonous night. Petty Officer John McCarthy, in charge of stores, blocked the gangway. The goods were passed up from the sampan and he checked the invoice. McCarthy complained that they had not brought enough potatoes, and said he would pay them the next day when the rest were delivered. It worked. The sampan departed, much to the relief of Kerans. It was probably the only time that McCarthy – *Amethyst* – got the better of the traders.

At 2100 Kerans went to the bridge, remaining there so that he could get his eyes used to the darkness. One hour later he was ready to give the order to sail but the moon was brighter than expected and he decided to wait a few minutes for it to pass behind a cloud. Then he spotted a merchant ship, fully lit, rounding Ta-Sha Island on her way down river. The ship, carrying passengers, was later identified as the *Kaing Ling Liberation*, owned by the Chinese Maritime Steamship Guild. Kerans thought it would be a good idea to follow her, especially as it was a difficult part of the river to navigate and he had no relevant charts. *Amethyst* went ahead on her port engine and the anchor cable was slipped, making little noise. The frigate's bows were thrown 45 degrees to starboard, turning in the right direction in less than 30 seconds. One heart-stopping moment came when yellow sparks spewed out of the funnel because of damaged brickwork in one of the boilers. Sentries on land would have seen the display, but *Amethyst* was soon on her way down river making about 10 knots in the wake of the *Kaing Ling Liberation*. The frigate was at action stations. Sailors manning 'B' gun and the Oerlikon were under orders not to fire first.

The Chinese ship was soon challenged by shore batteries, which were on both banks of the river. She answered a flare with the correct siren signal. A second flare went up, obviously intended for *Amethyst*, but Kerans ignored it and carried on. He spotted another vessel, smaller and fully lit, on his port bow. In the fading light it appeared to be a landing craft and it opened fire, sending shots across the frigate's bow in the direction of batteries on the south bank. 'My first impression was that he was trying to stop me and I was prepared to ram him if necessary,' Kerans reported. Seconds later *Amethyst* came under heavy artillery and small-arms fire. The ship was caught in crossfire from the landing craft, a battery on the north bank and three batteries on the south bank. The order 'Full ahead' was given but there was a big explosion forward of the bridge on the starboard waterline. Kerans thought the ship had been badly hit in the starboard engine or boiler room. 'We heeled well over to starboard and I thought it possible we might sink soon. I weaved heavily but it was some minutes before "full ahead" was reached and with the shallow water, steering was extremely difficult.'

Telegraphist French was once again on duty and Kerans told him to send the flash signal, 'I am under fire and have been hit.' Fortunately, it had been a near miss. French was not rating their chances of survival: 'We didn't expect to make half a mile, if we were asked truthfully. The guns were trained on us and we expected to be blown out of the water.' He had been told to maintain silence unless a message needed to be sent. But he kept contacting Hong Kong after the shelling. 'I decided on my own to send the symbols "OK" [not OKAY] every quarter of an hour. No call signs or anything like that but just "OK". Should we have had to abandon ship they could work out from their maps the position we were in from the last time I sent "OK".' This was an arrangement French made with his counterpart in Hong Kong, who would reply 'R', and no senior officers were aware of it.[10]

The *Kaing Ling Liberation* had switched off all her lights, turned towards the northern bank and stopped. *Amethyst* passed the ship with about two feet to spare, made black smoke and continued. The firing carried on for some time but the batteries were targeting their own ships. The *Kaing Ling Liberation* was ablaze and the landing craft appeared to have been hit. *Amethyst* returned fire though 'B' gun could not initially bear because of the list of the ship and got off only one round before Kerans ordered it to stop firing, fearing flashes would give away their position. The Oerlikon and Bren guns were firing.

The captain reported: 'There is no doubt that this gunboat [the landing craft] astern of me was part of the set-up to ensure my destruction. I considered a minimum of four batteries were firing at us.

The false silhouette and the complete darkening of *Amethyst*, and the confused situation with the *Kaing Ling Liberation* mainly assisted my slipping through this dangerous point. I decided now that I must continue my passage down at maximum speed regardless of navigational risk and the hazards involved as clearly they would be waiting for me with everything at their disposal.'[11] The frigate was doing about 22 knots.

There were anxious moments in the engine room. 'We didn't have a clue what was going on atop,' said Williams. 'Our job was to make sure the machinery was working perfectly. If we had had a breakdown at that time we would really have been in the soup. But everything ran perfectly. We had no problems at all. During our time in captivity we had spent a lot of time looking after the machinery.'[12]

On board *Belfast*, Brind and Madden, with charts spread out on the dining table, were waiting anxiously for news of *Amethyst*. At 'about 2200' a message marked 'emergency' had been received from the First Sea Lord, Admiral of the Fleet Lord Fraser, stating bluntly that no escape should be attempted 'without further reference to the Admiralty'. Brind replied that it was too late, adding: 'I have always thought his chances good provided Kerans personally confident.' There has been speculation that Brind decided on a Nelsonian response. Fraser's message might well have been received in time and fully understood but a reply was sent saying the original had been corrupted and it was necessary to repeat the signal, knowing that it would arrive too late. In London, Fraser was well aware of the political implications of failure. Brind shared the concerns but he was exasperated with the Communists and the time had come to resolve the issue one way or the other, tragedy or triumph.[13]

On board *Amethyst*, Lieutenant Hett was mainly responsible for the navigation. There were no charts covering the stretch of river from the spot where the frigate had been anchored to beyond Rose Island. Kerans had obtained a folio of Chinese naval charts before taking command but it was not complete and was out of date by the time of the escape. Hett had to rely on one of the ship's original charts, which had been torn apart during the attack on 20 April and afterwards pieced together, still showing bloodstains.

The echo sounder, the only navigation aid, behaved 'magnificently'. Soundings gave Kerans time to move to deeper water, with three fathoms the lowest reading. It was sufficiently light to make out the banks on either side and he kept the ship mainly in the centre of the channel throughout and as far from battery positions as possible. Only about 50 per cent of the buoys that should have been in the river were in position.

Amethyst slipped past Rose Island, scene of the tragedy on 20 April, surprisingly without incident. But as she approached Kiangyin, the former Nationalist naval base, there was another challenge with flares and the ship came under heavy fire. Kerans sent a flash signal reporting the new attack. There were no hits and the frigate carried on, laying a smoke screen and opening the range.

The next hurdle was a nearby boom. This was a relic of the Sino-Japanese War in 1937, a line of sunken merchant ships across the river, all below the surface. There was a narrow gap, normally marked by two flashing buoys. When *Amethyst* approached, only one buoy was flashing but Kerans chose the right side and she got through. Guarding the boom were Oerlikon batteries and a patrol craft, which opened fire but this was 'ineffectual'.

At 0149 on 31 July *Amethyst* had gone half the distance and at 0243 Kerans reported '100 up', marking the first 100 miles. Brind replied: 'A magnificent century.' Kerans knew that the destroyer *Concord*, positioned at the mouth of the Yangtze, had been detailed to help him. At 0309 he asked *Concord* to give him cover at Woosung. He was well aware that he could be almost in sight of freedom, open seas, but then face his biggest hurdle, the heavy guns of the forts at Paoshan and Woosung.[14]

Coxswain Frank had been in the wheelhouse since 2130 the previous evening. At about 0400 he got the order 'Hard a starboard' and then seconds later 'Hard a port'. *Amethyst* had sliced through a junk, which was seen at the last moment. Hett said: 'The Union Jack was still flying [at the bow]. The lookout on one side did report something ahead and we thought he'd seen the flag fluttering. It wasn't until we were right on top of it that we realised it was a junk and cut it in half. One half went down one side of the ship, the other half down the other side. I dare say there was loss of life but it was an accident.' There were probably no survivors. *Amethyst* was undamaged.[15]

Kerans would soon experience 'one of the worst moments'. He saw the searchlights at Woosung sweeping the area. Twice *Amethyst* was exposed to the glare of a searchlight but she was not fixed. The frigate sped on and, surprisingly, the big guns never opened up. First light broke at 0510 and *Amethyst* passed the quarantine buoy at Woosung. She had escaped. It was a thrilling moment for her weary crew. Frank probably summed it up: 'We had done. I cannot explain how I felt when the captain told me down the voice pipe. I don't really know whether I wanted to let the tears roll out of my eyes, jump for joy or just fall over. I do know that I felt jubilant.'

At 0532 Kerans sent the flash signal: 'Have rejoined the fleet. South of Woosung. No damage or casualties. God save the King.' Brind replied: 'Welcome back to the fleet. We are all extremely proud of your most gallant and skilful escape and that the endurance and fortitude displayed by everyone has been rewarded by such success. Your bearing in adversity and your daring passage tonight will be epic in the history of the navy.' Brind and Madden were not the only ones who had been following *Amethyst*'s dash down the Yangtze. Signals were being read through the night in Whitehall, Singapore and ships of the fleet. King George VI always took a close interest in naval matters and would get angry if he was not kept fully informed of events. He was told about *Amethyst* and sent the following signal to Brind: 'Please convey to the commanding officer and ship's company of HMS *Amethyst* my hearty congratulations on their daring exploit to rejoin the fleet. The courage, skill and determination shown by all on board have my highest commendation. Splice the mainbrace.' There were also messages of congratulation from the Admiralty – a much-relieved First Sea Lord – and the prime minister, Clement Attlee.

20

Salute to *Amethyst*

IT IS NOT CLEAR WHY the big guns of Woosung failed to open fire on *Amethyst*. The Nationalists may have put them out of action before retreating, or it is possible that the Communists occupying the forts feared a massive retaliation by British warships in the vicinity.

Amethyst carried on at speed to the Kiaotun light vessel, whose crew appeared on deck to greet the battered frigate, as did the ship's company of a Nationalist destroyer anchored close by. Freedom had come after 101 days. Shortly after 0800 *Amethyst* dropped her remaining anchor and asked the accompanying *Concord* to refuel her. But the swell was too great for the destroyer to come alongside, and Kerans decided to make for Alacrity anchorage. *Amethyst* was forced to continue at a slow speed because she was so low on fuel, and many of the men in the engine room were 'on their last legs', some having fainted. She eventually anchored at a sheltered spot and *Concord* refuelled her.

Concord's first lieutenant, John Roe, went across to *Amethyst* and asked what the frigate needed in the way of victuals. He did not get a warm reception from the captain. 'Kerans was almost dismissive of my enquiries,' Roe recalled. 'Yes, they would like beer and a few essentials but, no, there wasn't really anything else. A very cool, unforthcoming man who did not match up with the *Amethyst* we had known so well.'[1]

Kerans also asked for the loan of some engine room personnel, a signalman, a telegraphist and a watchkeeping officer. '*Concord* did everything to supply our immediate needs and was most helpful in every way,' he reported later. After resting his men – Lieutenant Hett was close to exhaustion – Kerans decided to sail at 2000, destination Hong Kong. The destroyer HMS *Cossack* replaced *Concord* as an escort.[2]

News of *Amethyst*'s escape was spreading quickly. Admiral Brind had taken the unusual step of ordering a press release during the early hours of 31 July when the ship was still in danger. The statement began: 'HMS *Amethyst* has been held hostage on the Yangtze since April 20, and has been on half rations since the beginning of July. At about 10pm last night she hauled her cable in defiance of her jailers to escape down river. She immediately came under heavy fire from shore batteries, which had been watching her for months and had frequently threatened her destruction.' It ended: 'At 2.30am she was still on her way down river. Although our hopes are high and all are indeed proud of her feat, she still has danger to negotiate.'[3]

In those early hours the Far East Station rang the main news agencies to give them the story. There was no answer at the Associated Press or United Press International. A clerk at the offices of Reuters said he could do nothing and suggested they phone correspondent Monty Parrott at his home. Parrott was asleep when his phone rang. He picked it up, listened briefly and then put it down. He thought he was dreaming. But it may have been a sobering moment because shortly afterwards instinct made him call back. Did you really ring me?

'Yes.'

And so Reuters got the scoop.[4] Later that day Brind sent a message to the Admiralty saying he thought Kerans was worthy of immediate advancement and a decoration for his services during *Amethyst*'s detention and his brilliant escape. On 1 August it was announced that the King had approved an immediate award of the Distinguished Service Order.

Amethyst's exploit would make headlines around the world. Frank Goldsworthy, a reporter on the *Daily Express*, had managed to get himself aboard the cruiser HMS *Jamaica*, which was steaming to meet *Amethyst* off the coast of China. Also on board was Vice Admiral Madden, who may have given an unofficial briefing. From the cruiser Goldsworthy filed a detailed story that became the front-page splash of the *Express* on 1 August. The first paragraph read: 'The little ship *Amethyst* owes her safety to two men. Now that the 1,430-ton frigate is back with the fleet, the secrets of her historic escape can be told.' The reporter named the two men as Kerans and Chief Engine Room Artificer Leonard Williams. Kerans apparently had been studying his only Admiralty chart – No 2809, Shanghai to Nanking – for three months, 'memorising every twist of the treacherous river so that his piloting would not fail in the great night dash'. In fact, Hett had been the navigator, and some of the crew felt he did not get enough credit.

Hett would later explain: Kerans was at the pelorus, conning the ship, I was beside him on the chart table navigating. We had lookouts and a messenger with us. Conducting a ship down a river at night in the dark without radar is a tricky job and we were fully occupied. For a normal ship in these circumstances there would be four or so officers on the bridge, a full communication staff plus lookouts, messengers and boatswain's mates.

Williams had performed wonders in the engine room. The Communists knew that *Amethyst* was built to do 20 knots. But they thought that because the ship had been so badly damaged she would not be capable of more than 12 knots in any escape attempt, 'which meant that one of their batteries would be bound to catch her in daylight, and could blow her out of the water'. Williams had sweated in the engine room to bring the speed up to more than 20 knots. In the event *Amethyst* touched 24 knots at one stage, helped by the current. At her home in Felixstowe, Suffolk, Williams's mother Elizabeth was quoted as saying: 'He's a chip off the old block. His father was in the navy in the First World War and joined up last time in the RAF at the age of 55.' Her husband Charles said: 'The whole neighbourhood is celebrating.' The parents of the telegraphist Jack French were also celebrating at Ashburton, Devon, along with the other locals. French's mother Elsie put up a large sign, perhaps prematurely, saying: 'Welcome home to our Jack DSM.'

In a comment piece that referred to the Dunkirk evacuation of 1940, the *Express* saluted the Little Ships: 'The men of the Little Ships smile knowingly to one another today. They share the delight, but not the surprise, of the landsmen whose hearts have been given a great lift by the news that the *Amethyst* is safe. Both the deed and the signal that announced it are in the tradition of the Little Ships of Britain, which specialise in tackling impossibilities with success.' The piece added: 'And a story speeds round the world that somehow more than makes up for the errors of policy which first put the *Amethyst* in her plight.'

The Daily Telegraph gave a full account of the 140-mile dash to freedom. It also carried a story from its Hong Kong correspondent:

It is expected here that the escape of the *Amethyst* will have a tremendous psychological effect on the Chinese masses, who have come to regard the Communists as invincible. But fears are expressed in some quarters that the Communists will not take the matter lying down, and pressure may be increased against Britons in Shanghai. The *Amethyst's* exploit has provided a great morale raiser among British and other western nationals in Hong Kong. The thrill of pride felt in the frigate's escape was clearly evident on the faces of most Britons in the streets and the feat formed the sole topic of conversation.

In a comment piece the *Telegraph* stated: 'To have navigated 140 miles of the treacherous Yangtze in the dark at high speed would have deserved praise; to have done so under almost point-blank range from shore batteries with the necessity of smashing a boom of unknown strength is a feat at which praise yields to something near astonishment.'

The Times noted: 'Had failure ensued and the *Amethyst* now be lying a wreck on the river bank, critics would have been quick to be wise after the event.' The newspaper reminded its readers of the decision to send the ship up the Yangtze on the eve of a major military offensive and 'this was asking for trouble'. The *Daily Mirror* referred to Kerans's 'Nelson touch', stating that he had acted without orders from either the Admiralty or the commander-in-chief.[5]

At 1600 on 2 August, north of Formosa, *Amethyst* and *Cossack* were met by *Jamaica*. Six hundred cheering sailors lined the upper deck of the cruiser, and a Royal Marines band played *Cruising Down The River*. Vice Admiral Madden sent a message to *Amethyst*: 'I am most proud that my flagship shares the honour of escorting your valiant ship to Hong Kong, where the commander-in-chief is waiting to welcome you back to the fleet.' Kerans replied: 'Thank you. It is a great moment.' The band struck up again with See The Conquering Hero Comes and For He's A Jolly Good Fellow. *Jamaica* ran up signal flags reading 'Welcome Back Tiddyoggie'. Then the sailors lining the upper deck kept roaring the West Country battle cry 'Oggie! Oggie!' A tiddyoggie is a pasty, and navy men from the West Country are nick-named 'Oggies' by their shipmates. Devonport was the home base of both *Amethyst* and *Jamaica*. The loudest roars came from 25 *Amethyst* men who had escaped after the 20 April attack. Lieutenant Berger, who had been badly wounded, was transferred to *Amethyst*, along with a large quantity of mail. Petty Officer William Freeman commented: 'We reckoned it was a hundred to one against escaping both shellfire and sandbanks but everyone was ready to go . . . It is a wonderful feeling to be free.' Kerans had made a special request. He wanted to sail into Hong Kong harbour with the seventy-two men who had shared his ordeal of more than three months on the Yangtze, and Madden agreed.[6]

Later that evening there was a serious problem with one of *Amethyst*'s boilers – No 2 – and the ship slowed down in time to avoid 'disaster'. The frigate stopped for 45 minutes before steam could be raised in No 1 boiler, and engine-room staff worked through the night to get the other boiler working. *Jamaica* offered to send over an engineer officer and ratings but Kerans declined. Later *Amethyst* signalled that she was shipping water aft and, with her reduced crew, found it difficult dealing with the problem. *Cossack* stood by with towing gear but the frigate was able to carry on in reasonable weather.

At 1000 on 3 August, *Amethyst* steamed into Hong Kong harbour 'to a tremendous welcome which none of us will forget'. Kerans took the precaution of asking for a tug to follow him in case his battered ship faltered. But she berthed without difficulty, showing fifteen shell holes on the starboard side, six on the port side and twenty-three on the upper deck. Some of her sailors were in borrowed uniforms, and *Jamaica*'s skipper, Captain Frank Ballance, himself a DSO winner, had given Kerans a length of the medal ribbon. Craft of all sizes greeted *Amethyst*, and planes of the RAF saluted her. Many thousands lined the waterfront in the rain.

Daily Express reporter Frank Goldsworthy had boarded *Amethyst* for the last leg of the journey. 'That arrival in Hong Kong was a great emotional experience,' he recalled. 'It brings a lump to my throat and tears to my eyes. Every ship in the harbour was hooting. There were fire floats with great jets of water. The crews of two cruisers were lining the rails to cheer us on our way. This was such a moment for these lads who had been 100 days isolated from the rest of the navy.'[7]

The governor of the colony, Sir Alexander Grantham, Admiral Brind, other service chiefs and local dignitaries were on the quayside. Fireworks exploded. As *Amethyst* secured, Brind sent the signal 'Manoeuvre well executed'. It was, according to Kerans, 'the most pleasing signal of all'.[8]

Brind paid tribute to the ship's company: 'You may not perhaps even yet fully realise what the exploit of HMS *Amethyst* has meant to our country. Failure in an endeavour to escape would have been disastrous with far-reaching effects on the Far East and the attitude of its peoples to the British.' He added: 'You have suffered much, but you are supremely fortunate in that you have each played a great part in a story which will be told and retold so long as the British navy is remembered – that is so long as Britain lives. You are an example too us all.'

The admiral made a comment that the men might have taken issue with later. He said: 'From the beginning I was anxious that you should eventually prepare to escape in this way, but I was even more anxious that I should say nothing which would force your captain's hand as the man on the spot.' According to Brind's staff officer operations, Commander Peter Dickens, and his first lieutenant, David Scott, the admiral had for a long time refused to consider the possibility of escape, thinking that negotiations would be successful. It was Dickens, believing from the start that there was only one option, who pushed the idea 'at every opportunity'. Kerans, too, would claim that escape had been on his mind from the outset but Hett, one of the few officers on board *Amethyst*, pointed out that the captain consistently refused to discuss the subject whenever others brought it up. If Colonel Kang had not agreed to allow the ship to have the crucial supply of oil fuel from Nanking, Kerans might well have left it too late to escape anyway.

Offers of hospitality from Hong Kong residents poured in, but there was one sour note as far as French the telegraphist was concerned. After the attack on 20 April the ship's NAAFI manager, John MacNamara, had handed out sweets and cigarettes to the wounded. This went on for 48 hours before sailors were told to start paying again. After *Amethyst* arrived in Hong Kong NAAFI bosses decided that the loss needed to be made up. 'They persisted to the nth degree that every penny had to be paid,' said French. 'This stuck in my craw. The fact is that they could have lost the whole lot of goods if we had scuttled the ship. And it went on and on until it was decided by the base in Hong Kong that the NAAFI would be paid from the sports club fund.'[9]

Robert Stone was one of the sailors who escaped after the initial attack, swimming to Rose Island. He ended up in Hong Kong and was assigned to anti-piracy patrols. He was on a patrol when *Amethyst* arrived in the colony. The next day he went on board to 'have a look round and see what I had left'. He was surprised to find most of his kit still there. 'I had a suitcase with some personal pieces. The kit in the lockers was no good, it had mildew. But everything basically was as I had left it. I was lucky. The only thing that was missing was a hammock, and they had used the hammocks to shore up the holes in the side of the ship. But that was no problem. I rejoined the ship's company, and then it was a case of getting the ship ready to sail home.'[10] Rumours spread that the Chinese Communists were so angry at *Amethyst*'s escape that they planned to sabotage the ship in Hong Kong. Extra sentries were posted and she was kept floodlit at night.

Before the escape there had been mounting pressure for the Admiralty to be more open about the ship's plight. Newspapers were aware of a considerable public demand for information. It was the job of the Chief of Naval Information, Captain Arthur Clarke, to try to block stories. He admitted: 'Again and again a personal appeal by myself or members of my staff had achieved the suppression of undesirable publicity in accordance with Admiralty policy.' But by mid-July Clarke had come to the conclusion that this censorship could not be continued for much longer. From Shanghai there was an increasing flow of stories from agency reporters and special correspondents. He warned: 'I think we may be in danger of one or more newspapers possibly taking the bit between the teeth. I suggest the Admiralty may also be in danger of searching questions in the House; conceivably initiated in consequence of next of kin complaints. I appreciate that the policy of "saying nothing" must have been given the most careful consideration. I only submit that a good deal of time has passed since the ship first got stuck in the river, and that a revision of policy may be even overdue.'[11]

Clarke's argument was shrugged off, his superiors noting that he worked for the Admiralty, not the media. Policy would be followed. Fortunately the escape gave him the opportunity to repay favours. He rose to the occasion, as one executive at the Press Association, the national news agency, gratefully acknowledged. Clarke's staff had weighed in with 'loads' of information. The executive noted: 'I have been particularly struck by the speed with which your department handled a first-class narrative . . .'[12]

On 31 July Brind, on board *Belfast*, had written a personal letter to the First Sea Lord, Admiral of the Fleet Lord Fraser. Brind's private thoughts appeared to be at odds with his public statements. When *Amethyst* was safely out of the Yangtze, the admiral sent the message: 'Your bearing in adversity and your daring passage tonight will be epic in the history of the navy.' However, he told Fraser: 'I had felt that a "break away" was definitely a practical operation, with nothing like so serious risks as would seem at first sight. Chinese field guns are not particularly well equipped for accurate shooting at night even at short range . . . The navigation, though difficult, was not by any means impracticable at night, particularly with a good sounding machine. Furthermore we knew that the Communists were moving ships at night for fear of air attack, so it seemed fairly certain the buoys were alight.'

Brind had serious doubts about *Amethyst*'s captain: 'At one stage I was convinced that Kerans was very nearly exhausted and near throwing in the sponge – and I do not blame him for he had an intolerable time.' The admiral explained about the lack of a secure code and the confusion over typhoon warnings and possible escape: 'He [Kerans] asked what seemed exceedingly stupid and unseamanlike questions about typhoons, and I felt that he must either be no sailor at all or that there must be something behind it.' Brind and Kerans were baffling each other. The admiral added: 'Kerans, in his endeavour to deceive Kang that he was far too frightened to think of breaking out, deceived me also into seriously doubting whether he [Kerans] had the stamina left for the job. Also my care not to blow the gaff deceived him into thinking that I did not contemplate a break away and was only considering fighting it out on the negotiation line!' Brind said he was very glad that the First Sea Lord's signal to stop *Amethyst* arrived 'just too late'.

The letter took some time to reach Fraser, and the First Sea Lord probably felt embarrassment that he had tried to halt something that was now seen as a triumph for the Royal Navy and Britain. His request also put a question mark over his much-quoted policy – leave it to the man on the spot. In a personal message to Brind, he said: 'Failure would have involved such complications that I felt I was duty bound to inform the government in advance and that is why I made my signal; I had not appreciated that it was likely to happen so soon otherwise, as you know, I should be the last to tie your hand. You know my motto – "Leave it as far as possible to the man on the spot" – and if there had been a failure we should still have supported you. I was indeed pleased when your signal came saying it was too late but it was an anxious night.' The insertion of 'as far as possible' was a revealing qualification. But he added: 'I give them all full marks.'

Fraser also commented on the civil war. The Nationalists were finished, but 'they were never much good for us', apart from Admiral Kwei, who could be regarded as a friend. It was important to preserve British interests in China, especially Shanghai, and if the Nationalists were offended 'they will have to lump it'. Britain's economic difficulties made world trade even more important.[13]

In a local radio broadcast, which was picked up by Radio Malaya, Brind put aside his private thoughts about Kerans and replaced his muted praise for the escape with another tribute to the ship's company of *Amethyst*, whose arrival in Hong Kong was 'a most inspiring sight'. He said: 'Lieutenant Commander Kerans has been under tremendous strain but he was cheerful and alert, giving great credit to the support of his officers, chief and petty officers and men. As always, not only did the leader inspire his subordinates but he himself was greatly fortified by them, a mutual effect which is not generally appreciated. The men looked very well and took all they had done as a matter of course. It was heartening to meet them and to hear how each one seemed to pass off credit to someone else on some pretext or other.'

The admiral referred to the circumstances of *Amethyst*'s captivity. She had every right to be on the Yangtze. The ship was sailing during a ceasefire between the Nationalists and the Communists, and she had the permission of the Chinese government. It was untrue that the frigate attacked PLA positions to help the Nationalists. *Consort*, *London* and *Black Swan* were involved in a 'humane mission' to provide medical supplies and to guide *Amethyst* back down river. 'There was never any intention to undertake an operation of war, their guns were fore and aft and they flew white flags,' said Brind. During her captivity *Amethyst* was under constant threat of destruction, and safe conduct was conditional 'on admission by me that the British were entirely to blame for the incident of 20 April'. This, of course, he could not possibly accept. Outlining the ship's escape, he pointed out that she came under heavy fire twice but replied with machine guns and only one round from one of her main guns. 'The Yangtze incident has now ended, and our thoughts are in the first place for the killed and wounded of all ships involved in the initial phase. The bearing and courage of the wounded, the sustained fortitude of those in the *Amethyst* and her gallant escape will long inspire the navy.'[14]

Brind's remarks went down well with the Foreign Office, which thought they struck 'just the right note'. But officials were keen to draw a line under the issue. Trade was the overriding factor. In a message to Ambassador Stevenson in Nanking, they pointed out: 'We feel strongly that we have a great deal to lose and nothing to gain by keeping this issue alive and we very much hope that from now on no new publicity will be initiated from our side. *Amethyst* is out but we still have a large stake in China. Our chances of eventually reaching some sort of recognition with the Chinese Communists are slender enough as it is and we do not want to jeopardise them further by embarking on a prolonged propaganda war if it can be possibly avoided.'[15]

But the Chinese were waging a propaganda war over *Amethyst* and specifically the destruction of the merchant ship *Kaing Ling Liberation*. General Yuan, the senior figure in the negotiations to try to free *Amethyst* and now no doubt seething with embarrassment, accused the frigate of opening fire on the ship, with the result that she caught fire and sank. *Amethyst* ploughed through passengers in the water 'calling for help' and fired on junks trying to rescue them, and 'the majority of several hundred passengers were drowned'. Many junks were also sunk. *Amethyst* carried on, taking advantage of rescue efforts by soldiers. The general accused Admiral Brind of insincerity over the negotiations. The PLA had shown a lenient policy towards the frigate's 'criminals', allowing them to receive letters, supplies and oil.

Yuan declared:

So the peoples of China and the whole world can see how imperialists committed misdeeds in reply to benevolence. Those on board the *Amethyst* made good their disgraceful flight at the expense of the sinking of the *Kaing Ling Liberation* and many junks and the murder of several hundred of our innocent brethren.

I am deeply convinced that all rank and file of the People's Liberation Army and all our brethren shall always remember to revenge the death of the victims and shall never forget or pardon the two barbarous acts committed by the British warship *Amethyst*. They shall never forget or pardon the British warships *London*, *Consort* and *Black Swan*, which abetted in the crime, nor the swindle of the British admiral Brind.

The general also complained that the British government was 'insolently' celebrating the escape. The New China News Agency called on the Chinese people to avenge the deaths of their compatriots on 20 April and 30 July.[16]

One Peking commentary stated: 'The whole proceedings of the *Amethyst* incident have deeply convinced the Chinese that imperialists, no matter their nationality, are so ruthless, hypocritical and disgraceful ... The fact is so clear that it was a British warship which intruded into a Chinese river and shelled Chinese troops. It is not a case in which Chinese troops intruded into the Thames and shelled a British warship.' Leading political figures in Peking also stepped forward to 'condemn the disgraceful act of British imperialism'. Shen Chun-ju, of the Democratic League, declared: 'The outrageous action of the *Amethyst* in sinking our merchantman and drowning our people while escaping in a hurry must especially be punished.' Kuo Mo-jo, described as a non-partisan democratic personage, said: 'This was a purely ruthless pirate act. The chieftains in the British imperialist piracy should delay their elation. We will certainly revenge the death of the passengers of the *Kaing Ling Liberation.*'

Local papers in Shanghai carried an article that said: 'After this incident [the sinking of the *Kaing Ling Liberation*] the prime minister, Attlee, and King George even sent their congratulations to the members of the sloop for their atrocious acts. The official report by the British foreign ministry and the British navy on the 31st was untrue.' The official report referred to was a joint press release from the Admiralty and the Foreign Office, giving a straightforward outline of *Amethyst*'s captivity and escape. The British consul in Shanghai, Robert Urquhart, was worried that the inflammatory remarks might lead to organised violence. But survivors of the *Kaing Ling Liberation* had arrived in the city and were not concealing the fact that they were fired on from the shore. 'Nevertheless the mob and predatory labour are on call to make trouble irrespective of any rights or wrongs,' the consul warned. There were foreigners in the city who urgently wanted to leave 'and the sense of strain is increasing'.[17] Nationalist warships were blockading Shanghai, severely restricting shipping.

The Communist version of the destruction of the *Kaing Ling Liberation* was, of course, nonsense. Survivors and next of kin were mobbing the Shanghai offices of the vessel's shipping line and claiming damages, 'brushing aside newspaper reports of British responsibility and saying that they know perfectly well the ship was fired on from shore'.[18] In his radio broadcast, Admiral Brind stressed that *Amethyst* had not fired at the merchant ship, and the Communist reports were 'quite untrue in all respects'. Brind repeated that the frigate fired only one round from the 4in gun she was using and that it was seen to hit the shore near one of the batteries. 'Those on board our ship say they clearly saw that the shore batteries were firing at one of their own ships and had set her on fire. These batteries continued their firing for about a quarter of an hour after all firing at the British ship had ceased. No more rounds were fired from the *Amethyst*'s 4in gun throughout the night because her captain decided not to reveal his ship in any way.' The Admiralty also issued an official denial. In Hong Kong, the government warned the New China News Agency that its reports claiming *Amethyst* sank the *Kaing Ling Liberation* were libellous, seditious and overstepping the limits of public security. The agency's director was warned that in the event of any further infringement 'appropriate steps would be taken against the organisation'.[19]

An interview with the captain of the *Kaing Ling Liberation* was published in *The Times* on 20 August. The captain, who was not named, said his ship loaded 400 tons of coal and beans at Hankow for Shanghai, and a large number of passengers boarded. After the ship passed Nanking she was attacked by Nationalist aircraft but all four bombs missed. Because of this attack most of the passengers disembarked at Chiangkiang to continue their journey by rail. Nearing the spot where *Amethyst* was anchored, flares suddenly lit up the *Kaing Ling Liberation* and she came under intense artillery and machine gun fire from the shore. The captain said the ship received several hits and was soon on fire and out of control. At this point he saw a big ship behind him, which was blacked out without any lights. He presumed this must have been *Amethyst*. Panic broke out on the *Kaing Ling Liberation* and passengers and crew jumped overboard, including the captain. He saw the other ship go past and he did not see her firing. The captain swam ashore. A Chinese naval craft put a boarding party on the *Kaing Ling Liberation*, which was anchored shortly afterwards. When the captain left to go to Shanghai, thirty passengers and ten of the crew were unaccounted for.

The captain was actually interviewed on 4 August by an Associated Press correspondent, who apparently had difficulty getting his story out. The Communist authorities discovered that the captain had talked to the reporter and arrested him. Urquhart, the consul, noted that the Communist version was getting less prominence in local papers on 5 and 6 August: 'If we get over 7 August without incident we may hope that the authorities are dropping the whole affair and I suggest we too need not go in for further defensive publicity.'[20]

Surprisingly, the Communists did not make any propaganda over *Amethyst*'s sinking of a junk as the frigate neared Woosung. Perhaps they were unaware of it. Ambassador Stevenson had feared that the accident would be exploited 'to the utmost'. He admitted: 'There is therefore a strong temptation to recommend concealing the fact in the hopes that it may never be known for certain by the Communists what happened to the junk. Experience has shown, however, the difficulty of preventing leakage of such news and I have consequently come to the conclusion that it would be better to release this information before the Communists can do so or members of the ship's crew inadvertently inform the press.' The ambassador suggested saying it was feared that an unlighted junk 'may have been run down'.

Stevenson, like his masters at the Foreign Office, was keen to focus on improving relations with the Communists. He hoped that *Amethyst*'s escape would remove 'a bone of contention and so will pave the way for more sober thinking and better understanding'.[21] There were, of course, all those business interests to think about.

21

The Cover-up

AMBASSSADOR STEVENSON WAS QUICK OFF the mark when he learned that the destroyer *Concord* had been involved in *Amethyst*'s escape. 'No – repeat no – publicity should be given to the fact that HMS *Concord* entered Chinese territorial waters,' he told the Foreign Office and Admiral Brind. The warning also went to British diplomats in Canton and Shanghai.

In a message marked 'emergency', Stevenson also advised:

> *Amethyst* in getting under way was forced to reply to fire directed at her by shore batteries. It should be stressed that she did so to the minimum necessary for self-protection.
>
> It might help to lessen possible repercussions upon British communities in Communist-occupied territory if public statements could stress that the escape of HMS *Amethyst* was due to the initiative of the officer in command in accordance with the best traditions of a sailor responsible for the safety of his ship and the welfare of the ship's company and that his intention to do so was not revealed to any of us out here. As the Communists have refused to deal with His Majesty's embassy in the matter, which they have in fact insisted upon treating as local issue for discussion between PLA and the Royal Navy, such a statement on our part is logical and cannot harm the persons concerned.[1]

In other words, Kerans would get all the blame if there were serious repercussions, despite the fact that the ambassador had suggested days earlier an escape might have to be attempted. Fortunately for *Amethyst*'s captain, the inept propaganda over the destruction of the merchant ship *Kaing Ling Liberation* quickly backfired and the Communists decided to save face and end their protests.

Stevenson's warning about *Concord* was taken seriously and a major cover-up took place, despite unintentional leaks. Over the years accounts of *Amethyst*'s escape have suggested that the frigate met the destroyer at the mouth of the Yangtze. Even the naval historian Professor Eric Grove wrote that *Amethyst* had 'safely passed' the forts at Woosung before seeing *Concord* 'just as dawn broke'.[2] This was not true. *Concord* played a much more significant role. Also covered up was the use of three other ships of the 8th Destroyer Flotilla, *Cossack*, *Constance* and *Comus*.

Soon after *Amethyst*'s escape Admiral Brind asked the Admiralty to issue a press release, which said the frigate met *Concord* 'after' passing the biggest fort at Woosung. But he was obviously uncomfortable about playing down the destroyer's important role. He had seen Stevenson's warning and later that day, 31 July, he sent another message to the Admiralty saying: 'I would suggest that, whilst we need not emphasise that *Concord* entered territorial waters, we should not hesitate to indicate she came to support *Amethyst* in dangerous waters after she had been subject to dastardly attack. We should not conceal fact that such action may involve entering territorial waters.' And he was not happy about Stevenson's 'we can blame Kerans' proposal: 'I hope that . . . we shall not give impression that it is naval practice to leave responsibility for such actions which may have international repercussions to young commanding officers.'

The Foreign Office and the Admiralty issued a joint statement on 31 July. It made no mention of the four destroyers, and referred to *Amethyst*'s escape in one sentence: 'In her passage down river HMS *Amethyst* came under heavy fire at least twice, and on one occasion was compelled to reply in self-defence.'

On 6 August Brind gave a press conference at his headquarters in Singapore. The admiral gave 'further details', without apparently telling journalists that they were off the record. The following day the *Sunday Tribune*, a newspaper published in Malaya, gave prominence to a story that began: 'If the frigate *Amethyst* had met with any serious trouble on her dramatic dash down the Yangtze, three destroyers of the 8th Flotilla, *Cossack*, *Constance* and *Comus*, would have blasted their way up the river to help her. A fourth destroyer, *Concord*, would have been detailed to silence the shore fort guns at Woosung.'

Strangely, only one national newspaper in Britain, the *Sunday Pictorial*, carried the story, revealing that 'a full-scale battle would have been unleashed by a waiting destroyer flotilla if the brave and battered little *Amethyst* had needed help'. The disclosure was too good for other newspapers to ignore. But Brind probably realised he had spoken too freely, and it raises suspicions that the Chief of Naval Information, Captain Arthur Clarke, might have acted once again to suppress 'undesirable publicity' by appealing to editors.

Even so, the Foreign Office was furious that the *Sunday Pictorial* had broken the story. A senior official, Patrick Coates, who had worked in China, complained: 'We, of course, had not previously heard of this plan, and to divulge it at this stage is criminal folly.' Coates was also upset that the *Sunday Express* revealed that *Amethyst*'s cat, Simon, had killed the large rat nicknamed Mao Tse-tung.

'I understand that we have already taken these matters up with the Admiralty,' Coates wrote. 'We have, as indicated on other papers, already taken up with the Admiralty the question of piping down on *Amethyst* publicity, with specific reference to a proposed ceremonial welcome to her in London, but that news too has leaked.'

Another official, Stanley Tomlinson, contacted the Admiralty and afterwards told Coates it was accepted there had been enough publicity about *Amethyst*. The Admiralty suggested that a junior officer in Singapore must have revealed the plan to attack the Woosung forts. Tomlinson was sceptical: 'One cannot but wonder whether the Woosung forts story was not, in fact, one of the "further details" given out by the C-in-C himself.' The Commissioner General for South East Asia, Malcolm MacDonald, confirmed that Brind did indeed reveal the story.[3] A few days later the Admiralty blamed three journalists, two American and one local, for a breach of confidence.

On 30 July Brind had sent a message to *Concord* warning that *Amethyst* 'may break out tonight'. The destroyer, already near the mouth of the Yangtze, should be ready 'to go above Woosung at night if ordered'. The other destroyers were told to close the entrance to the Yangtze at short notice. Brind ordered: 'Take no overt action yet as secrecy is vital.' Kerans was aware that *Concord* would provide cover for *Amethyst*, but he did not know that three other destroyers were primed to take action.

Amethyst began her dash down the Yangtze soon after 2200 on 30 July, and at 0145 the following day *Concord* headed for the Kiutoan light vessel, about 20 miles below Woosung. Thirty-five minutes later she was challenged by a Nationalist gunboat and told not to go any further. The order was ignored. The destroyer, travelling at 20 knots, reached the light vessel at 0255 and anchored, waiting for further orders. Brind signalled that she should continue further up river and engage the forts and batteries in the Woosung area if *Amethyst* came under attack. *Amethyst* was expected to pass Woosung near dawn, and at 0345 *Concord* continued her journey. A few minutes later *Amethyst* signalled that she was ahead of schedule. It was necessary for both warships to pass Woosung in darkness and, if the frigate had been delayed, they would have anchored at a safe spot and tried to break out the following night.

At 0445 *Concord* was nearing Woosung. She had been at action stations for nearly seven hours. On board *Belfast* in Hong Kong, Brind and Madden were concerned that at any moment they might receive signals from both ships saying they were under fire. There was a significant risk that *Amethyst* and *Concord* could be sunk. At 0503 *Amethyst* reported that Woosung was in sight. Twenty-three minutes later she said that she had seen *Concord*. The destroyer signalled, 'Fancy meeting you again', and Kerans replied, 'Never has a ship been more welcome'. *Concord* had picked up *Amethyst* on her radar a few minutes earlier. According to the HMS *Concord* Association, the ships met some four miles above the Woosung forts. The destroyer made a dramatic turn and appeared on the frigate's starboard side to shield her from the heavy guns. *Concord*'s main armament was trained on the biggest fort but its guns remained silent. *Amethyst* and *Concord* headed for the open sea. In *Belfast*, Commander Dickens, Brind's staff officer operations, poured champagne in celebration.[4] Action stations ended only at 0715. *Concord* had gone some 40 miles up the Yangtze. Despite Admiral Brind's revelations, the official version was soon accepted. *Concord* had met *Amethyst* at the mouth of the Yangtze . . .

With some irony, the Communists did not pursue the matter. It was the Nationalist government that complained. The Royal Navy was accused of 'a bellicose attitude'. China's ministry of foreign affairs revealed that *Concord* was challenged twice by Nationalist vessels but carried on sailing up river, at one stage without any lights. All foreign naval vessels needed permission to enter territorial waters, and at least 10 days' notice was required. The government was continuing to impose a blockade of shipping in an attempt to stop supplies reaching the Communists.

In a message to the British embassy, the ministry said:

The unexpected entry of the British naval craft *Concord* on the morning of 31 July into Chinese territorial waters already declared closed, without having first obtained the consent of the Chinese government, obviously violated the existing rules. The Chinese government regard this action of the *Concord*, irrespective of her motive and object, has virtually infringed the sovereignty of China. The ministry therefore have to lodge a strong protest to the British embassy, and to request the British government to issue to all British naval vessels instructions strictly forbidding the recurrence of similar incidents.[5]

A British diplomat in Canton told the Foreign Office that *Concord*'s action was 'a violation of sovereignty', but Ambassador Stevenson was in no rush to reply, referring to it as an 'alleged infringement'. The ambassador was more worried that the Communists would exploit the complaint. Stevenson wrote: 'The best line to take might be therefore to begin with reference to HMS *Concord* stating that necessity for the ship's journey up the river on this occasion was much regretted but it was hoped that the Chinese government would appreciate and sympathise with the special humanitarian objective of the rescue mission.' But he added: 'I prefer however the alternative of evading such argument as long as possible in the hope that the course of events … may obviate the necessity of any reply.'[6]

Stevenson was well aware that the days of the Nationalist government were numbered. The Communists held all the important cards. Officials at the Foreign Office did not take the protest seriously, one describing it as 'unnecessarily offensive' and adding: 'The longer we can delay a reply the better.' Stanley Tomlinson, who had already been involved in the cover-up, commented: 'I should have thought that from the point of view of the Chinese National government, *Concord*'s was more or less an innocent passage, and that their only real ground of complaint was because we had ignored their "blockade" regulations which, in fact, we have told them we consider to be illegal.'

Over the ensuing years the *Concord* cover-up has remained a controversial issue for former members of the ship's company who went to *Amethyst*'s aid. They believe their actions should have been recognised. In 2009, the year marking the 60th anniversary of the Yangtze Incident, the HMS *Concord* Association highlighted the grievance. The crews of *Amethyst, Consort, London* and *Black Swan* were all awarded the Naval General Service Medal with the clasp Yangtze 1949, or separate clasps if they already had the campaign medal. Why, asked the *Concord* men, were they not entitled to the award? The naval authorities pointed out that an awards committee had met in November 1949 and would have considered *Concord* along with the other ships, reaching the conclusion that she did not qualify. But this was not the case because at that stage *Concord* officially had not been in the Yangtze. The cover-up would last decades. The civil servant dealing with the association's complaint further enraged the *Concord* veterans by stating that they had not been in a war zone, despite the fact that the conflict between the Nationalists and the Communists was continuing. The ship's company, he argued, were not in any danger.

The association responded:

No danger! *Concord* had passed the Woosung forts, met *Amethyst* some four miles above the forts and had to pass her to turn round – the river was narrow there for turning. Having turned she caught up with *Amethyst*, and with *Amethyst* on her port side and the Woosung forts to starboard and with armament of both ships trained on the forts steamed past, thankfully without any incident, to the open waters. It was expected by the admiral and his staff aboard the flagship HMS *Belfast* that the Woosung forts would open fire, which is why the admiral had despatched *Concord* in the first place. Had they opened fire it was also expected that both ships would suffer damage and casualties.

The association had to wait until 1999, when previously secret documents were released, to prove that *Concord*'s role had been covered up. The destroyer's log was viewed at The National Archives in London. Also seen was *Amethyst*'s log, which aroused more suspicions. This log appeared to have a new cover and spine, and the last entry for 30 July 1949, the day of the frigate's escape, was timed 2043. The only entry for 31 July was 1215, recording that the ship had secured alongside *Concord*. 'Kerans would not have failed to record the events from 2200 on 30 July until 1215 on 31 July,' the association noted. 'What happened to the entries?'[7]

There were more revelations in the archives held at Churchill College, Cambridge. Among the papers of Rear Admiral Sir David Scott – Admiral Brind's flag lieutenant – were copies of all the naval signals sent during the night of 30/31 July. Even Kerans, in his final report on *Amethyst*'s detention and escape, made only a passing reference to *Concord*: 'At 0309 I asked *Concord* to cover me at Woosung at about 0530. I was not exactly clear as to where he was and I refrained from signalling him direct in order not to disclose his whereabouts.' He added: 'First light broke at 0510 and I passed the quarantine buoy at Woosung at 0525, five minutes ahead of my ETA, with *Concord* in sight.'[8]

After the mission the captain of the 8th Destroyer Flotilla, who was on board *Cossack*, asked for *Concord*'s log, which was not returned. The ship acquired a new log. She was not allowed to continue to escort *Amethyst* to Hong Kong. *Cossack* replaced her and *Concord* was sent on patrol towards Japan, so there was no chance of her sailors talking about their exploit on shore. In fact, *Concord*'s captain, Lieutenant Commander Nigel Rodney, told his crew that their mission had to remain secret.

Derek Hodgson, one of the sailors on board *Concord*, wrote of the tension crews experienced when they were at action stations:

When facing danger the ships would be converted into a series of watertight compartments, every door, hatch, porthole scuttle would be tightly clamped creating a gloomy almost airless steel box. Without any form of air conditioning what air there was, was piped through ducting which had an interior full of dust and muck drawn in from outside. Men would, in action, be confined to these areas for many hours, as in our case. A colleague and myself had the misfortune to be allocated the after magazine as our station and action station meaning that the only company to be had were high explosives and the knowledge that if the ship was hit by a shell, it would be unlikely that we could be let out. I do not want to appear over dramatic but do feel that, to form a proper conclusion as to risk, it is necessary to be fully aware of reality.

When the *Concord* sailed into the entrance of the river on 28 July we were only too aware of the circumstances prevailing. We, of course, knew what had happened to the four ships back in April, we were very conscious of the *Amethyst* still being held captive, we had been present at Woosung when Shanghai fell to the Communists so we knew that the land we could see on our port side was now completely in Communist hands. To add to this drama we had, during this period, often been buzzed by Nationalist aircraft and their ships made themselves known to us. Presumably it was to remind us that they had a blockade of the river in progress.

Our gun crews had been regularly drilling, cordite cartridges and shells were brought up from below and stowed ready for use. Damage control, medical and first aid parties were again briefed and stations allocated, the ensign and Union Flag staffs were taken down and battle ensigns were raised at the port and starboard yardarms.[9]

In November 2010 Hodgson asked his MP, Caroline Dinenage, to take up the matter with Minister of Defence Andrew Robathan, who had special responsibility for veterans. Robathan said a review had been carried out and confirmed that the file on the award of the Yangtze clasp to the Naval General Service Medal did not mention *Concord*. But he wrote: 'There are no plans to reconsider the qualifying criteria for this award.' He added: 'As previously advised the contention that the crew of HMS *Concord* were deliberately excluded from eligibility for this award is entirely speculative and is not sustainable in light of contemporary official records relating to the institution of this clasp.'

The minister appeared to be contradicting himself because, as he had already mentioned, the one file on the award did not make any reference to *Concord*. Robathan ended his letter: 'It was also considered that no further purpose would be served by continuing the correspondence between Mr Hodgson and the department . . .' According to Hodgson, the minister never bothered to reply to his letters.[10]

In December 2011 William Leitch, a navy veteran who was helping the *Concord* campaign, presented a petition to the House of Commons asking for a select committee to investigate the 'grievous injustice'. Leitch had already sent a similar petition to the Scottish Parliament and representations were made to the Ministry of Defence without success. Five years earlier his MP, Jim Devine, had approached the ministry. Rejecting the medal claim, Minister for the Armed Forces Bob Ainsworth stated incorrectly: 'By the time HMS *Amethyst* reached HMS *Concord*'s position at the mouth of the River Yangtze on the morning of 31 July 1949 she had succeeded in making her escape.'[11]

Amethyst men were guests of honour at a *Concord* reunion in 2000. Donald Redman, chairman of the HMS *Amethyst* Association, told the gathering: 'I can never understand why you, the *Concord* Forty Niners, did not receive the Yangtze medal. You were in a war zone, at action stations and were ready to risk your lives for shipmates who might stumble at the last hurdle. Your shipmates from the *Amethyst* will never forget that the crew of *Concord* were there ready to risk their lives if required.'

The survivors who fought at Trafalgar had to wait 45 years for an official medal. Veterans of the Arctic convoys during the Second World War faced an even longer wait. In December 2012 it was announced that they would finally receive the Arctic Star following a review of campaign medals by Sir John Holmes, a former diplomat. Holmes received a number of representations, including the case made by the *Concord* veterans.

Peter Lee-Hale, chairman of the HMS *Concord* Association, told Holmes: 'There can be no doubt in anyone's mind the 1949 crew were entitled to the medal and justice and honesty must now prevail and be seen to be done.' He complained that officials had 'consistently lied'.

Surprisingly, the Ministry of Defence was still arguing that *Concord* was not deliberately excluded in the original decision-making process. The ministry was also concerned about the administration and cost of supplying medals if groups of veterans successfully argued their case for various campaigns. It was estimated that the cost of issuing Yangtze clasps to *Concord* veterans or family members would be £1,000.

Holmes pointed out: 'The United Kingdom takes a distinctive approach to the award of military campaign medals, reflecting a strong view that medals must be awarded sparingly to maintain a highly prized currency.' But he said: 'It is also legitimate to ask whether a little more past flexibility would not have avoided some genuine grievances without opening the gates to a flood of vexatious correspondents.'

The review's recommendations included broadening the membership of the Committee on the Grant of Honours, Decorations and Medals, and setting up a military subcommittee to examine old controversies.

Holmes listed the main factors that should be considered when awarding a campaign medal. They included the risk and danger to life; the style and force of the enemy; and the physical and mental stress and rigours experienced by individuals. On the question of risk and rigour, Holmes commented: 'The idea is that campaign medals should only be awarded where deployed personnel have been exposed to a significant degree of risk to life and limb, and to arduous conditions, in excess of what might be expected as part of normal service duties . . .'

There is a rule that the issue of campaign medals should not be reopened after five years, but it was acknowledged that there could be exceptional circumstances. These included evidence that the issue was never properly considered at the time; significant new information; facts relied upon during the original decision-making process being shown to be unsound; and the original decision appearing to be manifestly inconsistent with those of similar campaigns. Tellingly, Holmes said a decision on whether to examine a particular case should not rest with the Ministry of Defence but with the honours committee.[12]

In January 2013 the former diplomat told the *Concord* veterans that their case had been rejected. He wrote: 'The first point to emphasise is that we fully accept that HMS *Concord* did indeed enter the Yangtze, and meet with HMS *Amethyst* there, and escorted her out of the estuary. There was obviously a degree of risk involved in this, given the shore batteries in particular, though fortunately the ships were not fired on in the event. The crew of HMS *Concord* can therefore be considered technically eligible for the clasp.'

Technically eligible. But not eligible. It was a baffling rejection. Holmes went on to say that the attempt to conceal *Concord*'s role was 'short-term' and it became 'public knowledge fairly quickly' that the destroyer had been in the Yangtze. He insisted that 'the authorities at the time took great trouble to identify precisely those people they wanted to reward for the Yangtze incident'. The dwindling band of veterans responded by declaring they would continue their campaign. 'We are not medal chasers but we would like public acknowledgement of the part we played,' said Derek Hodgson.[13]

Concord did not come under fire during the night of 30/31 July 1949, but with some irony she was attacked in August the following year – and replied. As she approached Hong Kong with 'peaceful intent', Chinese batteries on the islands of Tai Ta Mi and Ling Ting opened fire. *Concord* increased speed and zig-zagged but when the firing continued she answered with fifty rounds from her 4.5in guns, probably inflicting serious casualties and damage. Soldiers were seen fleeing from one battery. The Chinese fired a total of about 100 rounds. One rating was wounded but the destroyer did not take any direct hits. British diplomats in Peking were asked to make an urgent protest. Admiral Brind noted that visibility was good enough for *Concord*'s ensign to be seen. She was clearly a British ship, hoisting another ensign and Union Flag before returning fire.

However, John Hutchison, the newly installed charge d'affaires in Peking, warned that the Communists were likely to demand an apology and compensation, noting: 'I imagine that they would assert that the islands are Chinese territory, that *Concord* entered territorial waters without obtaining or seeking permission and without being under necessity for doing so, that she failed to stop when summoned by a warning shot and that her action in first trying to escape and in finally opening fire constituted a breach of international law . . . tantamount to a warlike act.'[14] A British warship, territorial waters, Communists opening fire first. It sounded familiar.

It emerged that *Concord* was using a channel generally regarded as 'an international highway' for merchant vessels and warships, and permission would not have been needed. Although the Nationalists had retreated to Formosa, tensions with the Communists remained high. The Nationalist blockade of ports had been effective. British shipping was harassed, with sixteen incidents between September 1949 and January 1950, which was why the Royal Navy remained active off the coast of China.

Britain had formally recognised the People's Republic of China that January, and talks were continuing to improve relations with the Communist government in Peking. There were fears that the *Concord* incident would jeopardise negotiations – and the interests of British companies. The growing crisis over the Korean War, however, would quickly overshadow the controversy.

22

Lieutenant Weston's Escape

AMETHYST'S FIRST LIEUTENANT, GEOFFREY WESTON, had an eventful time after leaving the frigate on 22 April. When Kerans rejected his pleas to remain on board, the wounded officer was taken by landing craft to Chingkiang. After some delay he managed to get a Jeep to the Nationalist naval headquarters, where he telephoned the embassy. Lieutenant Colonel Dewar-Durie, the assistant military attaché, came and arranged for him to go to a hospital in Nanking. Weston, who had a serious shrapnel injury, was driven to the local railway station and put on a train after being given a morphine injection by Charlotte Dunlap from the local mission hospital. The train, however, never arrived in Nanking because the retreating Nationalists had blown up part of the station. It stopped some distance from the capital, and an embassy official eventually found Weston in the early hours of 23 April. He was driven to Nanking's University Hospital.

'I had become very ill on the train, probably in consequence of Jeep journeys over cobbled streets, and could hardly speak or move,' Weston reported. 'After X-ray later the same morning the doctors pronounced that the piece of shrapnel – about matchbox size – had passed through the lung and entered the liver, where they proposed to leave it and where it still is. I wanted it removed but the surgeon replied that this would entail a very serious operation unnecessarily and he would only remove it if my condition deteriorated.'

The Communists occupied Nanking the next day. Captain Donaldson, the naval attaché, visited him and took away his uniform. Weston was having trouble sleeping: 'Ever since I was hit I have been unable to lie flat and have had to sleep sitting up or with my head on a desk or something. I can now lie at about 45 degrees.' By 12 May he had recovered enough to leave hospital. Stevenson invited him to stay at the embassy but the lieutenant was worried that he possessed only one suit, two shirts and a pair of pyjamas, 'insufficient for staying with an ambassador'. Most of his clothes had been destroyed when his cabin was hit. Donaldson replenished his wardrobe and he went to the embassy, where Lady Stevenson was 'a perfect hostess'. He did some work in the naval attaché's office, and played chess and bridge to pass the time. Weston learned that he had been awarded a Bar to his DSC, noting that 'many others deserve medals if I do'. In June he had this observation on the civil war: 'The Nationalists are more or less finished, but the Communists are waiting for the harvest to be got in before advancing any further. They do not want to conquer a starving country.' As the conflict continued, the behaviour of some of the foreign VIPs remaining in Nanking provided a source of amusement. The senior Canadian diplomat invited the Persian ambassador and others to lunch one day. The Persian envoy decided he had not been seated at the right place and refused to eat anything. His wife joined the protest. Western 'civilisation' baffled peasants fighting on the Communist side who had never seen a fan or an electric light before. Weston revealed: 'The other day one brought in some rice to a European house and went to wash it in a lavatory. When he asked how to get rid of the water he was told to pull the plug and was very indignant when his rice disappeared as well. There are also women in the army who wear uniform but do not actually fight. They are known as the Comfort Corps.'

Weston wanted to take a sampan down the river to rejoin *Amethyst* but Donaldson refused permission. The naval attaché thought the lieutenant should leave the country as soon as possible. Weston had been confined to Nanking, but in late June the Communists in the city lifted a ban on the movement of foreigners and he travelled to Shanghai, arriving on 30 June. He was still keen to reach *Amethyst*.[1]

On the night of 5 July, Kerans received a signal about Weston from the assistant naval attaché in Shanghai, Commander John Pringle. Kerans was left with the impression that the police in Shanghai had ordered the lieutenant to leave the city at short notice, but this may not have been the case. It was another dilemma. *Amethyst*'s captain feared that Pringle's plan to send Weston back to the ship might jeopardise the difficult negotiations with Colonel Kang, especially as the diplomat Edward Youde was about to be involved, a move of 'paramount importance'. Kerans tried to delay Weston's departure, and the matter was referred to Admiral Brind, who decided he should rejoin *Amethyst*.

Kerans assumed that Weston had important messages for him from the commander-in-chief, and it was hoped he would reach *Amethyst* without being noticed after arriving in Chingkiang. At that time the Communists were busy celebrating their military advances. To placate the uncompromising Kang, Kerans sent a letter explaining Weston's position, but due to the weather and 'local stupidity' it arrived too late. The interpreter Sam Leo was sent ashore to meet Weston, who was due to arrive by train in Chingkiang at dawn on 8 July.[2]

Weston did indeed have instructions from Brind, and he had also memorised a code for Kerans to use. He set off from Shanghai with two suitcases full of cigarettes, sweets, soap and other goods. With him was Commander Pringle's interpreter, Khoong. There were no problems on the journey but when they turned up at the station in Chingkiang sentries prevented them from leaving. 'They took me to an office where I argued for a few hours with Communist officers,' Weston reported.

> They said my pass was not in order and out of date, that Commander Kerans had not applied for permission for me to board and that it was an insult to Chinese national sovereignty that I should travel on Chinese national soil and so on. They said they would convene a meeting of the 'Amethyst Committee' to consider the matter and returned to say that it had been decided that I was to proceed straight back to Shanghai without leaving the station. All this was in Chinese through Mr Khoong. Although they could speak English they would not use it, except occasionally for abuse.[3]

Kerans recalled:

> Everything went wrong and it appears that the station authorities quickly got in touch with Kang and words were exchanged. Kang stated he could not consider the matter as it had not been discussed at any meeting. I realised that Kang had to a certain extent been short-circuited and confronted with a fait accompli. Regrettably, Shanghai too had been hasty, and if only I had been given time to obtain clearance at the Chingkiang end all undoubtedly would have been well. I am at a loss to understand why it should have been assumed that clearance in Shanghai was the only essential especially as the naval attaché Nanking himself had been at pains to point out clearance at Chingkiang was so essential and specially so, being a defended area. It was I fear entirely due to this affair that Youde's exit permit from

Nanking to Chingkiang was held up by Kang directly after he had given verbal clearance for his entry through Mr Leo.

Weston was detained for 12 hours. Then he was sent back to Shanghai with Khoong in a freight train. To Kerans's dismay Kang also stopped the Admiralty oil fuel from Nanking reaching *Amethyst*. Fortunately, it was a temporary setback, and it did arrive on 9 July.[4]

In Shanghai Weston tried without success to get police permission to return to *Amethyst*. He thought again about taking a sampan to the ship but realised that both banks of the river were too heavily guarded. He began work in the office of Commander Pringle, who was preoccupied with the *Amethyst* crisis, especially in trying to get supplies sent.

Weston learned of *Amethyst*'s escape in a BBC broadcast and was overjoyed. He noted: 'The British newspaper, the *China Daily News*, did not dare publish the news, but there was unreserved jubilation amongst the foreigners in Shanghai, which was by no means confined to the British community.' But Weston was now a wanted man, an *Amethyst* 'criminal'. After burning secret and relevant papers on the instructions of a British diplomat he went to ground.[5]

One of the people who helped to hide him was Wing Commander Peter Howard-Williams, the assistant air attaché. But Howard-Williams was urged by Ambassador Stevenson to leave Shanghai as soon as possible and go to Hong Kong. He went to a police station to obtain an exit visa but was told it could not be issued immediately. A few days later he was asked to return and this time an army officer, a Colonel Ch'eng, interviewed him. Howard-Williams was not allowed his interpreter and the questions were in Chinese until he made it clear he understood little, at which point the colonel, a defector from the Nationalists who had been trained in the United States, began speaking in 'perfect English'. He was asked about his movements, what military information he had obtained during the course of his work, his flying career, his views on the civil war and his favourite city in China.

'I was suddenly asked if I knew a Royal Navy officer in Shanghai called Weston,' he reported.

This question took me by surprise and I replied that I couldn't at the moment think of anyone by that name. Colonel Ch'eng wanted to know if Weston was still in Shanghai. It was a touchy moment as Lieutenant Weston was at that moment living in my flat and we had done our best to keep his whereabouts quiet. Something had to be done quickly and as soon as I had left the police station I made arrangements to move Geoffrey to another flat where he would be less likely to be caught. The American naval attaché, Commander Morgan Slayton, very kindly took him in and only just in time. The next day there were several officials round my flat asking the servants questions but they had arrived too late and Geoffrey was safe.[6]

At the end of the interview at the police station Colonel Ch'eng said he was not satisfied with some of Howard-Williams's answers. The exit visa was delayed. Commander Slayton found himself the target of anti-American feeling. Some 150 former employees of the US Navy in Shanghai, most of them Chinese, besieged the American consulate for several days. Slayton and other members of staff were not allowed to leave the building. The protesters, who demanded severance pay, were encouraged by Communist propaganda denouncing 'foreign imperialists' and 'bureaucratic capitalists'. Other pay disputes broke out in the city, with some demands going back years. The US State Department accused the authorities of permitting 'if not fostering, a pattern of extortion' against foreigners.[7]

Weston had no wish or reason to remain in Shanghai, but he could not, of course, obtain permission to leave. The British consul, Robert Urquhart, told him to continue to lie low until his escape could be arranged. The first opportunity was the British cargo ship ss *Edith Moller*, which had beaten the Nationalist blockade. 'However, the master was not keen to take me,' Weston reported. 'He had his own difficulties and was not even allowed to take passengers with permits and did not want to take me as a stowaway as his ship was to be searched before leaving.'

The lieutenant then asked a chief petty officer called Cunningham, who worked for Commander Pringle, and the interpreter Khoong to arrange with their Chinese friends for a junk to take him to the frigate HMS *Hart*, which was patrolling at the mouth of the Yangtze. On 10 August, in a room at the back of the consul's house on the Bund, he negotiated a deal with a fish merchant and a junk owner. The cost of hiring the junk was a large quantity of rice. It was arranged that the junk would rendezvous with *Hart* near Gutzlaff Island, and 'my junk would be distinguished by my white shirt at the masthead'.

The trip was planned for the next day but postponed after a tip-off that the Communists were searching all junks at Woosung. There were several arrests after arms were discovered. Soldiers were also checking vehicles travelling from Shanghai to Woosung. The fish merchant gave Weston daily reports on the patrols. On 15 August the lieutenant was given the all clear, and he met his helpers along with Khoong's 'numerous relations as cover' in a Shanghai street that afternoon. They left in a lorry, arriving in Woosung half an hour later without being searched.[8]

Weston, who had been given a special passport by the consul, noted: 'My only disguise consisted of being dressed in a dirty shirt and pair of shorts, being generally shabby and unshaven and wearing sunglasses and a Panama hat to simulate a Shanghai coolie. This would not have stood up to close scrutiny but my entourage of Chinese prevented my being closely observed. I believe there was only one other foreign resident at Woosung and Shanghai foreigners were not permitted there.' After waiting for the right moment in a 'native' restaurant Weston was taken to a sampan which went to a junk already under way. He was 'battened down in the hold' as the junk left the harbour. Later he emerged to find a 'happy' crew who shared their supper with him. The weather was squally but by dawn, with the tide in their favour, they were making good progress towards Gutzlaff Island.

The destroyer *Comus* had replaced *Hart* on patrol, and Weston spotted a warship. In the growing light he realised it was not *Comus* but a Nationalist ship enforcing the blockade. It was not a friendly sight. 'I made signs to the junk skipper to keep away and he put the junk about on a course clear of the warship, but the tide was setting more strongly and we continued to close. There were many other fishing junks near us but we were further to seaward than the others in order to make Gutzlaff. When about a mile away from her, the destroyer fired several bursts towards us with Oerlikon and machine guns and addressed us in Chinese over their loud hailer. This was evidently an order to close and about half an hour later we anchored astern, having failed to get alongside because of the tide.'[9]

A boarding party searched the junk and suspicions were aroused over the passenger with 'soft hands'. Weston was suspected of being a

Russian but he was able to prove otherwise. A request to allow the junk to continue was met with a refusal, and he was put on board the *Tai Kong*, an ex-American destroyer. Weston was told he would be taken to Ting Hai Island and he tried to argue with the captain but finally accepted that 'reason and argument seldom influence Chinese'. No doubt his experience at Chingkiang railway station was fresh in his mind. He learned that the Nationalist navy suspected its own army of trading with the mainland and there was also concern that Communist fifth columnists were being landed by junk on the Chu San islands. Weston pointed out that any junk involved in these operations would surely hug the coast but again his argument was ignored. The captain also refused to transfer him to *Comus* or to put him on Gutzlaff Island, or to even inform the Royal Navy of his whereabouts. Weston did not want *Comus* searching for him in vain.

A minesweeper replaced *Tai Kong* on patrol on 17 August. The junk was turned over to the minesweeper for 'further examination', and the destroyer sailed to Ting Hai harbour, arriving that afternoon. Weston said he was well treated on board, with the first lieutenant insisting on giving up his cabin. At Ting Hai he was seen by the captain of a destroyer flotilla and told he would be sent to Formosa on the next available ship, and the Royal Navy would be informed. He was accommodated in a Yangtze pilot vessel, which had been seized by the Nationalists shortly after the fall of Shanghai, and politely discouraged from going ashore during the day. Two ships sailed to Formosa without him, and on 19 August the captain of the destroyer flotilla said he would, in fact, be allowed to go to *Comus*. That evening he sailed in a destroyer for a midnight rendezvous with the British ship.[10]

'I was very glad to be back and to taste English food again and to be able to borrow some clean clothes,' he reported. *Comus* signalled that he had been picked up. It was made clear that Weston's escape should not be publicised. He was disappointed to learn that he would not be rejoining *Amethyst* in Hong Kong but would fly back to Britain in secret.

Comus had been searching for him for three days.

I believe that the refusal of the Nationalist navy to transfer me before, or to inform the Royal Navy or British consul at Canton that they had picked me up was due to their resentment at the presence of our guardship at the entrance of the Yangtze. They contended that the British guardship was inside the three-mile limit, which they measured not from the low water mark but from the Yangtze light vessel. Their officers continually tried to draw me on the question of their right to close the port of Shanghai, to which I replied non-commitally. Meanwhile I recorded on board HMS *Comus* or forwarded by signal all the intelligence I was able.

After a few days on board *Comus* he was landed near Kure, Japan, and a Sunderland flew him to Hong Kong. Kerans met him at Kai Tak with 'some gear salvaged from the wreckage of my cabin', and promising to settle his affairs in Hong Kong because Weston was not allowed to leave the RAF mess. The lieutenant even had to use another name. Early the next day a Dakota flew him to Singapore, where he met Admiral Brind and the chief of his intelligence staff. Later he travelled to Britain in a civilian plane.

A naval security officer was waiting for him at Heathrow but all the secrecy was in vain. Reporters and cameramen were also there. The security officer told Weston he could tell them anything up to the time of his escape, which he was not to mention.

'I felt I knew better and should not see any reporters at all,' Weston recalled.

But the security officer was quite right in that they were impossible to avoid. They were even waiting at my home and had been told I could answer limited questions. Apparently the *News Chronicle* had been told of my impending arrival by their Far East office. The BBC were told by the naval information department that my escape was secret and announced this on the news. This as I expected drew forth a protest from the assistant naval attaché Shanghai and I can only hope there will be no repercussions there. This escape would not have been successful without the constant support of Commander Pringle and Chief Petty Officer Cunningham and Mr Khoong, who each gave me great assistance at no little risk to themselves. [11]

During a spell of leave he was invited to the offices of the Admiralty's Naval Intelligence Division, which was 'anxious to hear at first hand of your experiences'.[12]

23

The Nervous Colony

AMETHYST'S ESCAPE AND THE ANGER of the Communists focused British minds once again on the vulnerability of Hong Kong. Reinforcements were being sent to improve the colony's defences, but it was thought advisable to keep publicity to a minimum. Britain wanted to deter aggression. It did not want to antagonise Peking. On 25 August Ambassador Stevenson in Nanking told the Foreign Office of the importance of restricting statements on 'warlike preparations'. The message had been taken on board by the Ministry of Defence and service chiefs, and the Foreign Office 'are doing what they can to influence the press, the news agencies and the BBC'. The Colonial Office asked the Governor of Hong Kong, Sir Alexander Grantham, to make sure that the colony's civil authorities showed the same 'reticence'.[1]

The problem of Hong Kong had been a headache for Prime Minister Attlee and his Cabinet for months. There was even the argument that the colony should be abandoned if the threat became too great. Sir Stafford Cripps, the Chancellor of the Exchequer, believed that post-war Britain, in the grip of austerity, could not afford to pay for the extra defence, and that the colony would be impossible to hold in the face of an attack by a massive Communist army. Attlee and the majority of his Cabinet did not take that view. Failure to face up to the challenge would seriously damage Britain's prestige throughout the region. Attlee thought 'the whole common front in Siam, Burma and Malaya was likely to crumble unless the peoples of those countries were convinced of our determination and ability to resist this threat to Hong Kong'.[2] Grantham was confident that the colony could be defended so long as the Soviet Union did not intervene.

Attlee and his defence minister, Albert Alexander, were hoping that Australia and New Zealand would see that it was in their interests to help with the colony's defence. New Zealand's premier, Peter Fraser, offered three frigates. His Australian counterpart, Ben Chifley, backed by foreign minister Herbert Evatt, rejected the appeal, arguing that Britain could be heading for a 'full-scale war' with China.[3] Chifley and Evatt had, of course, stopped the Australian frigate *Shoalhaven* from taking part in the Nanking mission in April, which led to *Amethyst* being chosen as the replacement.

In July 1949 British intelligence experts still believed that the return of Hong Kong was an important part of Chinese Communist policy. However, evidence obtained from Communist documents seized in the colony appeared to suggest that it was not an immediate plan. Trade and finance remained key factors: 'It is not impossible that the trading value of Hong Kong in British hands may in the immediate future be of such great importance to them that they may temporarily acquiesce in the status quo.'

In the event of an attack, it was estimated that 150,000 troops might reach the border with Hong Kong, but numbers could vary because of the narrowness of the front. Guerrilla raids were a threat, and the infiltration of agents in considerable numbers was probable. In the unlikely event of the entire Nationalist air force defecting, air raids on the colony would not involve more than forty medium and heavy bombers, supported by seventy fighter-bombers. The threat from the Communist navy had been 'dismissed rather too lightly'. It was thought the Communists had sixty-five ships, including six destroyers and seventeen gunboats. The Joint Intelligence Committee at the Cabinet Office in London reported: 'Although the efficiency of this force is thought to be low at present, it might be welded into an effective fighting force in a comparatively short time and might be of considerable nuisance value if employed against trade.'

The committee also noted that the Communists had not overplayed the propaganda card over the claim to Hong Kong: 'This restraint on the part of the vociferous and competent Chinese broadcasting system can only have resulted from orders from above. Furthermore, although Chinese Communist propaganda is constantly denouncing the "unequal" treaties with foreign powers, that governing Hong Kong has never yet been mentioned. These omissions are perhaps further indirect evidence in support of the theory that the Communists do not propose to take any immediate action to eject British rule from Hong Kong.'[4]

The intelligence experts made another assessment in August and concluded that if the Communists were going to attack the colony it would not be before mid-October. Communist forces were making steady progress southwards and westwards in China. The main threat to Hong Kong was the thrust on Canton by General Chen Keng's troops, who were advancing up the Kan valley. A subsidiary advance was being made in Fukien province.

Six armies of General Lin Piao had captured Chuchow and Changsha, and were advancing to Hengyang. A second group of five armies were fighting to the west of the Tungting lakes and along the Yangtze gorge towards Chungking. In addition, there were thirteen armies involved in operations in north-west China, driving towards Szechwan province.

The Joint Intelligence Committee reported:

It is probable these operations are designed to secure the important rice harvest in this province and ultimately to move on Chungking in conjunction with General Lin Piao's advance up the Yangtze gorge. It is considered this force is unlikely to be used for possible operations against Hong Kong.

We estimate that no substantial Communist forces are likely to arrive in the Canton area before the beginning of September, or before the end of September at the borders of the leased territories. From the military point of view it is unlikely that any possible threat to the colony would arise until the greater part of Kwantung province has been brought under control. This is unlikely to be effective before the latter half of October.

On morale in Hong Kong, there was this comment: 'The *Amethyst* incident has stimulated local Chinese morale and caused loss of face to the Communists.' The committee also looked at the situation in Shanghai, where many British nationals remained. The Nationalist blockade continued to be effective, with trade at a standstill. Six Liberator bombers had carried out 'an unusually accurate' attack on the dockyard.[5]

A bleaker picture had been provided by the British consul, Robert Urquhart, who reported that 'the opportunistic exploitation of capitalists in general and of the foreigner in particular is largely unchecked'. Urquhart was highly critical of the Communist officers in control of the city: 'They neither have administrative machinery nor the knowledge to cope with problems of Shanghai and have to refer constantly to Peking. Pending decisions from Peking the only people who know their minds are Moscow-type politicians and Shanghai racketeers. They have united effectively to exploit many ancient grudges against foreigners and the natural greed of the Chinese for loot . . .' He predicted that Peking would crack down on 'frothing extremists' who were trying to impress the new rulers. Shortages of food, fuel and raw materials were exacerbating the problem. 'American aircraft' of the Nationalist air force were dropping 'American bombs' on Shanghai and 'it could be fairly easy for agitators to direct popular wrath against imperialists'. Urquhart's comments were passed to admirals Brind and Madden.[6]

The threat to Hong Kong produced parallels with the Berlin blockade and the Cold War. In a telegram to Commonwealth prime ministers in September, Attlee noted: 'In some respects situation is similar to that which faced us – and to some extent still faces us – in Berlin. Just as we cannot foresee with certainty how future of Berlin will develop but are convinced of necessity of remaining there, so we are impelled to remain in Hong Kong without any clear indication of extent or duration of military commitments involved. In both cases the threat of Russian and Communist expansion necessitates holding what we have and not withdrawing.'

Lieutenant General Francis Festing, the newly appointed commander of British forces in Hong Kong, revealed that 'the building up of this place has gone exactly according to plan'. When completed, the gun density would be equal to that in London at the height of the wartime Blitz. There were so many soldiers that a commando brigade had to be accommodated at the Jockey Club.[7] One of the arrivals was Royal Marine commando Leslie Andrew Frank, the teenage son of *Amethyst*'s coxswain Leslie Frank. Father and son, who had not seen each other for more than two years, had an emotional reunion after the troopship *Georgic* docked. Marine Frank dashed down the gangway and grasped his father's hand. He had learned of the frigate's escape when his ship was in the Arabian Sea.[8]

The British intelligence warning that mid-October would be a critical time was remarkably accurate. On 15 October Chinese Communist troops fanned out along the border with the colony. They chased retreating Nationalist soldiers, some of whom surrendered their arms to Hong Kong police and crossed the frontier. Customs officers also fled, but businessmen at the key village of Shumchun quickly ran up the red flag. British forces put into operation phase one of their defence plan, a state of readiness with increased border patrols. There were 40,000 British troops in the colony. On alert in the harbour were the aircraft carrier HMS *Triumph*, the cruiser *Belfast* and six destroyers.[9]

The *News of the World* painted this picture:

An unending stream of army lorries rolls towards the border hills. Dispatch riders, darting at speed through the streets and hill country, are all armed with Sten guns. In the centre of the city gunners are training with mobile field guns. Far off an RAF reconnaissance plane is faintly visible in the half-haze. Now and again comes the deep-throated roar of a Spitfire. Wherever one turns there are signs of defence preparations. Steel booms up and down the river close all but a tightly guarded shipping channel against any possible incursion of unauthorised craft. And out in the countryside thousands of men – Commando troops in the green berets, kilted Highlanders, stocky Gurkhas, gunners, tankmen – are set out on the hillsides or snuggling down in the valleys behind.[10]

The United States sympathised with Britain's position but did not offer any direct help. This was probably a good thing because it did not add to complications with Peking. The Americans, with reservations, were backing the Nationalists and their new base, Formosa. In June 1950 President Truman may have deterred any Chinese Communist military ambitions towards Hong Kong by sending his navy's Seventh Fleet to the Formosa Strait.[11] The Nationalists would be a thorn in Mao Tse-tung's side for many years, but at that time he was more interested in helping to defeat the French in Vietnam and focusing on the developing war in Korea.

24

Kerans's Drunken Escapade

AS MILITARY CHIEFS STEPPED UP the defences of Hong Kong, community leaders were busy organising a full programme of entertainment for *Amethyst*'s crew, most of whom had been given twelve days' leave. An *Amethyst* cap tally appeared to be a guarantee of free drinks. The telephone of the fleet recreation officer was ringing almost continuously with offers of hospitality from residents and companies.

One of the events was the weekly lunch of the Rotary Club of Kowloon at the Peninsula Hotel. A party of forty sailors went along – and even Peggy the ship's dog was invited. It seemed that everyone wanted to meet the men from *Amethyst*. The lunch saw a record attendance of members. The club's vice president told the sailors: 'You have withstood hardship and trying conditions in having to deal with an unruly mob which knows no justice. We are proud of you.' He proposed a toast to 'our gallant friends'. Then members sang 'For they are jolly good fellows'. Loud and prolonged applause drew a bark from Peggy. Coxswain Leslie Frank replied on behalf of the sailors, admitting: 'The welcome we have received on our arrival has, I am afraid, overwhelmed us.'[1]

Messages of congratulation were pouring in to the Admiralty. The Chief of the Imperial General Staff, Field Marshal Sir William Slim, told the First Sea Lord, Admiral Fraser: 'On behalf of all ranks I send you the warmest congratulations on this magnificent feat which has yet again proved to the world that the courage, endurance and seamanship of the Royal Navy are, as ever, equal to any challenge.'[2] The message from the Norwegians was a typical example: 'Norway and the whole of the civilised world are proud of the achievement of HMS *Amethyst* in forcing her way out of the Yangtze River, through boom obstacles and minefields and in the middle of the night, in a daring bid to regain her liberty. We have all a deep admiration for the excellent way in which the escape was planned and carried out.'[3] The Chilean Navy expressed its admiration for the 'brilliant action', and the exclusive Roshanara Club in Delhi offered its 'warmest congratulations'. Even the French, who had suffered so many defeats at the hands of the Royal Navy in the past, contacted the Foreign Office to say 'how much they shared our rejoicing at the magnificent achievement of the *Amethyst*'.

The publicity resulted in a remarkable somersault by Australia's prime minister, Ben Chifley. It is worth recalling that Chifley refused to allow the frigate *Shoalhaven* to sail up the Yangtze, and he ordered that Australian warships were not to take part in operations off the coast of China. He also refused to help with the defence of Hong Kong. Most tellingly, when asked in his country's House of Representatives on 1 June about *Amethyst*'s captivity, he replied: 'It is not our problem to enquire what the Royal Navy does about its ships . . .' But Chifley was quick to try to share in *Amethyst*'s glory. On the day the frigate reached Hong Kong he sent a letter to the UK High Commissioner in Australia inviting the ship to pay a visit. He wrote:

The Commonwealth government and the people of Australia share the pride felt throughout the empire at the epic exploit of the sloop HMS *Amethyst* and would be very happy if Australia were given the opportunity of showing the captain and crew its appreciation of their effort. I should be grateful therefore if on behalf of the government of the Commonwealth of Australia you would convey a hearty invitation to the C-in-C Far East Station for the captain and crew of *Amethyst* to pay a visit to Australia as guests of the Commonwealth government. It is realised that the captain and members of the crew of *Amethyst* may wish to proceed at the first opportunity to their homes but the Commonwealth government would be quite prepared to await a visit when such would be most convenient to the Admiralty and the personnel concerned.[4]

It would not have escaped the attention of political observers that Chifley and his Labor Party were set to face a difficult federal election. Any positive publicity would be a bonus. Strikes and a belief that Chifley was soft on Communism had helped to undermine the former train driver's popularity. He did indeed lose power that year.

Admiral Brind and the Admiralty had no intention of sending Kerans and his men to Australia. The high commissioner, Edward Williams, was told to inform Chifley that his invitation was 'deeply appreciated' and it had been given 'very careful consideration', but 'with very great regret' it could not be accepted. In a letter to the prime minister, the high commissioner wrote: 'As you foresaw, Lieutenant Commander Kerans and the members of his crew are naturally anxious to return to their homes at the earliest opportunity – they are indeed very tired after their experiences – and it is difficult to say whether circumstances would make it possible for such a visit to be arranged later on.'[5] Perhaps Brind was taking revenge on Chifley for the Australian government's lack of co-operation.

Strangely, *Shoalhaven*'s captain, Lieutenant Commander William Tapp, was removed from his command soon after *Amethyst*'s arrival in Hong Kong. Captain Alan McNicoll, a George Medal winner and a future vice admiral, replaced him. A report on Tapp's conduct at that time did not suggest anything amiss: 'A sound, capable and reliable officer. He has done very well in command of HMAS *Shoalhaven* and has proved his initiative and capabilities on many occasions. His ship is clean, efficient and happy. He should do well in the higher ranks of the service.'[6] Tapp, who had been Mentioned in Despatches for his coolness under fire during the Second World War, soon found himself back in Australia, where he took up an appointment as executive officer of the shore base HMAS *Penguin* in Sydney. And before the month of August was out *Shoalhaven* returned to Australian waters. Had the friendly and chatty Tapp talked too much about the fate of *Shoalhaven* and *Amethyst*? It seemed that someone in authority no longer wanted Tapp and his frigate in the Far East. At that stage the Australian government's decision to block *Shoalhaven*'s Yangtze mission was not widely known. The next assessment of Tapp was less than complimentary: 'A hard-working, earnest and reliable officer who does his best to make the most of the average ability with which he is endowed. His comparative lack of the gifts which give a high standard of leadership is, to a great extent, compensated for by his deter-mination, application and rectitude.'[7] Later he was being described as 'neither brilliant nor of impressive appearance, but can be relied upon to do any job, however boring or unrewarding with complete thoroughness and cheerfulness'.[8] One senior officer pointed out that Tapp 'would never set the Thames on fire', and a rear admiral offered this opinion: 'A slow plodder – careful and trustworthy – he has reached his zenith. His appearance is as uninspiring as his thinking is slow.'[9] Tapp would not rise above the rank of commander, and most of his appointments after *Shoalhaven* were shore jobs. He left the Royal Australian Navy in 1963 and died in 1975, aged 59.

William Stenhouse Hamilton, an Australian diplomat in Nanking, probably summed up his government's attitude during the *Amethyst* crisis when he wrote years later:

In retrospect, the stationing of warships at Nanking seems a strange enterprise. In the event of substantial civil violence we locals would have had little chance of reaching a ship at Hsia Kwan [the dock area]. And how were other people to be prevented from swamping these quite small ships? Evidently there had been no real regard for the risks of entering a war zone. Puzzling also was an invitation I had received to cocktails on board HMS *London* at Nanking for 10 May with the Commander-in-Chief Pacific Fleet and Lady Boyd [Admiral Sir Denis Boyd was Admiral Brind's predecessor as Commander-in-Chief, Far East Station]. There seems no good reason for either to be in the area; and it seems also there was no awareness that major military activity was impending.

The *Amethyst* affair was a tragic accident waiting to happen. The courage of the crew and of the boy seamen, their resourcefulness and endurance, have been largely forgotten. But the lesson delivered so brutally has been well learned. No uninvited foreign warship has since entered the inland waters of China. More than that – it brought an ineradicable realisation that the days of contemptuous or even unthinking disregard of Chinese sovereignty were over.[10]

In Hong Kong in August 1949, dockyard workers were busy carrying out major repairs to *Amethyst* in preparation for her return to Britain. In London, the Chief of Naval Information, Captain Clarke, was busy trying to curb the press once again. The escape of *Amethyst* had excited the imagination of the austerity-suffering British, and the return of the ship was set to produce more stories. Clarke was keen that 'the public acclaim, and consequential press publicity, should be kept within proper bounds', in view of 'a potential danger of the matter becoming vulgarised'.

Clarke noted: 'If, and this seems to be a certainty, some form of public march in London takes place, then it would be a wise thing to make the purpose of the march one of assembling in a place of public worship to render appropriate thanksgiving. Such an inclusion would not preclude a luncheon for the participants with appropriate speeches, but by doing the traditional thing as well this would have a sobering effect upon both the press and the public and put things in a more reasonable perspective.'

He thought it would be a good idea if the First Lord or the First Sea Lord had 'a heart to heart talk with the more important editors', so that the dangers arising from 'uncontrolled adulation' could be explained. The editors could be invited to tea or a cocktail party at the Admiralty. If this took place in the boardroom, 'all the better'. Clarke reported that the City of London had made an informal approach about hosting a reception.[11] The Board of Admiralty decided that a working party should be set up to deal with all the arrangements for *Amethyst*'s return. Clarke was told that he would head the group.[12]

There was some press criticism of the Admiralty's apparent reluctance to announce plans. Sailors wounded in the Yangtze attacks had arrived in Southampton, but there was no official reception for families, who had been discouraged from going to the dockside. Press arrangements broke down in a muddle between the Admiralty and the Ministry of Transport. In a piece headlined, 'The people want no more bungling over *Amethyst*', the London *Evening Standard* declared: 'This off-hand treatment of men whom the nation wish to honour was inexcusable. The Admiralty must do better when Lieutenant Commander Kerans and his men arrive.' The newspaper suggested that after *Amethyst* reached her home port of Plymouth and the crew were given a spell of leave, the frigate should sail up the Channel to the Thames and moor in the Pool of London under the walls of the Tower to the city's cheers. 'There the *Amethyst* should lie, a triumphant symbol that the spirit of the men in the little ships who routed and burned the Armada, who won the victory of Trafalgar, who saved the flower of the British Army at Dunkirk, still flames brightly in the hearts of seafarers.' After being honoured in London *Amethyst* should then sail around Britain, visiting Hull, Newcastle, the Forth, Glasgow, Belfast, Liverpool and Bristol before returning to Plymouth. 'Everywhere the crowds will be waiting.'[13] The day after the *Evening Standard*'s plea, the *News Chronicle* reported: 'Naval circles in London do not incline to the view that *Amethyst* will be sent round as a "show ship" to the ports.'[14]

Invitations for *Amethyst* were still coming in. Air Chief Marshal Sir Frederick Bowhill, of the Honourable Company of Master Mariners, wrote to the First Sea Lord, Admiral Fraser, saying they would like to invite the frigate's officers to the livery company's headquarters ship *Wellington*, moored on the Thames in London. Fraser replied that the officers and men of *Amethyst* were being overwhelmed with invitations. He observed: 'In the navy we feel so many of these episodes occur which because they are not dramatic are unnoticed, such as our blockade of Palestine in which many feats of seamanship and endurance were performed. We have the greatest admiration of *Amethyst*'s feat in every way, but do not wish it to be overdone. They will probably march through London and lunch at the Guildhall and we think this should be sufficient before they take some leave and a rest.' The air chief marshal's invitation was passed to Captain Clarke's working party.[15]

On 9 September, a Friday, the commander of British forces in Hong Kong, Lieutenant General Festing, and the Commodore Hong Kong, Leslie Brownfield, went on board *Amethyst* to shake hands with Kerans and say farewell. The frigate had arrived in the colony to a great reception, but that afternoon she slipped away from the naval dockyard's east wall with little fanfare, homeward bound. A small crowd waved goodbye. Among them was Marine Frank, son of the frigate's coxswain. Also on shore was Lieutenant Commander Strain, the fleet electrical officer, who had endured *Amethyst*'s captivity after thinking he would only be taking a two-day trip from Shanghai to Nanking. Strain decided to complete his tour of service in the Far East rather than head home. Peggy the ship's dog had been found a good home in Hong Kong after crewmen weighed up the cost of keeping her in quarantine in Britain. But Simon the cat was still on board. A sampan exploded crackers as the newly-painted *Amethyst*, showing few scars, headed out to sea escorted by the destroyer *Concord* and the frigate *Hart*. On board *Concord* was Vice Admiral Madden, who must have experienced mixed emotions. So much had happened since 20 April. He sent *Amethyst* up the Yangtze, and he greeted her in *Jamaica* after the great escape. He also tried to stop Kerans taking *Amethyst* back to Britain.

Kerans was now a hero but his colourful past had not been forgotten. He was originally sent to the office of the naval attaché in

Nanking as a form of punishment – 'for disposal' – and his behaviour since arriving in Hong Kong had attracted unfavourable comments. Kerans's drinking was one of the problems. Madden came to the conclusion that *Amethyst*'s captain was unstable and he feared a scandal. He sent a personal message to Admiral Brind at his headquarters in Singapore advising that Kerans should not take the frigate home in view of all the publicity that was being generated. The commander-in-chief, well aware of Kerans's run-ins with authority, was not surprised to get the warning, but he was left in a quandary. Tragedy had been turned into triumph. Could the Royal Navy disown its newly-created hero? It was not an exaggeration to say that *Amethyst* had attracted worldwide attention. Should they relieve Kerans of his command? Brind was in such a dilemma that he asked the Admiralty for advice. Back came the reply that for 'political reasons' Kerans must remain *Amethyst*'s captain and bring the ship home.

Amethyst's first stop on the voyage to Britain was . . . Singapore. Brind decided to take a chance and carry on with the tributes. The frigate arrived on 14 September. That day the Governor of Singapore, Sir Franklin Gimson, held a reception for the ship's officers. In the evening there was a formal dinner party hosted by Brind at Admiralty House. Among the guests were the Commissioner General for South East Asia and army and air force chiefs. It was a prestigious occasion, and Lieutenant Commander John Kerans DSO was the guest of honour. There were drinks before dinner and all the guests had arrived by 2015 except one – Kerans. By 2030 he had still not turned up, and an embarrassed Brind decided he could not keep his guests waiting any longer. They sat down to dinner, with Kerans's place of honour empty. No one could fail to notice the absence. The conversation was hushed.

Shortly after the main course had finished a car came up the drive of Admiralty House and stopped at the main entrance. Brind's flag lieutenant, David Scott, went to investigate. It was a taxi. The engine was running and the Chinese driver sat motionless. Scott opened one of the doors and found Kerans lying on the floor covered in vomit. He was wearing a lounge suit. The driver was paid and stewards carried Kerans to Scott's room, where he was stripped and placed in a cold bath. Two minutes later he was lying on a bed being given a vigorous Chinese massage. Within five minutes Kerans was upright and dressed in one of Scott's white dinner jackets. He was able to speak. By this time the dinner was almost over and Kerans was advised not to enter the dinning room, which was across a hallway. But he insisted on going and walked unsteadily into the room, where conversation immediately ceased. He was shown to his place. Malcolm MacDonald, the commissioner general, said a few words of welcome and asked how he was feeling. There was no response. Kerans declined to eat anything and refused a glass of port. He sat in silence.

It would not be difficult to imagine Admiral Brind's thoughts. The guests were shown to the drawing room and they left early, apart from Kerans. It was decided that he would stay the night at Admiralty House and sleep off his hangover. But Kerans had other ideas. He announced loudly that he was 'going ashore' for a drink, and asked for a taxi to be called. Scott and Commander Peter Dickens tried to persuade him that it was not a good idea and he should go to bed. Kerans became aggressive and there was a heated argument. He wanted to go to The Tanglin Club – the secretary was an old friend and expecting him. Eventually Scott and Dickens decided they would drive Kerans to the club and keep an eye on him. When they arrived Scott went to order drinks. Kerans spotted the secretary and the pair dashed away, pursued by Dickens. They reached the secretary's office and the door was slammed in Dickens's face and then locked. Scott and Dickens had the task of getting Kerans back to Admiralty House, and they guessed rightly that they were in for a long wait. Another drinking session was under way. Hours later a steward carrying a large jug of water and glasses opened the door with his own key. Kerans and the secretary were unconscious, one in an armchair and the other on a sofa. Scott and Dickens carried Kerans to their car and took him back to Admiralty House, where he was put to bed. He was finally roused shortly before 0900.

Brind had gone to his office early and given instructions that Kerans was to appear before him that morning in uniform, with his sword and medals. A message was sent to *Amethyst* to get the uniform, sword and medals delivered to Admiralty House. Kerans duly appeared before a furious Brind and was given a severe reprimand. The incident was reported to the Admiralty. It was decided that Kerans should still be allowed to bring *Amethyst* home – those 'political reasons' – but the commanders-in-chief of the operational areas that the ship would pass through were told to take all necessary action to avoid the possibility of another scandal.

Amethyst's next port was Penang, followed by Colombo, Aden, Port Said, Malta, Gibraltar and finally Plymouth. 'What a voyage, everywhere a wonderful welcome,' Coxswain Frank wrote.

25
Welcome Home – 'Up To Standard'

ON THE EVENING OF 31 October, *Amethyst* was spotted heading towards Lizard Point and the English Channel on the last stretch of her journey to Devonport. Sailors rushed on deck when two RAF Sunderlands from the mainland flew overhead. In one of the planes was Flight Lieutenant Letford, who had made the dramatic landing on the Yangtze on 21 April. It was a poignant salute.

As *Amethyst* cap tallies were fixed to blue rather than white caps, the crew were facing a new round of celebrations, starting in Devonport and continuing with home events and finally a tribute in London. Brynley Howell, a 25-year-old stores assistant, who was among the wounded on 20 April, had not been to his home in Haverfordwest, Pembrokeshire, for three years. He was told that the town would be holding a civic reception in his honour and declaring a school holiday. Anthony Silvey, from Camberwell, South London, another stores assistant who had been wounded, wanted to get home for two reasons – 'to see my mother and to see Chelsea beat Pompey on Saturday'. Chelsea soon learned of their fan's devotion and invited Silvey to Stamford Bridge to meet the players, who presented him with an autographed football.[1]

At the Foreign Office in London, the Soviet spy Guy Burgess was once again complaining about publicity that would embarrass the Communists. He told colleagues: 'The BBC seem to be going to fall over backwards in the coming weeks to give the Chinese Communists prestige reasons for complaint. Given Hong Kong, these weeks are not well chosen. We have constantly asked the Admiralty to be more silent about their service and its feats of navigation, but on top of the now irreversible appearance of *Amethyst*'s unfortunate crew in a Lord Mayor's show, it now appears that they will be on air, constantly.' Burgess took particular exception to the BBC's plans for the ship's homecoming. The corporation had sent a correspondent, Frank Gillard, and an engineer to meet *Amethyst* at Gibraltar. They would be on board as the ship neared home waters, and Gillard planned to make a live broadcast when he was within range of a shore transmitter. Coverage would continue throughout the day of *Amethyst*'s arrival, with other reporters on Plymouth Hoe and at the dockside. Wynford Vaughan-Thomas, a well-known broadcaster, had been chosen to do the main commentary. This was all too much for Burgess, who suggested that a letter 'at the highest level' should be sent to the BBC urging cancellation of the coverage. He pointed out: 'It must be remembered that the corporation is universally held abroad to be even more official than *The Times* is wrongly supposed to be. The difference is, we can stop the BBC.' The threat to censor the BBC in such a blatant way did not appeal to Burgess's superiors, with one stating: 'Although we can – and do – advise the BBC overseas services, we can not interfere with what they say in the home programmes.'[2]

However, as *Amethyst* neared Devonport, the sailors were warned not to say anything critical of the Chinese Communists. The Foreign Office told the Admiralty:

> We are very anxious that nothing should be said which might unnecessarily complicate the present difficult situation in China. We are particularly anxious to ensure that criticisms of the behaviour of the Communists towards the *Amethyst* (outrageous though it undoubtedly was) are not allowed to become a part of the publicity programme. It could easily be explained to the ship's company that any criticism of the Communists in the press or on the radio would be likely to react unfavourably on their fellow countrymen still remaining in China.

The Admiralty sent the warning to Kerans: 'It is politically desirable that nothing should be said by ship's company which might aggravate present difficulties of HM Government in their relations with Communist China. For this reason criticisms of behaviour of Communists towards *Amethyst* should be avoided in interviews with the press and references to Communist behaviour should be limited to statements of fact.' The message was also sent to the Commander-in-Chief, Plymouth, Admiral Sir Robert Burnett.[3]

On the chilly, grey morning of 1 November, crowds gathered on shore to watch *Amethyst* sail into Plymouth Sound. At Devil's Point there were chants of 'We want Jack. Where's Jack French?' The hero telegraphist had plenty of admirers. Thousands of spectators gazed out from the Hoe. At Devonport the frigate, flying her battle-scarred ensign, berthed astern of the battleship HMS *Vanguard*, which signalled, 'Welcome. Well done.' Hundreds of relatives and friends were at the dockside, along with thousands of workers.

The Times reported: 'Every movement of her commanding officer, Lieutenant Commander Kerans, and of her crew as she berthed was visible as if she had been a pleasure steamer coming alongside a seaside pier. That was the first slight shock for the onlookers and a second was the youth of her crew, though experience proclaimed itself here and there in a war ribbon.'

Among the first to go aboard *Amethyst* were repatriated members of the crew who had been badly wounded. In a wheelchair was Leading Seaman Cyril Williams, who lost his legs in the attack. The official welcoming party, which included the First Lord of the Admiralty, Lord Hall, and the First Sea Lord, Admiral Fraser, was piped aboard, but 'the thin notes of the bosun's pipe could hardly be heard above the siren blasts from every ship in the harbour, the engines of low-flying planes and the cheering of people ashore and in small boats grouped round the frigate'. Then relatives swarmed on board. In his cabin Kerans was reunited with his wife Stephanie and three-year-old daughter Charmian and his mother.

In a speech punctuated by cheering, Lord Hall said:

With your comrades in HM ships *Consort*, *London* and *Black Swan*, you were confronted on the Yangtze with a situation and perils not to be expected in time of peace – an ugly situation which caused the loss of a number of precious lives. The tragic loss of gallant men we all deeply deplore. The dash down the Yangtze has fired the imagination of the entire Commonwealth and indeed of the free peoples of the world. It was inspiring and outstanding and in every way a very gallant exploit. But we know that your great test and ordeal came earlier when you were isolated in the river, confined to your ship, suffering many physical discomforts and, which was the worst, a period of great uncertainty. The Royal Navy during its centuries of existence has passed through troublesome times, but whatever tasks have been pressed upon it the British people have had implicit faith that the navy will do its job and do it well. You have yet again justified this trust. The qualities of steadfastness, initiative and courage of the Royal Navy today are as great as at any time in the past.

Tens of thousands of people, some standing twenty deep, lined the route as *Amethyst*'s officers and men, led by a Royal Marines band, marched from the dockside to Royal Parade, where they were formally welcomed to Plymouth by Lord Mayor Francis Leatherby and Admiral Burnett, who declared: '*Amethyst*, well done. Up to standard.' The ship's company carried on marching to the landmark Duke of Cornwall Hotel for a civic lunch. With them was Dr Fearnley, who had left the RAF after his national service. Children waved flags and mothers cheered 'till they cried'.

At the hotel reception, where Drake's Drum was on display, emphasising the tradition of the Royal Navy, Kerans stressed: 'From the very word "go" in the Yangtze it has been co-operation, and the essence of all naval service is team work. Without that loyalty and co-operation behind me I should never have been able to achieve what has been achieved.' One report noted: 'Plymouth and Devonport gave the ship's company a reception such as has not been given to any other within memory. It was even greater than that accorded to the *Ajax* and *Exeter* after the Battle of the Plate.'[4]

That evening Jack French arrived back at his home town of Ashburton, Devon, where hundreds turned out to greet him. There was another civic reception, and French admitted he was 'lost for words'. Later relatives and friends crowded into his parents' cottage, where the telegraphist signalled, 'Now for a nice cup of tea, mum.' His admirers had sent him 300 letters, forty telegrams and a dozen parcels.[5]

On 16 November it was the turn of a foggy London to salute *Amethyst* and some of the sailors from *Consort*, *London* and *Black Swan*. At Horse Guards Parade 270 officers and men representing the four ships were inspected by Prime Minister Attlee, Minister of Defence Alexander, Lord Hall and Admiral Fraser. There were thousands of spectators. The sailors marched to nearby St Martin-in-the-Fields for a memorial service, which cost the Admiralty one guinea – for the organist. Then, led by Royal Navy and Royal Marines bands, they continued along the Strand and Fleet Street, which were lined with enthusiastic crowds, to Guildhall for a lunch hosted by the Corporation of London.

The Daily Telegraph reported: 'From the November gloom the crews passed into the mellow light of Guildhall amid whose splendours they were given the hospitality traditionally accorded by the City to Britain's illustrious men.' The guest list included seventeen admirals, Field Marshal Sir William Slim and Marshal of the Royal Air Force Lord Tedder. So much for previous attempts to keep the celebrations low key. The Lord Mayor, Sir Frederick Rowland, told the sailors their 'victory could not have been won but for a display of grit determination and devotion to duty which had moved the whole world to wonder'.[6]

The next day all the officers and men, many probably nursing hangovers, headed to Buckingham Palace for a presentation of awards. They were paraded in three sides of a square in the ballroom, with the fourteen to be decorated drawn up in front. A Guards band played the national anthem as King George VI, wearing the uniform of an admiral of the fleet, and the Queen entered. The King and Queen walked along the ranks, pausing frequently to engage in conversation.

They spoke to Gerard Devany, the air gunner of the Sunderland that swooped on the Yangtze to deliver Dr Fearnley. Before the palace visit Devany had been told to report to the Air Ministry for a briefing, which was also attended by Group Captain Jefferson, who had helped to organise the Sunderland mission, the pilot, Flight Lieutenant Letford, and other members of the crew, and Fearnley. 'Someone with rings on his sleeve and up to his elbow told us how to behave,' Devany recalled.

> I don't know the reason but it was most important that we did not have any guns on board. This was a joke because we were fully armed and we used them. Dr Fearnley was now a civilian and he just laughed out outright. But chief high and mighty turned quite nasty and told us to do as we were told. Next he came out with the real joke of the century. He said, 'You are going to the palace to receive the DFC [Distinguished Flying Cross] from the King. Flight Lieutenant Letford will go up to the dais to receive it, but it is for all of you'. More suppressed mirth.

The King asked Devany if he had opened fire during the Yangtze mission. 'No, sir,' he replied.[7]

Before presenting the awards the King gave a speech in which he said: 'In these difficult times it is not always easy to feel confidence regarding the ideals by which we try to live. By your conduct you have shown that the old qualities which have sustained this country through the centuries are still alive. Your bearing has been that which I expect from all ranks and ratings of the Royal Navy, and has given strength to the faith of many people throughout the world.'

Kerans received the Distinguished Service Order, as did Commander Robertson of *Consort*. The newly promoted Commodore Cazelet of *London* was given a Bar to his DSO. Lieutenant Weston received a Bar to his Distinguished Service Cross, and the medal was awarded to Lieutenant Berger, Commissioned Gunner Smith of *London* and Dr Fearnley. The DSC was an unusual award to a former RAF officer. Flight Lieutenant Letford was already a holder of the Distinguished Flying Cross and he received a Bar. Among the others honoured were the *Amethyst* men French, Frank and Williams, who were each given the Distinguished Service Medal.[8]

With the exception of the Bar to the DFC for Letford, Admiral Brind made the recommendations for awards. Surprisingly, the First Sea Lord thought Vice Admiral Madden should have been honoured. Madden had admitted that he blundered in sending *Amethyst* up the Yangtze, and he also ordered the rescue attempts by *Consort*, *London* and *Black Swan*. But the Admiralty accepted that it was right to make these attempts, which were 'gallantly and correctly carried out'. In Admiral Fraser's view it therefore followed that 'credit is surely due in the first place' to Madden, who was, of course, on board *London*. Fraser thought that any award to Madden should not be less than the DSO, which was awarded to the captains of *Consort* and *London*. He was also keen that Madden should become the Second Sea Lord.

The First Sea Lord was advised that it would 'not look good' to give Madden a knighthood 'which is about all that can be done'. The vice admiral already had a CB (Companion of the Order of the Bath) and a CBE (Commander of the Order of the British Empire) and 'was well down the scale for a ration'.[9] The matter was left open. But the following year Madden was appointed the Second Sea Lord, and in the King's birthday honours of June 1951 he was knighted – Knight Commander of the Order of the Bath. In September 1952 he was promoted full admiral.

The attack on *Amethyst* produced a four-legged hero, Simon, and the cat was honoured during the ship's time in Hong Kong. He was awarded the Dickin Medal, the 'animal Victoria Cross', by the People's Dispensary for Sick Animals. It was the first time a cat had received the honour 'for conspicuous gallantry or devotion to duty' while serving with the armed forces. Simon's citation read: 'Served on HMS *Amethyst* during the Yangtze Incident, disposing of many rats though wounded by shell blast. Throughout the incident his behaviour was of the highest order, although the blast was capable of making a hole over a foot in diameter in a steel plate.' Kerans apparently wrote the citation. The medal had been instituted in 1943 and awarded sparingly, pigeons and dogs being the main recipients. The PDSA sent a length of the medal ribbon attached to an elastic collar for Simon to wear 'pending the award of the actual medal'. The cat quickly became a celebrity and pictures of him went round the world. Letters, gifts and toys poured in for him. When *Amethyst* returned to England the cat had to go into quarantine for six months. An anonymous letter to the Admiralty warned that Simon was so famous he was in danger of being stolen 'and exhibited in the black market'. But Simon would suffer a different fate. He picked up a virus and, weakened by his wounds, died on 28 November. Cards, letters and flowers arrived at the quarantine shelter in Surrey 'by the truckload'. The Dickin Medal was due to have been presented on 11 December at a ceremony attended by Maria Dickin, the PDSA's founder, and the Lord Mayor of London. Able Seacat Simon was buried with 'naval honours' at the PDSA's animal cemetery in Ilford, Essex. He had also been awarded the Blue Cross Medal 'for useful services to human beings when in difficulties'.[10] Jack French was critical of Britain's strict quarantine laws: 'I think Simon died because he lost the company of sailors. He was quite content to be aboard the ship. They could quite easily have left him on the ship and he could have gone on the next commission. I firmly believe he died of heartbreak. He pined away.'[11]

The euphoria over *Amethyst* was not shared by everyone. Admiral Sir Hugh Tweedie, who had once been the senior naval officer on the Yangtze, urged 'a commonsense review of the facts and remember that we are not really celebrating a victory, but the last of many unhappy defeats in the Far East'. He added: 'To those who have served on the river and remember the days when the White Ensign was the symbol of law and order and justice on its whole 2,000 miles of water [*sic*], not only for the foreigner but for the thousands of Chinese who make their homes on the banks – it is hard to understand why the rather ignominious dismissal of that same White Ensign should be treated as a victory.'[12]

On 21 November 1949 the Chief of Naval Information, Captain Clarke, thought it necessary to remind the First Sea Lord of how well Kerans had been handling all the publicity. When Clarke first met Kerans, he noticed that he was 'under a nervous strain'. Clarke explained: 'Since then I suggest he has continued to keep on an even keel, and he has displayed admirable qualities of modesty and self restraint. I certainly know how hard he had worked to ensure that his officers and men came up to scratch, what trouble he took with his speeches and over all the other details of the unavoidable public appearances of himself and his company. In all this the poise, charm and natural behaviour of his wife also struck me and others.' There had not been any reports of 'incidents'. Clarke suggested that a personal note of appreciation from the First Sea Lord would be 'a comfort and an encouragement to them'.[13] Admiral Fraser did send a brief note congratulating the couple on the 'dignity and ability' with which they had handled the publicity. He told Kerans: 'I appreciate that your officers and men have also borne themselves well which reflects great credit on you.'[14]

Within days of *Amethyst*'s escape there had been talk of making a film about her exploit. The Fifth Sea Lord, Vice Admiral Maurice Mansergh, was enthusiastic and asked the Chief of Naval Information, Captain Clarke, to explore the possibility. David MacDonald and Lieutenant Colonel Arthur Rawlinson, who both worked for a major film company, the Rank Organisation, were approached. MacDonald had directed *Desert Victory*, a 1943 documentary about the campaign against Rommel's Afrika Korps in North Africa. The response was positive: 'They consider that the *Amethyst* story has the makings of an excellent film, which would be not only of good commercial value for the company undertaking it, but also excellent for British prestige and for British naval publicity all over the world.' A film similar to *Desert Victory*, lasting around 70 minutes, was envisaged. The head of the Rank Organisation, J Arthur Rank, would be approached. If he turned the idea down, the director and producer Sir Alexander Korda would be sounded out. It was made clear that only a 'first-class film company' could be involved, and the idea needed to be kept confidential 'on account of the political angle attaching to the *Amethyst* episode'. And the Foreign Office would have to give its approval.

J Arthur Rank did show interest and liked the idea of a film along the lines of *In Which We Serve*, a 1942 production directed by Noel Coward and David Lean. The film, which also starred Coward, was inspired by the exploits of the destroyer HMS *Kelly*, commanded by Lord Mountbatten, which was sunk during the Battle of Crete. Captain Clarke thought an 'up-to-date *In Which We Serve*' would be good for recruiting. If the navy offered full facilities, the company would be obliged to allow the Admiralty to keep a check on the production, making sure it remained 'on the tram lines'. Another company was interested in making a documentary.[15]

There was no film deal, probably because the Foreign Office objected on the grounds that the subject was still too sensitive at a time when Britain was trying to establish diplomatic relations with the Chinese Communists. However, a film called *Yangtze Incident* did appear in 1957. It was made by British Lion Films, in which Korda had a controlling interest. Directed by Michael Anderson and produced by Herbert Wilcox, it starred the popular actor Richard Todd as an apparently flawless Kerans. The River Orwell in Suffolk became the Yangtze and *Amethyst* was taken out of mothballs in Devonport for a starring role. Another frigate, HMS *Magpie*, was also used. The film was based on a book by Lawrence Earl, *Yangtze Incident, The Story of HMS Amethyst*, which had been written with the co-operation of Kerans, who acted as a technical adviser during filming.

The battle scenes were realistic, but the Royal Navy almost sank *Amethyst* in the process, something the Chinese Communists had failed to do. A team of experts, led by Lieutenant Max Reid, were sent from the Portsmouth shore base HMS *Vernon* to carry out the special effects. The 'experts' blew a hole in the hull, which flooded the engine room. Reid's son Mark explained:

> Their equipment was crude in the extreme and included a car battery and a board fitted with nails as their demolition panel. The incident which cracked a plate in the ship's side resulted from a moored underwater charge during an extended pause in filming. By the time

the lighting or make-up specialists had given their approval to continue filming the charge had drifted against the ship's side and the resulting damage sent a couple of matelots racing to the local fire station to borrow a pump – most of the ship's equipment had already been removed.

The water was pumped out and filming resumed the next day but the incident had been witnessed by a former captain RN who had retired to the River Orwell and had immediately phoned a friend at the Admiralty. My father was summoned back to HMS *Vernon* to explain himself but returned later that day, a somewhat chastened special effects expert![16]

Yangtze Incident, with its patriotic theme, was a cinema success, but the makers had largely ignored the background to the attack on *Amethyst* and the political dimensions. There was artistic licence. The Woosung forts were seen opening fire on the frigate, for example, and the official line that *Concord* had not entered the Yangtze was repeated. The role of *London* and *Black Swan* was underplayed.

26

The Case against China

BOTH THE ADMIRALTY AND THE Foreign Office realised that 'sooner or later' they would have to argue the *Amethyst* case and the question of compensation with the Chinese Communists. It was likely to be later. Experience had shown that any negotiations were certain to be difficult. In August 1949 it was evident that the Communists would win the civil war and seize power. That would give rise to the thorny question of establishing diplomatic relations. On 10 August the Foreign Office told the Admiralty that it was important to get detailed accounts of the attacks on *Amethyst* on 20 April and 30 July as soon as possible 'before memory becomes dimmed and imagination runs riot'. Members of the ship's company should be asked to make signed statements.[1] There were also the attacks on *Consort*, *London* and *Black Swan*.

On 15 August the Admiralty replied that it had already started collecting evidence. In early July sailors who escaped from *Amethyst* after the 20 April attack were asked to give statements, as were officers and men from the other ships. A key issue was who opened fire first. Since *Amethyst*'s escape other members of the crew had been asked to give statements, which were not sworn but witnessed by an officer.

A full report was being written by Kerans. It was pointed out: 'We had thought of drawing attention to the fact that the CO in writing his Report of Proceedings, and the senior naval authorities in their covering remarks, should bear in mind that it might be made public. We did not do so, however, partly because we thought this unnecessary, and partly in order to avoid any imputation of influencing the evidence. However, if you or your legal adviser think this desirable, we will do this.'[2] Kerans's report would be closed to the public until 1980, although some parts were kept secret for much longer – and originally not due for release until 2025.

On 31 August the Far East Station informed the Admiralty that it had collected a number of statements – forty from *Amethyst*, fourteen from *Consort*, twenty-eight from *London*, including six Royal

Marines, and twelve from *Black Swan*. Lieutenant Henry Mirehouse gave a statement, disclosing that some of the officers on board *Amethyst* were well aware of the danger as the frigate sailed up the Yangtze. 'The ship's company were closed up at action stations at about 0830,' Mirehouse stated. 'I was told, either just before or when I arrived on the bridge, that this was because we were approaching a recognised crossing which the Communists might be expected to use if they attacked the south bank.' If *Amethyst* knew about the crossing point, then Vice Admiral Madden also must have been aware of it. As the *Sunday Pictorial* pointed out on 24 April: 'The British have the finest intelligence system in the world, and it is impossible to believe that naval units were sent up the Yangtze without possessing information on the disposition of forces likely to be hostile. Were they, therefore, sent on their mission in spite of the existence of such information?' The captain, Lieutenant Commander Skinner, was also aware that the Communist ultimatum to the Nationalists expired that day. Mirehouse confirmed that the Communists on the north bank opened fire first, about 45 minutes after the ship closed up. 'There is no doubt that we were the target as there was no other vessel in the vicinity, indeed I doubt whether there was one in sight at the time, and we were I should say quite four cables from the south bank. I think all the projectiles fired on this occasion were explosive, as the range must have been upwards of one mile, and explosions were clearly audible as the shells hit the water. I estimate that about 30 shells were fired, most of which fell on the port side within two cables of the ship. The firing continued for about two minutes.'

Skinner gave the order to return fire but the gunnery control officer reported that the target was very hard to find. The captain said something to the effect, 'Do the best you can'. There were fleeting puffs of smoke on the shore. Then the firing ceased, 'and I am almost certain that we did not fire a single round on this occasion'.

The main attack came about half an hour later. Mirehouse stated: 'My first intimation that we were being fired on was a metallic clang as of a bullet striking the ship – I heard no explosion – followed immediately by a scream, coming I thought from the starboard Oerlikon position. There is no doubt that the enemy fired first.' Shortly afterwards Mirehouse and others were wounded when two shells apparently hit the bridge at the same time. 'Either before or just after he was wounded, I heard the captain order a white flag to be hoisted, but I was unable from where I was lying to see whether this was flying or not.' The Communists continued firing. Mirehouse was taken to the quarterdeck. 'I had been struck by the cheerfulness and apparent nonchalance of the stretcher party who had brought me down from the bridge, and of those I had seen on the quarterdeck.'[3]

Commissioned Gunner Alec Monaghan pointed out that the firing eased during the first attack when the two large Union Flags were unfurled on the sides of *Amethyst*. Of Lieutenant Weston's decision to get many of the ratings ashore to save lives after the ship ran aground, Monaghan stated: 'Approximately 65 men jumped and started to swim. The river was then raked with machine gun fire and also where the men were swimming was shelled by the battery. Approximately five were killed. The ratings who reached the shore were then taken inland by Nationalist troops. The wounded, about 15, were still on the quarterdeck and in a very bad state. The Communists prevented any of us rendering assistance by shooting as soon as we showed ourselves. Consequently the wounded had to lay for six hours till dark without attention or water.' He added: 'The conduct of the men was remarkable considering 40 new ratings had joined the ship only a week previously.' Monaghan paid the following tributes: Weston 'for carrying on though in considerable pain'; Lieutenant Berger 'for being carried from his stretcher on to the bridge each time the ship moved'; Electrical Artificer Lionel Chare 'who worked himself to a standstill repairing all emergency lighting then tending the sick all night'; and Surgeon Lieutenant Alderton 'who, until he was killed, went everywhere unflinchingly, administering first aid'.[4]

Petty Officer David Heath, in his statement, said that *Amethyst* hoisted two white flags but the firing continued. At one point during the attack he found many sailors on the upper deck being issued with rifles and small arms. 'We lay down on the starboard side in the lee of the motor boat, Bofors guns' support and X gun which by this time had been hit on at least two occasions and had ceased fire. Whilst we were laying down in the lee of the motor boat a shell landed in the vicinity killing two stokers and one able seaman and wounding a couple of others. These were dragged over the port side and the idea of defending the ship with small arms was tacitly dropped.'[5]

Michael Fearnly, the RAF doctor, was asked to give a statement and he related how he had ended up in Monaghan's sampan after the Sunderland flying boat landed near *Amethyst* on 21 April. The flight lieutenant had threatened the sampan's panicking occupants with Monaghan's revolver when they tried to head straight for the shore. He did not mention this episode and, with a touch of humour, simply stated that 'the sampan consented to take me to the ship'.[6]

Lieutenant Hett gave an account of the attacks on *Amethyst* during her escape, confirming that once again the Communists had opened fire first. As the frigate followed the merchant ship *Kaing Ling Liberation* two flares were set off. Soon after the second flare the Communists fired. 'There can be no doubt to me that the batteries were waiting for us as they gave practically no time to reply to this challenge,' Hett stated. And no warnings were given when the Communists opened fire further down river.[7]

The Admiralty was busy weighing up how the *Amethyst* case could be pursued. It was important to obtain redress for the 'wrongs' inflicted upon the ship and to maintain the rule of law and discourage similar attacks. Clearly, the Communists had opened fire on the frigate without provocation and she was forcibly detained, with 'suffering so inhumanely inflicted upon her crew'. There was plenty of evidence to support the charges. Also, the ship had the permission of the Nationalist government to sail up the Yangtze. But should the claim against the Communists be pursued or dropped?

A report pointed out: 'An important factor in this, of course, will consist of political future developments, many of which are hard to foresee. These will, anyhow, have to be dealt with by the Foreign Office. It is not proposed to argue about these at the moment. One obvious factor in which the Foreign Office and the Admiralty will agree is the general desirability of maintaining both international law and justice, and our own national honour and prestige, which here coincide.'

The Admiralty was still smarting from the Corfu Channel attacks of 1946. Communist Albania opened fire from the shore on the cruisers HMS *Orion* and HMS *Superb* on 15 May 1946. No damage or casualties were inflicted. The British government demanded a public apology but none was given. A much more serious incident took place on 22 October when the cruisers HMS *Mauritius* and HMS *Leander* and the destroyers HMS *Saumarez* and HMS *Volage* were sailing up the channel.

Saumarez struck a mine, which blew off her bows. *Volage* took the destroyer in tow but also hit a mine. She too lost her bows. Both ships remained afloat and eventually ended up, stern first, in Corfu harbour. Forty-four men were killed and many more wounded. The Admiralty saw it as a 'particularly humiliating loss of face'. In the November the navy carried out a minesweeping operation in the channel, and Albania protested to the United Nations. Shortly afterwards Britain accused Albania of laying the mines and demanded reparations. The International Court awarded Britain nearly £1 million, but the Albanians refused to pay, and the case was not finally settled until 1996.

The Admiralty report on *Amethyst* stressed: 'It therefore seems essential, in the interests of the Royal Navy, that claims against perpetrators of such aggression should be pressed by all means, as long as possible, and with the greatest possible publicity, with the object both of humiliating the original aggressors and discouraging repetitions for the future. Thus, from the purely Admiralty point of view, there appears to be a strong argument for continuing to press redress of wrong in the *Amethyst* case.'

There were several options for pursuing the case. A joint commission would mean appointing special representatives of the two parties. But this was unlikely to work with an 'aggressive' Communist state. Mediation by a third party historically had not been very successful. An international commission of inquiry under the Hague Conventions was a possibility, but there might be difficulties in agreeing on the composition. International arbitration, also under the Hague Conventions, would allow judicial decisions and the award of damages. However, there could be difficult questions of international law that the arbitrator might not be competent to answer. Past experience had shown that the United Nations Security Council was an unsuitable body to carry out either a judicial or fact-finding role.

The best option appeared to be the International Court. But the court could only deal with disputes between states. The report noted: 'The Chinese Communists are not a state and have so far shown great skill in avoiding the external responsibilities of statehood. Moreover, if and when they do claim to be a state, great complications as to their official recognition will arise, and, if such recognition arises, the Foreign Office legal advisers say they will automatically obtain China's seat (and right of veto) in the Security Council. In fact, there are a number of confusing factors and no clear solution can be foreseen.'[8] As events turned out, the People's Republic of China had to wait until 1971 for United Nations recognition.

On 23 August 1949 the Admiralty realised that it would probably have to delay any major action until the Communists formed a 'responsible' government, but in the meantime it was important to keep the 'pot boiling'. Officials wanted to serve a writ on the Communists but there were problems doing even that: 'They don't open the front door if you ring. They don't read your letters if you post them. Knocking on the back door and delivering a message that way would hardly achieve our main object.' When a decision was taken on the right kind of inquiry, pressure should be kept up on the Communists by using the press, 'whispering through the back door', and keeping other governments informed.[9]

In October the Admiralty told the Foreign Office that it had collected a number of witness statements, and a complete series of the commander-in-chief's reports on *Amethyst* and the other ships would be available shortly. This material would provide the basis for a claim by the government. The Admiralty hoped that the case would not be dropped. It listed the options for pursuing the matter, saying it favoured the International Court.[10]

It was clear from the Foreign Office's reply in November that any progress would be painfully slow. The answer appeared to be contradictory: 'The first step must certainly be to raise the matter through our representatives with the Chinese Communist authorities, and the course to be pursued thereafter must depend on the Communist reaction to an approach of this nature. We cannot, therefore, raise the matter until we have succeeded in establishing some form of relations with the Communist authorities.'[11] And that really was the end of the matter, as Albert Blackburn MP discovered when he asked a question in the House of Commons in March 1951. Foreign Secretary Herbert Morrison admitted that no claim against the Chinese Communists had been made. The Foreign Office had quietly buried the case.

A Foreign Office briefing document stated: 'There is no doubt that however deplorable this incident and unjustified the Chinese attack on this ship, no prospect whatsoever of obtaining compensation exists, and the Chinese would almost certainly once more raise their own claims. Politically it would be undesirable to raise this issue since it could only serve to embitter relations which are already bad. Full diplomatic relations with the Chinese government have, of course, not yet been established.'[12]

In November 1949 the Foreign Office insisted it needed to establish 'some form of relations' to make any progress, yet by March 1951, when that had been done, it still did not want to press the case. Perhaps surprisingly, the Admiralty accepted that 'up to the moment it is obvious that the time has not yet arrived for raising such issue'. It never would arrive. The Foreign Office and the Admiralty may have been too cautious. Even Mao Tse-tung expressed surprise that the British government had not made a formal protest.[13]

27

Mao's Trap

WHEN NEWS OF THE ATTACK on *Amethyst* was reported in Britain, there were immediate suspicions that the frigate had sailed into a Communist trap. National newspapers were quick to question the wisdom of sending *Amethyst* up the Yangtze when Mao's forces were about to launch a major offensive across the river at Nationalist positions on the southern banks. As *The Daily Telegraph* pointed out: 'If it is entirely clear that the attack on the *Amethyst* by Chinese Communist artillery was unprovoked and indefensible, it is also clear that the possibility of such an attack might, and indeed should, have been foreseen.' The *Sunday Pictorial* was more damning: 'As more of the facts reach London it has become pitifully obvious that: the British authorities were caught unawares; the whole position along the Yangtze River was gravely misjudged; men in high places have blundered.'[1] Unsurprisingly, Admiral Brind did not share these views. He saw the attack on *Amethyst* as an unfortunate accident. The commander-in-chief was quoted as saying: 'The shelling of the sloop *Amethyst* and the destroyer *Consort* by Chinese Communists was not a deliberate hostile act. The excitement when blood is up between two forces often involves a third in disaster.'[2] Neither *Amethyst* nor *Consort* had opened fire first and they were attacked at different locations. Explaining away the two attacks as the result of some kind of panic may have stretched credulity. These were battle-hardened and disciplined soldiers on the northern banks of the Yangtze. The 'blood is up' explanation falls down further when the attacks on *London* and *Black Swan* and the Sunderland flying boats are taken into account. All the attacks were calculated.

In 2005 Jung Chang and Jon Halliday revealed in their book, *Mao, The Unknown Story*, that the Communist leader had given orders that any foreign warship on the Yangtze could be attacked if it appeared to be a threat. 'Treat them as Nationalist ships,' Mao declared. *Amethyst*'s fate was sealed even before she left Shanghai. However, the attacks on

Amethyst and *Concord* alarmed Stalin, who feared that Western powers might finally take military action in China's civil war, with the Cold War opening up on a new front. Soviet forces in the Far East were placed on alert, and Stalin urged Mao to pull back from a possible confrontation. According to Jung and Halliday, Mao had to 'tone down his aggressiveness'. He issued new orders to 'avoid clashes with foreign ships. No firing at [them] without the order of the Centre. Extremely, extremely important.'[3]

Mao was aware that *London* and *Black Swan* were being sent to help *Amethyst*, and a message went to General Su Yu that the ships should not be attacked unless they interfered with the river crossing. The message arrived too late.[4] Despite Stalin's concern, Mao was no doubt pleased that Britain had been confronted in this way. US ambassador Stuart recorded: 'Commercial and naval ships of foreign countries, principally British, had long sailed up and down this mighty river at their own unbridled will, but now at last they had been bravely challenged and routed.'[5] The use of the word 'bravely' was curious. The Communists were not under threat and, as has been shown, warships were easy targets for land-based artillery in the confines of the river. The point about the symbolism of the 'old' China was taken up by the Communists, with the New China News Agency declaring: 'The British imperialists must understand that China is no longer the China of 1926 when British naval vessels bombarded Wan Xian [Wanhsien]. She is no longer the China of the days when Great Britain and the United States jointly bombarded Nanking in 1937. The Yangtze River now belongs to the Chinese people and the PLA and no longer belongs to servile and weak traitors.' The Wanhsien incident saw the rescue of crews of British steamers who had been seized by a warlord's soldiers. There were wild propaganda claims that British gunboats had attacked the port of Wanhsien, killing up to 5,000 Chinese. The Nanking incident was also a rescue operation, when an Anglo-American flotilla laid down a protective barrage to help evacuate westerners during anti-foreign rioting.

Under the Moscow Declaration of December 1945, Britain, the US and the Soviet Union agreed on a policy of non-interference in the internal affairs of China. At the Labour Party conference in Blackpool on 9 June 1949, Foreign Secretary Bevin reiterated the policy, stressing: 'We have never, since we have been in office, intervened in Chinese internal affairs.' It was not an accurate statement. Mao was right to have suspicions about Britain and the US. Both nations had been giving military aid to the Nationalists.

America's General George Marshall, one of the architects of victory in the Second World War, gained first-hand experience of the civil war. President Harry Truman had sent him to China in December 1945 in an attempt to persuade the Nationalists and the Communists to form a coalition government. The mission was a failure, with Marshall returning home little more than a year later to be appointed secretary of state, a post that left him with the vexed question of whether the Nationalists should continue to receive US aid. Chiang Kai-shek still enjoyed the support of many Republican politicians. As well as getting large sums of money, Chiang had been given American military advisers. In May 1947 Marshall reluctantly agreed to lift an arms embargo and ask for the release of a $500 million loan that had been agreed the previous year. Increasingly, Marshall viewed the Nationalists as a lost cause. In February 1948 he stated: 'It can only be concluded that the present government evidently cannot reduce the Chinese Communists to a completely negligible factor in China. To achieve that objective in the immediate future it would be necessary for the United States to underwrite the Chinese government's military effort, on a wide and probably constantly increasing scale, as well as the Chinese economy. The US would have to be prepared virtually to take over the Chinese government . . .'[6] But two months later Congress passed another package – $338 million in economic aid and $125 million in military aid. This was in addition to the $1.4 billion that the Nationalists had received since the end of the Second World War. Among those urging more money for the Nationalists was Admiral Badger, who had refused to send any of his warships up the Yangtze. Badger and General David Barr were the new heads of the US military mission to the Nationalists. Mao could not have been unhappy with the US stance on aid. The demoralised, inept and corrupt Nationalists were losing about 40 per cent of their supplies to the Communists.[7] So the Americans, in fact, were arming both sides. Austerity Britain was not in a position to hand over large sums of money but it did have warships to spare. The British government would be involved in some embarrassing decisions, highlighted by the case of HMS *Aurora*.

In 1944 the naval attaché at the Chinese embassy in London, Captain Chow Ying-Tsung, had sent the Deputy First Sea Lord, Admiral Sir Charles Kennedy-Purvis, a 'shopping list'. The captain's letter was brief and to the point.

> *I have been instructed by the Generalissimo* [Chiang] *to enquire whether the British Admiralty are prepared to make available to the Chinese Navy the following vessels:*
> 1 *A modern light cruiser of five to six thousand tons suitable for training as well as operational purposes.*
> 2 *Destroyers, submarines and coastal craft.*[8]

The request was referred to Minister of Defence Alexander and the Foreign Office. Alexander was in favour and so was the then foreign secretary, Anthony Eden, who told him: 'So far as I am concerned I am only too glad to find some field in which we are able at this difficult time to strengthen relations with China. I therefore welcome the offer which according to the draft reply you are now prepared to make to the Chinese.' The Nationalists were, after all, fighting the Japanese. The US also offered warships – four destroyers and four gunboats.[9] The Admiralty could not spare ships at such a critical point in the war against Germany and Japan. However, in 1946 Attlee's government decided it would still give warships to the Nationalists, despite the fact that the war against Japan had ended and Britain had agreed to the Moscow Declaration. By that time the Nationalists and the Communists were back fighting each other on a major scale.

That year the Admiralty handed over the corvette HMS *Petunia*. But the survivor of the Battle of the Atlantic would find the questionable navigating skills of Nationalist sailors too great a challenge. In March 1947 *Petunia*, renamed *Fubo*, sank after colliding with a merchant ship off the coast of Formosa with the loss of all hands. An Admiralty report noted: 'The Chinese had not insured the vessel and the Treasury therefore agreed that she should be formally regarded as a gift to China.' Two months later the British government decided that the light cruiser *Aurora*, the destroyer HMS *Mendip*, two submarines and eight harbour-defence launches would be transferred to the Nationalists under a complicated loan agreement. Chiang did not want to pay for any of the vessels, insisting they should be gifts. The Nationalists argued that Britain had seized several of their ships in Hong Kong during the Second World War and that they were owed compensation. The Admiralty decided that the 'awkward case' could be settled with the transfer of *Aurora* and the other vessels. The Treasury agreed to the 'tidy arrangement'.[10] Bevin sealed the deal at a meeting with the Chinese ambassador in London. The ambassador 'expressed the gratitude of the Chinese government for this material aid which he welcomed as a further proof of our long-standing friendship and co-operation'.[11] In the case of *Aurora*, it was agreed that the Nationalists would pay around £100,000 for the Chinese crew of more than 600 to be trained in Britain. This money probably was never paid.

The difficulty of dealing with the Nationalists was highlighted in an Admiralty report:

> The Chinese throughout tended to refer to these ships as gifts and continued to show great reluctance to sign any loan agreement, notwithstanding that a draft had been presented to the Chinese government in the autumn of 1947. It was, in fact, only shortly before the date provisionally fixed for the transfer of HMS *Aurora* that it proved possible to induce them to give consideration to the question of formal terms. Abandonment of the offer at so late a stage would have been politically most unfortunate, but it was eventually agreed, with the concurrence of the Treasury and the Foreign Office, that the ships should be transferred outright to the Chinese, the United Kingdom receiving as consideration the abandonment by the Chinese government of a claim against the Admiralty of some £300,000 to £350,000 in respect of the loss on war service of certain Chinese maritime customs vessels whilst on Admiralty requisition.[12]

It is surprising that no one in the British government seems to have questioned the wisdom of supplying arms to one side in a civil war, while at the same time professing to be neutral.

Aurora distinguished herself in the Second World War, most notably during the Mediterranean campaign, but she suffered an undignified end after being given to the Nationalists. Renamed *Chongqing* (*Chungking*), the cruiser sailed from Britain for China on 26 May 1948 under the command of an experienced captain, Deng Zhaoxiang. When she reached Hong Kong, nearly one third of her engineering ratings deserted. The cruiser carried on to Nanking, where Chiang and other leading Nationalists celebrated her arrival by paying a visit. *Chongqing*'s first mission – with Chiang on board – was to give support to troops retreating on the Shandong Peninsula and along the north coast. The military reverses and a lack of pay further undermined the crew's morale and, unknown to the captain, Communist sympathisers, led by one Wang Nishen, were planning a mutiny. By November 1948 the ship, based in Shanghai, was guarding the Yangtze. There were further desertions, and soldiers and dockyard workers were recruited as replacements. The Communist sailors had formed a 'liberation committee', and on the night of 24 February 1949, after breaking into the ship's small-arms locker, the group confronted the captain. Threats persuaded Captain Deng and some of his officers to sail the ship to Yantai on the Shandong Peninsula, which was occupied by the PLA. For most of the crew it was a shock. They had no idea that they were defecting to the Communists. *Chongqing* was carrying Nationalist funds, a large quantity of silver coins. The money, apparently with Mao's approval, was used to persuade many of the crew to remain on board and work with the Communists. Captain Deng and others were no doubt aware that their careers in the Nationalist navy had come to an abrupt end anyway. Chiang's anger at the loss of his prize after such a short time can be imagined. On 2 March a reconnaissance plane spotted *Chongqing* and B-24 bombers began targeting her. Members of the crew who remained loyal to Chiang threatened to take over the ship, and PLA soldiers were sent to quell the unrest. The cruiser sailed for another port further north, Huludao, where the entire crew faced 're-education'.The Nationalists kept up their hunt, and the ship was again attacked on 19 March, without any hits. But two days later a bomb seriously damaged the stern, and most of the crew abandoned the ship. The cruiser was out of fuel and unable to reply to high-level air attacks. It was decided to scuttle her. The *Chongqing* capsized at her moorings. On 23 April, three days after the attack on *Amethyst*, the Nationalists' Shanghai flotilla – a destroyer, three destroyer escorts, a gunboat, five landing ships and eight auxiliaries – defected to the Communists.[13] In April 1951, with the help of Russian experts, an attempt was made to salvage *Chongqing*. The hull was in good condition, and the ship was raised in the June and towed to a shipyard at Dalian, which had a dry dock. The Russians decided after closer examination that it would not be economical to return the cruiser to service. *Chongqing* was stripped of some machinery and weapons. Her engines ended up in a local factory. In November 1959 the hull was towed to Shanghai and used for fresh water storage. In 1964 it was given to a shipping line to accommodate workers on coastal projects, and later abandoned. The remains of the former *Aurora* were finally broken up in about 1990.

The destroyer *Mendip* was loaned at the same time as the handover of *Aurora*. *Mendip* was transferred 'free of charge' for a period of five years, but the Nationalists were expected to pay all maintenance costs. One of the conditions of the loan: 'The government of China undertake to restore the vessel to His Majesty's government at any time during the period of the loan upon receiving from His Majesty's government three months' notice to do so.' In the wake of the *Aurora* fiasco, the Royal Navy repossessed *Mendip* – renamed *Lingfu* – in June 1949. The crew who took over came from *Consort*. But a few months later the destroyer was sold to the Egyptian navy. Under the name of *Ibrahim el Awal*, she was seized by the Israelis after attacking the port of Haifa in October 1956. With some irony the Israelis added her to their navy with the name *Haifa*. The ship that ended up serving four navies was scrapped in 1972.

The Nationalists did not receive any submarines from the Royal Navy despite a complaint from the Chinese Embassy in London that they had been promised. The Nationalists pointed out that they were in 'urgent need' of two 'S' class boats. More than sixty 'S' class submarines had been constructed for the Royal Navy and, despite wartime losses, some were surplus. The Admiralty no doubt felt it had been generous enough. And there must have been serious doubts about the competence of Nationalist submariners. The First Lord of the Admiralty, Lord Hall, made it clear to Minister of Defence Alexander that submarines 'cannot be made available until 1951 at the earliest'.[14] By that time, of course, the picture had changed completely.

Hundreds of sailors trained by Britain and the United States for the Nationalists ended up forming the nucleus of China's Communist navy. In 1950 they underwent a heavy programme of indoctrination, forced to read the works of Mao and to 'write their autobiographies and self-criticism'. Those who passed went on to naval schools for further training. Deng Zhaoxiang, the captain of the *Chongqing*, was among the men who proved adept at survival. In 1953 he still regarded himself as 'British navy' but despite this admission – and a liking for 'afternoon tea' – he earned promotion. In 1977 he was appointed the deputy commander of China's north sea fleet.[15]

28

The Tragic Sam Leo

ONE MAN WAS 'SACRIFICED' WHEN *Amethyst* broke out on that July night. Sam Leo, Kerans's loyal interpreter. On 28 May 1949 Leo, who worked as an interpreter and a translator for the naval attaché in Nanking, had volunteered to help *Amethyst*'s captain in negotiations with the Communist authorities, which were usually led by the obstructive Colonel Kang. Leo, also known as Liu Chin-tseng, worked tirelessly throughout June and July. Kerans, of course, had decided he could not risk taking Leo into his confidence over the escape plan. Hours before the frigate's bid for freedom the interpreter was sent ashore with instructions to collect 'urgent' medical supplies from the mission hospital in Chingkiang. Kerans provided him with a covering letter for Kang, and Fearnley the RAF doctor had listed the supplies that were supposedly needed in an attempt to add authenticity to the request. At no time was Leo aware that Kerans planned to try to escape. As the captain pointed out: 'It was one man's life against the rest of us on board.'[1]

On the morning of 31 July, as *Amethyst* sighted freedom, the Communists were quick to seize on the innocent Leo. He was arrested and taken to Nanking, where he was placed in detention. For three days he was kept in irons and threatened with death, falsely accused of helping the ship's escape. Leo would face months of 're-education', during which some of his 'fellow students' were taken out and shot. His health deteriorated.[2]

Ambassador Stevenson and the naval attaché, Captain Donaldson, recognised the important part Leo, who had a wife and two sons, played in helping Kerans's negotiations and supported the idea of giving him compensation. On 5 September Donaldson sent a telegram to the director of naval intelligence at the Admiralty recommending 'generous compensation' and the payment of Leo's salary during his time in detention. Stevenson sent a copy of the telegram to the Foreign Office, which ended up on the desk of Guy Burgess, the Soviet spy, who commented: 'His [Leo's] anxiety as to exactly what might happen to him in Communist Chinese hands (who must have been convinced not without some excuse that he was being used to throw dust in their eyes and that he was consciously part of the escape) must have been terrible even though in the surprising event he was not too badly treated.' Burgess also thought Leo deserved generous compensation, which was presumably a matter for the Admiralty. But he wondered if the interpreter had been 'thoroughly indoctrinated' and whether 'other threats and proposals' had been a condition of his release. With great irony, Burgess questioned the wisdom of continuing to employ Leo as an interpreter in the naval attaché's office, where he would have access to sensitive material, and advised 'some less critical role'. Other Foreign Office officials were happy to learn later that the Admiralty might agree to pay the compensation rather than their department.[3]

Kerans obviously felt guilt over the fate of Leo because on 21 November he recommended him for an award. The recommendation stated:

He did much to help me, not only in correct translations but in his very sound advice on Chinese cosmogony and Communist methods of dilatoriness and intransigence. In addition his cheerful manner and quiet confidence did much to help and reassure the ship's company that everything possible was being done. He was of immeasurable assistance to me in obtaining the entry of stores, mail and fresh food. His loyalty to the Royal Navy was of a very high order, and though he was finally taken prisoner by the Communists to undergo political indoctrination, I do not consider that Communism will even now have much effect upon him. Throughout the negotiations he remained as neutral as was possible and clearly pointed out to the Communists that he was there purely as an interpreter and a translator.

As well as supporting compensation, Stevenson recommended that Leo should be awarded an honorary MBE (Member of the Order of the British Empire) of the civil division. The Admiralty agreed that it would be a 'most appropriate award', and 'we would be prepared to put forward the recommendation if, or when, the Foreign Office consider there is no objection politically'.[4]

The Foreign Office, still keen to improve relations with the Communists because of British business interests, was not enthusiastic, with one official pointing out: 'The auspices are far from being favourable and I think we can only bring it up in six months' time for reconsideration.' Another official noted that conditions needed to improve.[5] Leo received £1,000 in compensation from the Admiralty but he was never awarded the MBE. He did not go back to his job in the naval attaché's office, supposedly because of his poor health as a consequence of his treatment by the Communists. But sadly, he was viewed as a security risk and the British embassy – and other embassies – would not employ him. With his compensation Leo bought a salt business but that failed when the Communists decide to control the sale of salt. On 29 September 1954 he died. Leo had been receiving regular medical treatment since 1950 and his health deteriorated sharply in the final months.

His widow got in touch with the British embassy, now located in Peking, and pointed out that his medical expenses had been heavy and that in 1953 the family had started selling their belongings to pay for them, also borrowing from relatives and friends. As a result, the family were in debt. Leo's widow appealed for financial help from Britain. In a letter to the Foreign Office's Establishment and Organisation Department in November 1954, the Nanking embassy pointed out:

> From time to time we get appeals from widows of former pensioners or recipients of recurring gratuities for money to meet funeral expenses or pay debts. It has been our practice to refuse any payment in these cases since to act otherwise would be to create what might well be an expensive precedent. We think, however, that in the special circumstances of Mr Leo's case some further payment should be made. His service was exceptionally meritorious and, through no fault of his own, the compensation already paid him, although generous, did not fulfil its object, which was to provide adequately for himself and for his family for his remaining years. Mr Leo's case is really not at all on a par with other cases of old-age pensioners. He volunteered for the job in *Amethyst*, at great and obvious risk to himself and his dependants. As a result of this he became unemployable by ourselves or by any other foreign embassy in China – no western government could take the risk of taking him on after his 're-education'.

It was recommended that Leo's widow should be given £200 as 'a final compassionate grant'.[6] The Far Eastern Department of the Foreign Office supported the idea of a payment, but other officials were cautious, pointing out that Leo was an Admiralty employee. It was 'extremely important' not to allow the case to set a precedent.[7]

In January 1955 the Foreign Office sent a copy of the letter from the embassy to the Admiralty, noting: 'We consider that Peking have a very good case for some payment being made. If this had been our responsibility, we should certainly have supported the application, and hope that you will be able to seek Treasury approval for the additional payment.' The Admiralty was advised to tell the Treasury that in 1949 the ambassador had recommended Leo for an MBE, which was not awarded for 'political reasons'.[8]

The correspondence had been sent to the Admiralty's M (Military) Branch, which decided that it should be dealt with by C E (Civil Establishment) Branch. C E Branch had been involved in the original payment of £1,000 to Leo. However, it emerged that a similar claim had been made by another Chinese national – his name was not revealed – for 'recognition of services rendered by him to officers of HMS *Amethyst*'.[9]

C E Branch had just asked the Treasury for approval to make a payment of £1,000 to the man, who was forced to flee China, apparently leaving his wife behind. In view of Leo's 'undoubted valuable services to us and the unfortunate consequences for him, it would seem churlish not to attempt to alleviate his widow's present plight'. There was concern about setting a precedent, but if other officials at the Admiralty agreed, an approach to the Treasury for a payment of £200 would be made.

By April 1955 the question of a payment to Leo's widow had not been settled. The embassy in Peking contacted the Foreign Office again because it had received a further letter from her and she 'appears to be in desperate straits'. C E Branch delayed contacting the Treasury about Leo's widow. There had been some argument over the proposal to give the other man £1,000. In the end the Treasury decided it would approve a payment of only £500.

In July Admiralty officials agreed to ask the Treasury to give Leo's widow £200 in view of the strong recommendations from the embassy in Peking and the Foreign Office. Leo had, in fact, signed an agreement that no further claims would be made by him or on his behalf, and one official pointed out: 'The loss of much of the original £1,000 gratuity in a salt business was presumably one of the hazards of life under Communist rule and can hardly be attributed to the fact that he was an ex-employee of the British government.'[10]

On 29 July one C A Pace of C E Branch wrote a lengthy letter to one P L Smith at the Treasury seeking approval for an ex-gratia payment of £200 to Leo's widow and explaining the background. Pace acknowledged that it was unusual to make a payment to a widow of a former employee who had been compensated already.

> But on the other hand, this is undoubtedly a very exceptional and possibly unique case in as much as Mr Leo's imprisonment by the Communists, which in turn led to his decline in health and ultimately we assume to his death, was due entirely to his connections with HMS *Amethyst* and the escape of the ship from the Yangtze. In compensating Mr Leo to the tune of £1,000 we recognised that his health had been impaired by his imprisonment and that his prospects of earning a living had deteriorated, but it would I think be true to say that the £1,000 was not intended to cover the cost of regular medical attention after his release from prison.

Smith at the Treasury replied on 10 August and was entirely unsympathetic, writing:

> We are not happy about the grounds on which Mr Leo was paid £1,000 and this further application does not make us any happier. I am far from convinced that Mr Leo did in fact perform service of an exceptionally meritorious character and when the skipper of the *Amethyst* put him ashore he did so in the best interests of Mr Leo. That is past history of course but it must influence us in the present case. So far as I can judge there is no reason on 'good employer' grounds why you should pay anything to Mrs Leo.

C E Branch sent a copy of Smith's letter to the Far Eastern Department of the Foreign Office on 16 August. The Admiralty regarded it as 'a rather strange reply'. But the entire matter was passed back to the Foreign Office, with the suggestion that the £200 payment could be made from funding known as the Foreign Office Vote.

The Treasury response did not go down well with the Foreign Office either. The Foreign Office told C E Branch: 'We are far from satisfied with the way in which the Treasury have turned down your application and are not prepared to let the matter rest where it is. We are ourselves convinced that Mr Leo was a very good servant of Her [His] Majesty's government who fully deserved the original award.' The Admiralty was urged to take the matter up again with the Treasury. The suggestion that the Foreign Office might care to pay the £200 was not well received. 'Although we have a very real interest in this case, we cannot see any good reasons for trying to make it a charge on the Foreign Office Vote nor any prospect of success if we did so. Payment when it is made must, of course, relate to the original payment to Mr Leo. On these grounds it should be borne on the Admiralty Vote.'[11]

Pace of the C E Branch was back in touch with Smith on 13 September, telling him of the Foreign Office's displeasure. It was now accepted that it would be 'administratively convenient' for the payment to Mrs Leo to come from the Admiralty Vote. Smith was asked to reconsider his views. The Treasury official took nearly two months to reply. Smith was not backing down. He wrote:

The statements and arguments in support of the payments to or on behalf of Mr Leo have been so conflicting that we consider it worthwhile to restate the position. In January 1950 we approved the payment, ex-gratia, of £1,000 because there were some grounds for accepting the view that Mr Leo had suffered physical and mental impairment affecting his earning capacity as a result of his experiences. He was therefore given the benefit of the doubt, which would not have been given to an employee of HMG in this country where we should have insisted on medical evidence in support of the payment. Subsequent correspondence in which it was proposed that Mr Leo should be re-employed certainly tended to suggest that our original doubts were extremely real.

Smith pointed out that there had been an undertaking that no further claims would be made. Such undertakings would be worthless if additional payments were made. Smith concluded: 'Against this background and my opinion that we are under no moral or legal obligation to Mrs Leo and my further opinion that non payment would not harm us politically and payment would not help us politically to any measurable extent and would be likely moreover to excite other claims I come to the conclusion that we cannot agree to any further payment being made.' And there the matter appears to have ended. Mrs Leo did not get her £200. Her fate is unclear.

Much of the official correspondence relating to Sam Leo was originally closed until 2031, a surprising 82 years after *Amethyst*'s escape. It was released only because of requests under the Freedom of Information Act 2000. The name of the other Chinese man who helped *Amethyst*'s officers remains secret, presumably because there are still relatives living in China.

29

Looking Back

IN THE MONTHS THAT FOLLOWED *Amethyst*'s escape John Kerans had time to reflect on the ship's ordeal, and in February 1950 *The Naval Review*, the Royal Navy's independent and restricted forum, published an article by Kerans on some of the less publicised points. The account is a good illustration of the resourcefulness that was necessary for day-to-day survival on the Yangtze. These are edited extracts:

CO-OPERATION. This was in evidence right from the start when the embassy in Nanking became aware of the disaster that had overtaken *Amethyst*. The commander-in-chief of the Nationalist navy, Admiral Kwei Yung-chin (now in Formosa) offered every facility and help that he could to assist *Amethyst*'s wounded; his orders were quickly conveyed to the Nationalist army authorities in the immediate neighbourhood of Rose Island, where the ship had grounded.

Later in Shanghai the US authorities placed the hospital ship *Repose* from Tsingtao at the Royal Navy's disposal. By this time the Nationalist army had successfully evacuated by train from Changchow (about 15 miles due south of Rose Island) some 60 ratings who had been ordered to evacuate the ship when under fire to avoid further loss of life; due to minefields they could not rejoin her.

The very ready assistance of the Royal Air Force in Sunderlands from Hong Kong was of the highest order. The Yangtze is not an easy place to land in, and Communist gunfire did not assist matters. The help of the RAF medical officer [Flight Lieutenant Michael Fearnley] was invaluable and things might well have been difficult without his presence.

MORALE. There is no doubt that this was the most important point of all to consider from the word go; an incident of this nature which came with such suddenness is bound to affect those concerned in various ways. From all the evidence that I have gathered, there is everything to show that morale was of a high order, in spite of the extreme youth of many ratings. When I joined on 22 April, though, it was near breaking point. After three days under fire and with little rest, this was not surprising. In addition, the presence of 17 dead on board for over 56 hours was a depressing influence. In spite of all, they were prepared for the last rites by a valiant team of petty officers and a few junior ratings. Eventually, when the ship's company realised the situation and the hopelessness of movement either way, there was a distinct hardening of determination to stick it out and face the future with equanimity and confidence.

I decided that a strict service routine must, and would be, adhered to from the beginning. This continued throughout and with watchkeeping every day and night on the bridge as well as consider-able damage repairs, this kept the men fit and physically tired.

Non-working hours were hard to fill. We were lucky to have a fairly plentiful supply of gramophone records. No attempt by officers was ever made to institute recreational games for ratings. This bore fruit and it was not long before they made their own entertainment. I have felt that there is nothing more a sailor dislikes than being organised into whist drives or other such ideas, which eventually finish up as a dismal flop.

The ship's company were always kept fully informed (as far as possible) of the outcome of all my meetings with the PLA. I did, however, never at any time give them any assurance that events would be speedy – it was a personal opinion, which became truer as time unfortunately wore on. Certain selected chief and petty officers were given access to the ship's signal log each day. This did much to help morale and gave petty officers a clearer knowledge of the issues at stake, and acted as a deterrent to the proverbial false 'buzzes'.

In addition, the knowledge that everything possible was being done by all authorities elsewhere to extract *Amethyst* gave the ship's company added assurance and confidence. The ability to receive and send telegrams helped immeasurably (265 were despatched during our 101 days internment). Inability to send outgoing mail was unfortunate but we did receive three bags towards the end of June. For reasons best known to the PLA they were well censored and pilfered. The presence of two domestics and a cat and a dog, which had somehow survived the shelling, tended to produce an air of normalcy in messdeck life.

VICTUALLING. This was an important problem from the beginning and needed much care and attention as it was considered essential to provide a balanced diet, with as much additional variety as stocks permitted, to give some compensatory advantage in the circumstances we had found ourselves. Fortuitously *Amethyst* was well stocked, having just left Hong Kong, and in addition was carrying flour and frying oil and other provisions for the embassy in Nanking to replace emergency stocks that the lengthened stay of *Consort* had depleted.

Mercifully the forward galley remained intact and was in constant use throughout; there was thus no difficulty in baking bread and the provision of hot meals. Casualties amongst cooks (whites as well as Chinese) were nil, which was salutary. By bartering with supplies of flour, frying oil, soap, duffel coats, sea boots and other articles we were able to augment our fare with eggs and potatoes. Later on we were able to obtain Communist money (Jen Min Piao, which translated means People's Money) and increase our purchases. For large amounts I was able on occasions to use Hong Kong currency. Whichever way one looks at it we lost heavily on the rate of exchange, and their prices were as the opposition wished. Perhaps I reached the limit when after three months I discovered Shanghai-brewed beer was available in Chingkiang by paying approximately 12s 6d per bottle. I was determined that the ship's company would have some amenities, leaving final payment until later. The commander-in-chief kindly allowed public money to be used and eventually the station central amenities fund reimbursed the crown. This gave a great morale boost. The daily issue of rum continued as usual – stocks of this were sufficient for many months ahead. This is not surprising when 25 out of the 68 were under 20 years of age.

When I went on half rations at the beginning of July the seriousness of the situation was very quickly brought home to many ratings. This mainly concerned conservation of cold room stocks and butter, milk, sugar and tea. Looking back on it now there was sufficient calorific value at each meal not to cause undue anxiety; the main trouble was lack of variety. A careful tally was kept on each item each week and the limiting dates of each article were reassessed. By the end of August it was estimated that starvation would have been very close. Still I was preparing to go on quarter rations early in August. Difficulty in maintaining morale might have been hard. Lack of food was one of my reasons for the break-out.

MACHINERY. Everything ultimately depended on damage control and refitting and maintenance of all machinery. Amongst the wounded who were evacuated were *Amethyst*'s engineer officer [Lieutenant Ernest Wilkinson] and chief ERA [Stanley Roblin]. In addition the chief stoker [Owen Aubrey] was drowned and others were killed, wounded or evacuated. It was a depleted engine room staff that remained, but mercifully the majority were petty officer stoker mechanics backed up with sufficient hands to run machinery. Considerable credit is due to the senior ERA [Leonard Williams] who kept up the efficiency of his department, with the electrical officer [Lieutenant George Strain] in overall command.

I cannot stress too highly how important knowledge of damage control is when disasters such as this occur, especially ship knowledge. It was unfortunate that large drafting changes had taken place in *Amethyst* only a few days previously. The important points that come to my mind are accurate damage control markings and dispersion of lockers and fire-fighting equipment. A more simplified form of markings on doors and fans should, I feel, be introduced. Young ratings are inevitably going to forget what the various letterings stand for in time of emergency. The dangers of ratings painting over rubber on hatches and doors are still too evident wherever one looks in spite of all that has been said in training. Only time and constant supervision will eradicate this very important detail. There is no doubt that our peacetime damage control must be maintained as near to the wartime scale as habitability allows.

FUEL. The vital factor throughout our detention. *Amethyst* left Shanghai on her fateful journey with full tanks. A small amount was lost by pumping to refloat her after grounding. By the time I joined her on 22 April approximately 270 tons remained. No attempt was made in the early days at conservation since the situation was dangerous and fluid. On 28 April contact had been made with the Communists ashore, and with the realisation that time meant nothing to the PLA steps were initiated to curtail consumption. As time wore on the hours without power became greater – at the end we were shut down for as long as 59 hours without steam. This was grim and was accentuated by the extreme heat the Yangtze experiences in July. I consider we could have exceeded this period and shut down for 72 hours at a time with strict rationing of fresh water.

The only power during these periods was a 24-volt battery supply from the lower power room for the emergency WIT set and a few pinpoints of light in my cabin and on the messdecks. To live in a 'dead ship' is an experience which none of us is likely to forget. Our lowest average daily consumption of fuel was a ton a day.

STABILITY. The forward ballast tank and X magazine (X gun was destroyed anyway) were flooded when the ship was light instead of flooding oil fuel tanks. The two after ones were flooded earlier on. I hoped to keep as many tanks free of Yangtze water and its large amount of sand whilst there was any hope of fuel replenishment.

The world has never seen a good deal of the damage caused to *Amethyst*'s upperworks since all that was practicable was cut away. To increase stability many heavy weights were struck below – the best examples of this were the damaged Bofors and certain radar equipment. A blackboard was kept in my cabin throughout with details of fuel of all types remaining in each tank, fresh water, main items of food and limits of endurance in each case.

NEGOTIATIONS. In all, 19 meetings took place with the Communist military authorities. Of this number eight were preliminary 'skirmishes' with the opposition ashore near *Amethyst* or on board. The remainder were all on shore and for the most part in Chingkiang at General Yuan's headquarters. These meetings were held with a very thin veil of amicability and rigid formality. The general's appearances at the table were few and always of short duration. The negotiating powers were handed over to Colonel Kang, who had two interpreters well indoctrinated in Communist ideologies. Everything I said at these meetings was religiously taken down in full, in English and Chinese. At some meetings I had the attention of the press and propaganda section of the PLA. Thus I am well documented. The keenest photographer was a female who one day actually ventured out in a sampan from the local village to photograph *Amethyst* at all angles. The local garrison commander, Captain Tai Kuo-liang, who acted as my personal bodyguard, also attended each meeting. But apart from writing reams he was never allowed to say a word. Funnily enough we used to converse in French. The progress of the meetings can fairly be summed up as representing a sine curve; at one meeting some hope for safe conduct was given, but the next would speedily dash it.

COMMUNICATIONS: That the main WIT office was undamaged in the shelling was indeed fortunate and even more so that an electrical officer [Lieutenant Strain] was on board. This officer belonged to the senior officer's frigate at Shanghai and was on passage to Nanking in order to repair *Amethyst*'s radar. No sooner had he done this than circumstances were such that destruction of classified radar equipment was ordered for security reasons. Telegraphist French became the sole wireless operator left in *Amethyst*. He did well, and it speaks highly of West Country physique and guts that he stood up to continuous watchkeeping for so long. Two electrical ratings were eventually trained to read our call sign and simple procedure. By special arrangements with the flagship or Hong Kong continuous watch was always maintained, and the telegraphist rested accordingly.

It is fairly certain that the opposition were eventually reading our messages, and considering we were on the same wavelength for many months, it is perhaps not surprising. The need for caution was paramount. Lack of codes and ciphers were undoubtedly my severest handicap and in the end a reasonably secure but limited method was adopted. Rising temperatures in July began to tell on the telegraphist, and there is no shadow of doubt that his mental capacity in reading traffic was falling rapidly. There was unfortunately little we could do when shut down to alleviate conditions. This was one of my paramount reasons that escape was the only solution.

LEADERSHIP. One small but important item was fully borne out by this tragic incident. There is absolutely nothing wrong in the leadership of the chief and petty officer of today. A good many had undertaken disciplinary courses and the merit of these is most fully justified. Chief and petty officers are the important 'link in the chain', and no stone should be left unturned to encourage these men to remain in the service.

PUBLICITY. Considerable publicity was given to our escape and eventual passage to the United Kingdom, and again at Plymouth and London. Some quarters have voiced disapproval of this course, especially as *Black Swan* and *Consort* did not come home too.

However, it took place, and we had to face it. Taking an overall view it has really done the Royal Navy little harm, and perhaps our recruiting figures may show an increase.

I have received between 700 and 800 letters and cables from all parts of the United Kingdom, the Commonwealth and many foreign countries. Many and diverse peoples have written, and in this country of ours it evinces an unswerving loyalty and faith in the hope for a resurgence of more amenable times. This in itself gives much encouragement for the future.

The final honour we were accorded was to appear in Buckingham Palace before His Majesty the King and the Royal Family. Each rating had one friend or relation present (those with gongs, two). Two comments by parents which appeared in the press are a fair summing up: 'The Queen smiled at me – was all I wanted' and 'Our son joined up two years ago, and I never could have dreamed that he would get us inside the palace in that time'.

CONCLUSION. The last nine months have been difficult but unforgettable times. It was a situation that has no parallel in history and, it is hoped, will not occur again. From the youngest to the oldest the situation was faced with poise and confidence, which was indeed salutary. This was my greatest asset. The spirit of leadership and devotion to duty by those under my command was fully exemplified throughout; this after all is the fundamental basis of all our training and everything that the Royal Navy has stood for in the past and stands for in the present and the future.

Co-operation was predominant from the start to the finish, and that no link in the chain was broken augurs well for the future, and speaks much of the Royal Navy's basic training. Prayers to Almighty God were not overlooked in our routine during those weary and trying days last summer. There is an ingrained sense of religion deep down in most of us, apparent more in some than in others. How easy it could have been as the empty days wore on to be discouraged and adopt a fatalistic outlook.

Our prayers were answered, and escape was achieved without loss of life and serious damage. Faith is not the least of the lessons to be learnt when in adversity.[1]

30

The Fading Hero

AT THE BEGINNING OF 1949 John Kerans's future in the Royal Navy had not looked promising. His run-ins with authority left him a marked man, listed 'for disposal' before taking up his appointment as an assistant naval attaché in Nanking. But twelve months later his star was shinning brightly, in spite of the drunken episode in Singapore. Kerans was a national hero, awarded the Distinguished Service Order, and now a full commander, even though he had held the rank of lieutenant commander for less than three years. For the Royal Navy he had turned disaster into triumph, and saved Admiral Brind and Vice Admiral Madden, in particular, from further embarrassment.

However, his heroic status and speedy promotion may not have endeared him to some of his fellow officers. The navy's many brave acts and sacrifices of the Second World War were fresh in the memory. The year 1950 began promisingly enough for Kerans. He was sent on a staff course at the Royal Naval College, Greenwich, and he may have harboured thoughts of rising to high rank. Greenwich was followed by a desk job at the Admiralty, head of naval intelligence for the Far East. But the lure of the sea was too much for Kerans and he pushed for another command. A destroyer would have seemed a fitting choice, given his rank and status. Kerans, in fact, ended up with a humble minesweeper, HMS *Rinaldo*. Perhaps he had lapsed into his old ways, perhaps he was being given a message. After wartime service *Rinaldo* was paid off at Portsmouth and placed in reserve, later being used for training and Home Fleet duties, a far from glamorous role. Kerans took command in January 1953 but he had not been on board long when he wrote to his wife Stephanie revealing he was 'somewhat depressed' because of a serious stomach bug. He experienced loneliness and, out of character, began writing long letters to Stephanie, though in the June there was good news, the birth of his second daughter, who was called Melanie, despite press speculation the name might be Amethyst.

In 1954 Kerans returned to the Far East as the naval attaché in

Bangkok. This time Stephanie was with him. The job also entailed covering Phnom Penh, Vientiane, Saigon and Rangoon, but Kerans did not impress some of his colleagues. Commander David Hunter, who worked with him, would comment: 'His reputation was not good in the Far East. In fact, it used to be said that Kerans was famous for two things – he had the biggest balls in the Royal Navy and he was the stupidest officer in the Royal Navy. I cannot vouch for one of these accolades but I did encounter him professionally when the second did not seem too unlikely.'[1]

The posting should have lasted two years but Kerans was sent back to Britain in 1956 after suffering dysentery. The following year he went on a senior officers' technical course in Portsmouth. In reality, his career was going nowhere, and in 1958 he faced the shock of learning that he would be forced to retire from the navy, at the age of 43. The family moved from Littlehampton in Sussex to a leafy part of Purley, on the outskirts of London, with Kerans using his gratuity of £5,500 to buy a pleasant detached house. But he found it difficult to get a job and even resorted to placing an advertisement in newspapers offering his services. In an interview with the *Daily Express*, he said: 'I don't know at the moment what I am going to do. My gratuity from the service doesn't go far these days and if I don't find a job quickly we shall find it hard to eat.'

He took a course in business administration and became a door-to-door salesman offering life insurance. It must have been strange for people to open their front door and find the hero of the *Amethyst* trying to sell them a policy they were unlikely to want. Kerans decided it was the quickest way 'to lose your friends' and quit the 'degrading' job. The construction firm George Wimpey gave him employment as a trainee manager. He was sent to Sunderland to work on a new steelworks, and happened to mention in a local newspaper interview that he was interested in politics. He ended up standing as the Conservative candidate for The Hartlepools in the 1959 general election – and winning the seat from Labour with a narrow majority.[2]

During his term as a Member of Parliament he asked hundreds of questions in the House of Commons on a bewildering variety of subjects – nursery school places, unemployment, visits to Royal Navy ships by sea cadets, the closure of sub post offices, the number of police dogs in London, the width of loads on lorries, the treatment of leprosy, school discipline, immigration, coal mining, chimes on ice cream vans, the slaughter of grey seals. No subject seemed to be off limits, but whether such enthusiasm impressed his political masters is open to question.

Trips to his constituency were time-consuming, and Kerans wanted a seat nearer his home in Purley. But there were no offers, and he did not stand at the next general election. A lengthy spell of unemployment followed. He worked briefly for stockbrokers in London and then found himself placing more newspaper advertisements seeking employment. In 1967 he was appointed bursar at his daughter Melanie's boarding school in Surrey, but he was sacked after seven months, the responsibilities over finances proving too great for a man with no accountancy training. 'Things got into a terrible mess,' he confessed. He was back looking for a job. Two years later the Civil Service came to his rescue, with a role in the Service Pensions Appeals Tribunal. He seems to have enjoyed this work, commuting from Purley to central London and checking the claims of ex-servicemen.[3]

Kerans retired when he reached the age of 65, and he and Stephanie moved to a terraced house in Oxted, Surrey. Over the years he had been asked many times to talk about the Yangtze Incident. He became bored with the story, and 'heartily sick' of discussing China. But he was left wondering if he could have made more of his naval career after 1949. In Nigel Farndale's book, *Last Action Hero of the British Empire*, Melanie describes her father as generous, amusing and sentimental – but also dogmatic, can- tankerous and intolerant. Three years after retirement Kerans was diagnosed with bowel cancer and later he endured throat cancer. He died on 11 September 1985, aged 70, after 'much distressing illness'. Many former members of *Amethyst*'s crew went to his funeral at St Peter's Church in the village of Tandridge, near Oxted. The hero of the *Amethyst* was buried in the churchyard.[4]

In 2001 a bizarre story about Kerans appeared in *Time* magazine. Journalist Anthony Paul claimed that the commander had been a secret agent in the mould of James Bond. Paul interviewed him in the late 1970s for *Asiaweek* magazine, and Kerans revealed that he was sent to spy on the Americans in Formosa in January 1949. With Chiang Kai- shek's Nationalists facing defeat in mainland China, the British government apparently wanted to know the extent to which the United

States was helping to build the island fortress of Formosa. The Americans, rightly fearing that British intelligence had been infiltrated by Communist sympathisers, were reluctant to share information. Kerans travelled to Formosa on 'a seaside vacation' and while swimming off the west coast photographed US ships 'disgorging massive supplies of military material'. He was caught in a forbidden zone on the east coast and thrown into jail. After a few days 'discreet bribes restored his freedom'. Paul said he agreed not to publish the story until he had confirmation from the Admiralty, which never came. 'But I have no reason to disbelieve Kerans,' he wrote. 'And more than half a century after the activities he described, I see no need to remain silent.'[5]

Unlike Kerans, Lieutenant Peter Berger, one of *Amethyst*'s wounded, did go on to achieve high rank. Berger was Fleet Navigating Officer, Home Fleet, from 1956 to 1958, and afterwards the navigator of the Royal Yacht *Britannia*. From 1962 to 1964 he commanded the frigate HMS *Torquay* in the Dartmouth Training Squadron, 'where a twitch of his famously bushy eyebrows was sufficient to admonish any wayward cadet'. He became the first non-submariner to command the Clyde nuclear submarine base. He rose to the rank of vice admiral and received a knighthood in 1979, the year he was appointed Flag Officer Plymouth. Berger retired from the navy in 1981 and died in October 2003, aged 78.[6]

Amethyst's gallant first lieutenant, Geoffrey Weston, had perhaps the strangest career move – he joined the army. In 1950 it was made clear to him that he could not remain in the navy because of his shrapnel wound, which prevented him from going to sea. He would carry the piece of metal in his liver for the rest of his life. Weston decided to study law and went to Clare College, Cambridge, later winning a Fulbright scholarship to Kansas University. He was called to the Bar, Lincoln's Inn, in 1954, but he still missed the navy and offered his legal services to the Admiralty, which turned him down. Weston's next port of call was the War Office, and he was immediately offered a short service commission with Army Legal Services in the rank of captain. The commission became a regular one, and he went on to serve in Cyprus, Germany, Hong Kong and Northern Ireland. Much of his service involved the prosecution of cases before courts martial. He also gave advice on the legal aspects of military operations. Weston must have been the only army officer to wear the navy's Distinguished Service

Cross and Bar. He also had an unusual collection of campaign medals – the Naval General Service Medal with clasps Malaya and Yangtze 1949, the General Service Medal (1918) with clasp Cyprus, and the Campaign Service Medal (1962) with clasp Northern Ireland. He retired from the Army Legal Corps, as it became known, in the rank of brigadier in 1981. His father Percy had been a brigadier, serving in both world wars and winning the Distinguished Service Order and two Bars and the Military Cross. Weston was described as 'a true eccentric who needed the discipline of the services to pit his idiosyncrasies against'. One report noted: 'It says much for the army that it tolerated such a non-conformist for so long. He had a first-class legal brain but was probably a better administrator than advocate, as he tended to become too personally involved in his cases.' Despite his shrapnel wound and a fondness for cigars and brandy, he played a 'violent' game of squash and loved winning. He also enjoyed chess, bridge, cricket and fast cars, which he 'drove slowly'. He was an insomniac spending nights listening to classical music 'not always to the delight of fellow mess members'. His Savile Row suits were rarely dry-cleaned and 'bore a permanent layer of cigar ash'. Weston died in May 1993, aged 71.[7]

Leonard Williams, the cool head in *Amethyst*'s engine room, had the most challenging of naval careers. He was in the Yangtze gunboat HMS *Dragonfly* when she left Singapore on 14 February 1942, the day before the island fell to the Japanese. *Dragonfly* and her sister ship HMS *Grasshopper*, both packed with civilians, were attacked by around twenty-five fighter-bombers south of Singapore. *Dragonfly* took two direct hits and sank within 10 minutes. After several hours in the water Williams and a few others reached Singkep Island, where *Grasshopper* had managed to beach. After a long journey by boat, road and rail most of the survivors – and a dog called Judy – reached Padang on the opposite side of Sumatra, only to be taken prisoner on 17 March. As Williams put it, 'thus began years of the most horrific labour, torture, starvation and every degradation the Japanese could inflict on us'. He was taken to a camp at Medan, northern Sumatra, along with Judy, who had become a mascot. In June 1944 he was among 800 prisoners being sent to Japan in the cargo ship *Harukiki Maru*. Judy had been smuggled aboard in a sack. In the Strait of Malacca two torpedoes from the submarine HMS *Truculent* sank the ship, and about 180 prisoners lost their lives. Williams escaped, as did Judy, who was credited with saving lives by pushing debris towards men struggling in the water. The dog was later awarded the animal VC, the Dickin Medal. Williams ended up back in Sumatra, working on the Pekan Baru to Muara death railway, which went through 140 miles of mostly jungles and swamps. More than 100,000 Indonesian slave labourers and around 6,000 prisoners of war were forced to build the line, which was completed on 15 August 1945, the day that Japan surrendered. Countless thousands had died. 'Every sleeper laid cost lives,' said Williams. 'Surviving prisoners were in a terrible state of health, emaciated and needing medical help for tropical diseases.'

Amethyst must have been the least of his ordeals. With Simon the cat receiving the Dickin Medal, Williams had the distinction of serving with two animal VCs. After the Yangtze Incident he enjoyed more peaceful times. He was in the cruisers HMS *Cumberland* and HMS *Devonshire* in the Mediterranean and the West Indies. In 1953 he was among those chosen to join the Royal Yacht *Britannia*, which was nearing completion at the John Brown shipyard, Clydebank. Williams was the first to start the ship's engines, and then followed 12 'wonderful' years, with three round-the-world trips. He left the navy in 1964 and taught in the engineering and naval architecture department at Portsmouth Polytechnic for 20 years. Williams died in December 2006, aged 87.[8]

The Yangtze Incident did not harm Admiral Sir Patrick Brind's career. In 1951 he was appointed the first Commander-in-Chief, Allied Forces, Northern Europe, as part of the newly formed North Atlantic Treaty Organization. That year also saw him created GBE (Knight Grand Cross of the Most Excellent Order of the British Empire). He died in October 1963, aged 71. Brind's Nato deputy, General Sir Robert Mansergh, paid this tribute: 'With characteristic thoroughness and unfailing courtesy he created, in a remarkably short time, an efficient command, training and operational organisation which worked smoothly mostly and happily always. An international, closely integrated force is never easy to control, but Pat Brind achieved this and laid the basic foundation of what today is one of the major defences of the west.' Mansergh also saluted the admiral's 'adherence to Christian principles, his delightful manner and impressive presence'.[9]

Madden's career also prospered. He returned home early from the Far East to become Second Sea Lord in 1950, later receiving a knighthood and becoming a full admiral. Admiral Sir Alexander Madden's last appointment before retiring in 1955 was Commander-in-Chief, Plymouth. He died in September 1964, less than a year after Brind's death.[10]

David Scott, Brind's flag lieutenant during the *Amethyst* crisis, had been involved in the famous 'man who never was' deception during the Second World War. Scott was first lieutenant of the submarine HMS *Seraph* when she carried out Operation Mincemeat in April 1943, depositing a corpse wearing the uniform of a Royal Marines officer off the coast of Spain. Attached to the body, which had been kept in a metal container packed with ice, was a briefcase with fake secret documents. The body was found, and the Spanish, who assumed they had an air crash victim, duly passed on the documents to the Germans. The ruse worked. The Germans diverted forces from the defence of Sicily. The Royal Marines officer was actually a Welsh vagrant who had been found dead in London. In October 1942 *Seraph* had rescued the French general Henri Giraud from a beach near Toulon. Giraud had refused to be saved by the Royal Navy because of the British attack on the French fleet at Mers-el-Kebir. When he boarded *Seraph* she was flying the Stars and Stripes, had a temporary US Navy captain and Scott and the rest of the crew were speaking with dubious American accents they had picked up from watching films. Giraud, apparently none the wiser, was taken to Gibraltar to meet General Eisenhower, who wanted him to help with the invasion of French North Africa. Scott was also involved in the Corfu Channel disaster of 1946 when the destroyers *Saumarez* and *Volage* were badly damaged by Albanian mines, with heavy casualties. He was second in command of *Volage*, which went to *Saumarez*'s aid only to suffer a similar fate. But *Volage* towed the other destroyer to safety, and Scott was commended for his superb seamanship and courage. In 1953 Scott achieved the first submerged transatlantic crossing by a diesel submarine using a snorkel. Twenty years later he became deputy controller of the Polaris programme. He was later knighted and left the navy in 1980 in the rank of rear admiral. Scott died in January 2006, aged 84.[11]

The Soviet spy Guy Burgess, who monitored *Amethyst* and the events on the Yangtze so closely, also tried to influence policy on China during his time in the Foreign Office's Far Eastern Department. He argued for early recognition of the Communist regime, and persuaded his superiors to put pressure on the Americans and the French to do the same. The Labour politician Tom Driberg noted: 'Because of his knowledge of Communism he became, in effect, the department's political analyst of the Chinese revolution. His colleagues knew China – he knew Marxism. It was a happy partnership.' Cambridge-educated Burgess opposed the move to increase military forces in Hong Kong. He acknowledged that the Chinese Communists could overrun the colony but insisted they would not. Because of his stand the department found itself in a major dispute with the War Office and the Colonial Office. Soon after the start of the Korean War in June 1950 Burgess was sent to the British embassy in Washington to liaise with the US State Department on Far East policy. According to Driberg, he experienced an 'agonising' time. Burgess found his new colleagues ignorant and incompetent, and he fell out with a senior diplomat, Sir Hubert Graves, who removed him from his specialist role. Burgess's state of mind was not helped by concussion he suffered after a colleague pushed him down a stone staircase during an argument. Heavy drinking and fast driving – he was stopped for speeding three times in one day – did not endear him to the American authorities. Burgess was recalled to London.[12] In May 1951 he fled to the Soviet Union with Donald Maclean. They belonged to the Cambridge Five spy ring, whose other members were Kim Philby, Anthony Blunt and someone who has never been positively identified. The son of a naval officer, Burgess had been born in *Amethyst*'s home, Devonport. He went to Britannia Royal Naval College, Dartmouth, but he never took up a career in the navy after an eyesight problem was uncovered. Burgess, who disliked life in the Soviet Union, died in 1963, aged 52.

Clement Attlee, who lost the 1951 general election and saw his Yangtze critic Winston Churchill return as prime minister, made a remarkable journey in August 1954. He went to Peking and shook hands with Mao. It was the first time that the Communist leader had met a Western statesman since coming to power. President Richard Nixon would make a similar trip nearly 20 years later and claim a diplomatic triumph. Attlee was still leader of the Labour Party and took along some of the faithful, including Aneurin Bevan, for the eighteen-day visit to China. He had three hours of talks with Mao, which he described as 'vigorous but quite friendly'. Mao branded the United States as China's 'chief enemy' and railed against the emerging

South East Asia Treaty Organization. At a dinner days earlier Attlee told his audience: 'We know how much China has suffered in war', adding that Britain had lost 'the flower of our youth' in two world wars.[13] In his talks with Mao it does not appear that the former prime minister mentioned the attacks on *Amethyst*, *Consort*, *London* and *Black Swan* and the high number of casualties. Nor, apparently, did he mention the 1,078 British service personnel who were killed in action during the Korean War, which began during his premiership and ended in stalemate the previous year. Mao and Stalin were the driving forces behind the war.

And *Amethyst*? When filming of *Yangtze Incident* finished in 1956, the frigate was towed back to Devonport. In January 1957 she went to a local breaker's yard. The film was released shortly afterwards. As cinema audiences watched the Yangtze drama unfold, *Amethyst* was being ripped apart.

Appendices

Appendix 1: Ships in Action

HMS *Amethyst*
Class: modified *Black Swan* destroyer
Pennant number: U16, later changed to F116
Builder: Alexander Stephen, Govan
Laid down: 25 March 1942
Launched: 7 May 1943
Commissioned: 2 November 1943
Displacement: 1,350 tons
Length: 283ft
Beam: 38.5ft
Draught: 11ft
Speed: 20 knots
Complement: 192
Propulsion: Parson geared turbines driving two shafts
Armament: 6 x 4in guns, 4 x 40mm Bofors guns, 2 x 20mm Oerlikons
Scrapped: 1957
The frigate was the seventh Royal Navy vessel to bear the name
   Amethyst. Battle honours: Cerbere 1800, Thetis 1808, Niemen
   1809, China 1856–60, Ashantee 1873–4, Heligoland 1914,
   Dardanelles 1915, Atlantic 1945 and Korea 1951–2.

HMS *Consort*
Class: 'C' class destroyer
Pennant number: R76
Builder: Alexander Stephen, Govan
Laid down: 26 May 1943
Launched: 19 October 1944
Commissioned: 19 March 1946

Displacement: 1,885 tons, 2,545 tons full
Length: 362.75ft
Beam: 35.75ft
Draught: 11.75ft
Speed: 32 knots
Complement: 186
Propulsion: geared turbines driving two shafts
Armament: 4 x 4.5in guns, 4 x 40mm Bofors guns, 4 x anti-aircraft
    mountings, 8 (2 x 4) tubes for 21in torpedoes
Scrapped: 1961

HMS *London*
Class: 'County' class heavy cruiser
Pennant number: C69
Builder: Portsmouth dockyard
Laid down: 23 February 1926
Launched: 14 September 1927
Commissioned: 31 January 1929
Displacement: 9,750 tons, 13,315 tons full
Length: 633ft
Beam: 66ft
Draught: 21ft
Speed: 32 knots
Complement: 784
Propulsion: geared turbines driving four shafts
Armament: 8 x 8in guns, 8 x 4in guns, 8 x 21in torpedo tubes
Scrapped: 1950

HMS *Black Swan*
Class: *Black Swan* destroyer
Pennant number: L57, later U57 and F57
Builder: Yarrow Shipbuilders
Laid down: 20 June 1938
Launched: 7 July 1939
Commissioned: 27 January 1940
Displacement: 1,250 tons
Length: 299.5ft
Beam: 37.5ft

Draught: 11ft
Speed: 19 knots
Complement: 180
Propulsion: geared turbines driving two shafts
Armament: 6 x 4in guns, 8 x 2pdr pompoms
Scrapped: 1956

HMS *Concord*
Class: C class destroyer
Pennant number: R63, later D03
Builder: John Thornycroft, Southampton
Laid down: 18 November 1943
Launched: 14 May 1945
Commissioned: 20 December 1946
Displacement: 1,885 tons, 2,545 tons full
Length: 362.75ft
Beam: 35.75ft
Draught: 11.75ft
Speed: 32 knots
Complement: 186
Propulsion: geared turbines driving two shafts
Armament: 4 x 4.5in guns, 4 x 40mm Bofors guns, 4 x anti-aircraft
    mountings, 8 (2 x 4) tubes for 21in torpedoes
Scrapped: 1962

Appendix 2: *Amethyst's* **Ship's Company**
Killed or died of wounds:
Alderton, John, Surgeon Lieutenant
Aubrey, Owen, Chief Petty Officer Stoker Mechanic
Baker, Thomas, Sick Berth Attendant
Barnbrook, Maurice, Boy 1st Class
Barrow, William, Stoker Mechanic
Battams, Charles, Ordinary Seaman
Crann, Leslie, Stoker Mechanic
Driscoll, Albert, Ordinary Seaman
Griffiths, Dennis, Ordinary Seaman
Hicks, Sydney, Electrician's Mate 1st Class
Maskell, Victor, Stoker Mechanic

Morgan, Dennis, Stoker Mechanic
Muldoon, Patrick, Stoker Mechanic
Sinnott, Patrick, Ordinary Seaman
Skinner, Bernard, Lieutenant Commander
Tattersall, Edmund, Probationary Writer
Thomas, David, Ordinary Seaman
Vincent, Albert, Able Seaman
Winter, George, Ordinary Seaman
Wright, Reginald, Ordinary Seaman
Three Chinese, including a Yangtze pilot, also died

Wounded:
Anderson, Thomas, Stoker Mechanic
Bannister, Samuel, Stoker Mechanic (returned to ship)
Berger, Peter, Lieutenant
Canning, Leonard, Stoker Mechanic
Crighton, Arthur, Leading Seaman
Davies, Amos, Able Seaman
Davis, Dennis, Cook (S)
Fletcher, Ronald, Stoker Mechanic
Howell, Brynley, Stores Assistant (remained on board)
Loving, Bryan, Stoker Mechanic
Maddocks, George, Stoker Mechanic (remained on board)
Marsh, Samuel, Boy 1st Class
Martin, Keith, Boy 1st Class (returned to ship)
Mirehouse, Henry, Lieutenant
Morrey, Frederick, Stoker Mechanic
Nicholls, Rosslyn, Petty Officer
Potter, Ronald, Able Seaman
Redman, Donald, Able Seaman
Richards, Ronald, Able Seaman
Rimmington, Albert, Ordinary Seaman
Roberts, Brian, Boy 1st Class
Roberts, Dennis, Signalman
Roblin, Stanley, Chief Engine Room Artificer
Silvey, Anthony, Stores Assistant
Stevens, Gwilyn Leading Seaman
Tetler, Maurice, Ordinary Seaman

Weston, Geoffrey, Lieutenant
Wharton, Douglas, Signalman
Wilkinson, Ernest, Lieutenant (E)
Williams, Cyril, Leading Seaman
Williams, Edward, Ordinary Seaman
Williscroft, Kenneth, Ordinary Seaman

Non-wounded who took part in the evacuation of 20 April 1949:
Aldridge, Thomas, Able Seaman
Ashford, John, Able Seaman
Bailey, Ronald, Ordinary Seaman
Bowles, George, Petty Officer
Calcott, Raymond, Able Seaman
Clarkson, Lawrence, Yeoman of Signals
Cook, Derek, Telegraphist
Crocker, William, Leading Telegraphist
Davies, Ronald, Able Seaman
Dawson, Kenneth, Able Seaman
Donaldson, William, Able Seaman
Eddleston, Ronald, Able Seaman
Ferrett, Joseph, Leading Signalman
Ferrier, David, Able Seaman
Gibson, Robert, Stoker Mechanic
Gill, Donald, Able Seaman
Graham, Gerald, Engine Room Artificer 3rd Class
Hackman, Clive, Boy 1st Class
Harratt, Norman, Able Seaman
Haveron, Hugh, Able Seaman
Heath, David, Petty Officer
Heighway, Percy, Joiner 3rd Class
Higgins, Stewart, Stoker Mechanic
Hiles, Norman, Ordinary Seaman
Johnston, James, Able Seaman
Lees, Leslie, Ordinary Seaman
Mewse, Leonard, Chief Petty Officer Telegraphist
Monaghan, Eric, Gunner (left in Sunderland flying boat on 21 April)
Morrison, George, Ordinary Seaman
Mortimer, Ernest, Electrician's Mate 1st Class

Morton, John, Boy 1st Class
Mulley, Kenneth, Able Seaman
Mullins, Thomas, Leading Seaman
Mustoe, Eric, Able Seaman
Osbourne, Alfred, Able Seaman
Pitman, Horace, Able Seaman
Porter, Donald, Able Seaman
Quinn, John, Ordinary Seaman
Sampson, Arnold, Able Seaman
Stapleton, Albert, Stoker Mechanic
Stone, Robert, Telegraphist
Thomas, James, Signalman
Todd, Matthew, Able Seaman
Traylor, Bruce, Able Seaman
Turner, Robert, Able Seaman
Wakeham, Brian, Able Seaman
Warwick, Walter, Ordnance Artificer 2nd Class
Watson, Thomas, Leading Seaman
Webb, John, Petty Officer
Williams, William, Able Seaman

Men who stayed on board until *Amethyst*'s escape:
Augustyns, Denis, Leading Stoker Mechanic
Bannister, Samuel, Stoker Mechanic
Bell, David, Able Seaman
Blomley, Hugh, Electrician
Brown, Arthur, Stoker Mechanic
Bryson, James, Able Seaman
Cavill, George, Cook (S)
Chare, Lionel, Electrical Artificer 4th Class
Connor, Leonard, Petty Officer Stoke Mechanic
Day, Jack, Able Seaman
Delve, Kenneth, Ordinary Seaman
Donnelly, Malachy, Electrician's Mate 1st Class
Fearnley, Michael, Flight Lieutenant (joined ship 21 April)
Fellows, Albert, Stoker Mechanic
Frank, Leslie, Petty Officer
Freeman, William, Petty Officer

French, Jack, Telegraphist
Garfitt, William, Leading Seaman
Garns, Albert, Petty Officer Stoker Mechanic
Grazier, Bernard, Ordinary Seaman
Griffiths, George, Petty Officer Cook (S)
Harris, Henry, Ordinary Seaman
Hartness, George, Leading Seaman
Hawkins, Charles, Stoker Mechanic
Hett, Stewart, Lieutenant
Holloway, Eric, Mechanic 1st Class
Horton, Sydney, Boy 1st Class
Hutchinson, Roland, Able Seaman
Irwin, Vernon, Electrician
Jones, Donald, Able Seaman
Jones, John, Ordinary Seaman
Jones, Peter, Ordinary Seaman
Kay, Raymond, Able Seaman
Keicher, Charles, Able Seaman
Kerans, John, Lieutenant Commander (joined ship 22 April)
Logan, George, Petty Officer Stoker Mechanic
Macdonald, Duncan, Leading Stoker Mechanic
MacNamara, John, NAAFI manager
Maddocks, George, Stoker Mechanic
Martin, Keith, Boy 1st Class
McCarthy, John, Stores Petty Officer
McCullough, Raymond, Able Seaman
McGlashen, Ian, Engine Room Artificer 2nd Class
McLean, James, Able Seaman
Mitchell, Robert, Able Seaman
Munson, Ernest, Ordinary Seaman
Murphy, Jeramiah, Chief Petty Officer Stoker Mechanic
Murphy, John, Ordinary Seaman
Nolan, James, Ordinary Seaman
Ormrod, Thomas, Leading Stoker Mechanic
Parish, Colin, Boy 1st Class
Parnell, Wilfred, Boy 1st Class
Paul, George, Electrician's Mate 1st Class
Pearce, Albert, Stoker Mechanic

Ray, John, Ordinary Seaman
Rees, Trevor, Ordnance Artificer 4th Class
Roberts, Dennis, Ordinary Seaman
Rutter, Jack, Leading Radio Electrical Mechanic
Saunders, Eric, Able Seaman
Shaw, Bernard, Boy 1st Class
Smith, William, Shipwright 4th Class
Strain, George, Lieutenant Commander (L)
Townsend, Thomas, Able Seaman
Venton, William, Petty Officer Stoker Mechanic
Walker, Jack, Able Seaman
Wells, Richard, Able Seaman
White, Alfred, Petty Officer
Williams, Albert, Ordinary Seaman
Williams, Leonard, Engine Room Artificer 2nd Class
Wilson, Denis, Able Seaman
Winfield, Kenneth, Stoker Mechanic
Wright, Gordon, Able Seaman

A total of about fourteen Chinese – stewards, cooks, tailors, laundrymen – were on board when *Amethyst* was attacked

Appendix 3: Casualties for *Consort*, *London* and *Black Swan*
Killed or died of wounds:

Consort
Akhurst, John, Petty Officer Telegraphist
Gifford, Raymond, Stoker Mechanic
Gurney, Maurice, Chief Petty Officer
Hutton, Christopher, Able Seaman
Iredale, Dennis, Ordinary Telegraphist
Jenkinson, Sidney, Ordinary Seaman
Moir, William, Leading Seaman
Morton, Albert, Petty Officer
Theay, Charles, Ordinary Seaman
Tobin, John, Electrician's Mate

London
Arkell, James, Leading Seaman
Ellwood, Arthur, Able Seaman
Fisher, William, Marine
Foley, James, Able Seaman
Grice-Hutchinson, Charles, Lieutenant Commander
Harrison, Edgar, Able Seaman
Jarvis, Lawrence, Marine
Jones, Sidney, Ordinary Seaman
Lane, John, Ordinary Seaman
Pullin, William, Able Seaman
Roper, Alec, Petty Officer
Shelton, Harry, Able Seaman
Stowers, Patrick, Chief Petty Officer Writer
Walsingham, Stanley, Ordinary Seaman
Warwick, Geoffrey, Ordinary Seaman

Wounded:
Consort
Adams, K, Leading Signalman
Addis, A, Telegraphist
Attridge, C, Able Seaman
Bevan, P, Leading Seaman
Brewer, J, Boy 1st Class
Brown, J, Electrician
Butcher, G, Stoker Mechanic
Chambers, W, Leading Stoker Mechanic
Cox, K, Leading Telegraphist
Davies, L, Stoker Mechanic
Donaldson, A, Petty Officer Cook
Duffin, L, Ordinary Seaman
Flanagan, F, Stoker Mechanic
Fleet, W, Able Seaman
Ford, S, Ordinary Seaman
Greening, H, Petty Officer
Holdsworth, P, Leading Signalman
Robertson, I, Commander
Rose, S, Leading Stoker Mechanic

Tootell, J, Able Seaman
Williams, W, Able Seaman

London
Banfield, Robert, Stores Assistant
Bansall-Allan, Frederick, Petty Officer
Barnard, G, Marine
Barwick, A, Boy
Bayes, V, Ordinary Seaman
Blenkin, T, Leading Writer
Brewer, C, Ordinary Seaman
Brewis, C, Able Seaman
Brown, J, Ordinary Seaman
Cazalet, Peter, Captain
Clark, Edwin, Able Seaman
Dalrymple-Kelly, J, Sergeant
Deeks, H, Marine
Gale, A, Chief Petty Officer
Hall, C, Ordinary Seaman
Head, J, Marine
Hipwell, William, Petty Officer Airman
How, B, Marine
Ingham, Robert, Sub Lieutenant
Main, T, Stoker
McCarthy, R, Marine
Meikle, R, Able Seaman
Melia, T, Able Seaman
Morris, Stuart, Stores Assistant
Pearce, L, Able Seaman
Pike, Ronald, Stoker Mechanic
Piper, E, Stoker Mechanic
Prescott, Walter, Able Seaman
Pulling, R, Leading Writer
Sabin, Charles, Able Seaman
Searle, G, Marine
Spence, W, Able Seaman
Warr, Norman, Marine
Watts, R, Boy

Wells, James, Mechanic 1st Class
Wilmhurst, Edwin, Petty Officer Writer
Wilson, A, Able Seaman

Black Swan
Dickson, A, Ordinary Telegraphist
Esplin, K, Boy 1st Class
Fowler, G, Ordinary Seaman
McKenzie, T, Telegraphist
Potter, A, Boy 1st Class
Reeves, M, Ordinary Seaman
Tincombe, D, Boy 1st Class

Appendix 4: Awards

Awards to Amethyst
Distinguished Service Order
Lieutenant Commander John Kerans

Bar to Distinguished Service Cross
Lieutenant Geoffrey Weston

Distinguished Service Cross
Lieutenant Peter Berger
Flight Lieutenant Michael Fearnley RAF

Member of the Order of the British Empire
Lieutenant Commander (L) George Strain

Distinguished Service Medal
Acting Petty Officer Leslie Frank
Telegraphist Jack French
Engine Room Artificer Leonard Williams

Mention in Despatches
Surgeon Lieutenant John Alderton (posthumously)
Electrical Artificer Lionel Chare
Petty Officer William Freeman

Lieutenant Stewart Hett
Stores Petty Officer John McCarthy
Boy 1st Class Keith Martin
Lieutenant Commander Bernard Skinner (posthumously)
Ordinary Seaman Reginald Wright (posthumously)

Awards to Consort
Distinguished Service Order
Commander Ian Robertson

Distinguished Service Medal
Leading Stoker Mechanic Tony Johnson
Chief Petty Officer Henry Robinson (awarded the George Medal in
    1942)

Mention in Despatches
Ordinary Seaman Ivan Bennett-Bound
Lieutenant William Bonner
Able Seaman Albert McKee
Acting Leading Telegraphist Robert Miller

Awards to London

Bar to Distinguished Service Order
Captain Peter Cazalet

Distinguished Service Cross
Commissioned Gunner Reginald Smith

Distinguished Service Medal
Able Seaman Alan Dudley
Bandmaster Frederick Harwood

Mention in Despatches
Chief Petty Officer Stoker Mechanic Henry Fletcher
Corporal William Hart
Chief Petty Officer Thomas Learmouth
Chief Writer Patrick Stowers (posthumously)

Surgeon Commander Wilfred Taylor

Awards to Black Swan
Mention in Despatches
Ordinary Seaman Graham Fowler
Commander Richard Hare
Surgeon Lieutenant William Owen
Chief Petty Officer Telegraphist Reginald Stovell

(Awards announced in *The London Gazette* of 6 May, 5 August and 1 November 1949.)

Appendix 5: Timeline of Main Events

Edited version of timeline compiled by Lieutenant Commander John Kerans. Some of the times before he joined *Amethyst* are approximate.

19 April 1949
0800 *Amethyst* leaves Holt's Wharf, Shanghai.
1632 Anchors Kiangyin for the night.

20 April
0510 *Amethyst* weighs and proceeds up river.
0638 Anchors due to fog.
0734 Ship weighs and proceeds up river.
0836 Under fire from starboard side. Jacks unfurled. Battle ensign hoisted at masthead.
0850 Firing ceases. Ship not hit.
0930 Under fire from starboard beam and hit.
0935 Ship runs aground on Rose Island and still under heavy fire. Commanding officer and almost all bridge and wheelhouse personnel killed or seriously wounded. First lieutenant, Weston, though seriously wounded assumes command.
1000 Lieutenant Weston orders all life-saving equipment to be lowered and ship to be evacuated to the south bank.
1015 Medical officer and sick berth attendant killed.
1100 All confidential books are burnt and confidential equipment destroyed. Main steam shut down.

1115 Sniping at ship.

1430 *Consort* in sight. Unable to tow off *Amethyst* and continues down river.

1700 Nationalist soldiers offer assistance in evacuating wounded. Offer not taken as it is hoped to refloat ship and proceed Nanking.

1930 Raised steam.

2245 In W/T communication with Hong Kong. Discharged oil fuel and lightened ship.

21 *April*

0015 Ship refloated.

0045 Under small-arms fire from north bank.

0130 Ship anchors.

0915 Nationalist army personnel arrive on board to offer medical assistance.

1000 Lieutenant Commander Kerans and assistant military attaché Lieutenant Colonel Dewar-Durie leave Nanking by road for Chingkiang.

1045 Nationalist naval craft offers assistance. Not taken as *London* due 1130.

1130 Ship weighs ready for *London*'s arrival with *Black Swan*.

1150 Ship anchors. Opposition too heavy for ships to reach *Amethyst*. About 50 ratings leave Wutsin by train for Shanghai.

1330 Kerans and Dewar-Durie reach Chingkiang.

1530 Nationalist army medical officer and two orderlies arrive on board.

1630 Sunderland aircraft lands near ship and is fired on. RAF medical officer only and a few supplies reach ship. Gunner Monaghan caught in aircraft, which returns to Shanghai. Ship shifts berth.

1800 Kerans and Dewar-Durie reach Tachiang village.

1830 Nationalist medical officer leaves ship to arrange evacuation of wounded.

2130 He returns to ship with sampans.

2200 Evacuation of wounded begins.

2350 Kerans and Dewar-Durie with medical team reach coast. Communists cross Yangtze and land to east of Kiangyin during the night.

22 April

0100 Kerans and Dewar-Durie leave the coast by sampan to board *Amethyst*. Last of the wounded except first lieutenant leave ship.

0130 *Amethyst* moves further up river. Kerans and Dewar-Durie unable to reach ship and return Tachiang.

0235 Ship anchors and is immediately fired upon, this time by Nationalists. Shifts berth again one mile down river.

0345 On shore Lieutenant Commander Skinner and one able seaman succumb to their wounds.

0510 Fourteen seriously wounded men and medical party leave Tachiang for Chingkiang in lorries.

0715 Kerans and Dewar-Durie return to Chingkiang.

0830 Wounded reach Chingkiang.

1000 Wounded arrive at station. Train late.

1100 Four more wounded reach station.

1210 Train leaves for Shanghai.

1315 Sunderland aircraft lands near *Amethyst* and is fired upon. Aircraft returns Shanghai without disembarking anyone.

1500 Kerans reaches *Amethyst* in Nationalist naval craft. Lieutenant Weston evacuated to Chingkiang mission hospital. Dewar-Durie remains in Chingkiang.

1534 Kerans ordered by Vice Admiral Madden to assume command of *Amethyst*.

1630 Buried at anchor 17 dead (11 Church of England, five Roman Catholics and one Chinese).

1800 Communist crossings reported to the east of Nanking. Rapid deterioration of situation.

2010 Vice Admiral Madden signals to be prepared to evacuate *Amethyst* and sink her.

2145 Preparations completed to beach and destroy ship.

2200 Nationalist navy evacuate Chingkiang. Quiet night.

23 April

In fog at daylight.

0900 Fog lifts. Nationalist forces in area withdrawn.

1200 Communist activity on starboard side. Ship shifts down river two miles and meets accurate battery fire.

1245 Anchors close to south bank. No hits.

1500 Communist crossings ahead and astern unopposed. Vice Admiral Madden approves destruction of ship if no alternative and evacuation to Shanghai.

2145 Chinese naval units pass down river. Heavy fire between ship and batteries.

24 April

Wardroom partially flooded and top weight jettisoned to right ship.

1000 Ship on even keel.

Diplomat Youde's mission into Communist territory fails to achieve safe passage for *Amethyst*. Civilian junks appear free to move on river at will.

25 April

Communist troop movements in vicinity of ship. Make good damage and lessen fire risks.

26 April

Crossings ahead and astern of ship.

1330 Three soldiers and two civilians on land endeavour to make ship send out boat. This is not possible.

1515 Soldiers make further efforts. Decide to risk whaler as weather calm. Interview takes place with Communist major and a senior rating.

27 April

1200 Junk arrives with soldiers. Interview takes place ashore between Lieutenant Hett and a battery commander.

1 May

Clocks advanced one hour (zone 9).

2 May

1730 Interview takes place on board between Kerans and Communist officer from local garrison.

3 May

1200 Fresh eggs bartered for rice and flour as a result of help from local Communist soldiers.

5 May

AM Trader brings fresh potatoes and a request from local garrison commander for Chinese (Cantonese) on board to visit Chingkiang area commander.

6 May

PM Lieutenant Hett calls on local garrison commander to hasten safe conduct. Nothing learnt.

8 May

AM Local garrison commander visits Kerans. Coaxes ship's Chinese to accept area commander's request to go ashore next day. No news from Nanking.

9 May

Amethyst's Chinese return from burial service on Chiso-shan Island. No reactions except all glad to be back.

17 May

Kerans has interview with local garrison commander on board. No result.

18 May

AM Lieutenant Hett visits local garrison commander to hasten interview with area commander.

PM Kerans presented on board with PLA's formal demands for settlement of Yangtze Incident.

22 May

PM Receive order from Admiral Brind to deliver personal message to General Yuan.

24 May

PM Kerans has first meeting with General Yuan and Colonel Kang.

Safe conduct will not be given until Royal Navy takes responsibility for incident.

25 May

PLA return two wounded ratings, Bannister and Martin, to the ship. Both recovered.

29 May

Sam Leo, an interpreter at the British embassy, Nanking, joins *Amethyst*.

31 May

Kerans has meeting with Colonel Kang at village opposite ship. No progress.

3 June

Kerans has meeting with Colonel Kang on Silver Island. Deadlock.

12 June

Further meeting with Colonel Kang on Silver Island.

15 June

Meeting with Colonel Kang at village opposite ship.

18 June

Meeting with Colonel Kang, who is anxious for Admiral Brind's views on previous meetings.

20 June

Meeting at Chingkiang headquarters with General Yuan. British side accused of insincerity and delaying tactics.

22 June

Further meetings at Chingkiang headquarters. General expresses opinion incident can be settled by an exchange of notes. Mail clearance for Shanghai granted.

24 June

Three bags of mail reach *Amethyst* from Shanghai.

28 June

Kerans ill.

30 June

Clearance for fuel from Nanking. Difficulties over wording of notes acceptable to the Communists.

1 July

Interpreter Khoong from the assistant naval attaché's office in Shanghai reaches ship with emergency medical supplies and charts but latter are confiscated. *Amethyst* nearly hit by two large merchant ships in darkness (no lights on *Amethyst* as power is off).

5 July

Meeting at village opposite ship with Colonel Kang. Attempt made to get diplomat Youde as an additional interpreter. Some hopes of early safe conduct.

8 July

Lieutenant Weston ordered back to Shanghai by PLA at Chingkiang after attempting to rejoin *Amethyst*. Hitch arises in Nanking over exit permit for Youde after verbal clearance at Chingkiang.

9 July

Usable fuel remaining 65 tons. Fuel from Nanking arrives PM (54 tons). Last valve on transmitter for Type 60 W/T gone.

11 July

Final draft exchange note presented to Communists at Chingkiang meeting but refused after very lengthy and difficult talks. Youde's entry refused. Replenishment refused. Kerans receives personal abuse for attempted entry of Lieutenant Weston. Situation grim. Kerans unable to see General Yuan. *Amethyst* receives virtual ultimatum.

13 *July*
Lengthy memorandum received for General Yuan from Admiral Brind.

17 *July*
Part of emergency naval stores from Shanghai reach *Amethyst*.

22 *July*
Metting at Chingkiang headquarters. General Yuan refuses entry of the naval attaché, Captain Donaldson, and will only accept Admiral Brind's signature on Kerans's authorisation to negotiate. Deadlock.

25 *July*
Typhoon passes over Yangtze centre within about 50 miles of *Amethyst*. No damage.

30 *July*
0800 Total fuel remaining 55 tons.

Notes and Sources

Chapter 1

1. HMS *Amethyst*'s final report of the Yangtze Incident, Phase 1, Lieutenant Commander John Kerans, 30 November 1949, and Imperial War Museum interview with Townsend, 6 March 2000.
2. Imperial War Museum interview, 23 May 1990.
3. Imperial War Museum interview, 9 March 2000.
4. Imperial War Museum interview, 25 October 1990.
5. Imperial War Museum interview, 3 January 2001.
6. Imperial War Museum interview, 29 May 1996.
7. Report by Lieutenant Geoffrey Weston, 8 October 1949.
8. Report by Lieutenant Peter Berger, undated.
9. Imperial War Museum interview, 8 August 2000.
10. Christopher Lew, *The Third Chinese Revolutionary Civil War, 1945–49*, Chapter 1, and Stuart's memoirs, *Fifty Years in China*, Chapter 11.
11. Information removed from HMS *Amethyst*'s final report of the Yangtze Incident, Kerans, 30 November 1949, and originally not due to be made public until 2025 (ADM 116/5740B, The National Archives, Kew, London).
12. *South China Morning Post*, 21 April 1949.

Chapter 2

1. Telegram, 4 December 1948.
2. Telegram to the Foreign Office, London, 18 December 1948.
3. Cablegram from Australia's Department of External Affairs to its legation in Nanking, 3 June 1947.
4. Messages from the Commander-in-Chief, British Pacific Fleet to the Admiralty, 30 August 1945 and 16 September 1945.
5. Report by the Director of Plans, 15 September 1945. The Director of Plans at that time was Captain E Langley Cook, but the report may have been compiled by his predecessor, Captain (later Admiral Sir) Guy Grantham, who left the post in July 1945.
6. Ibid.
7. Report by the Admiralty's M Branch, 14 September 1945.
8. Memorandum for the Board of Admiralty – 'Composition of the Post War Navy', 12 September 1945.
9. Obituary of Stevenson, *The Daily Telegraph*, 24 June 1977.
10. Report by Madden to the Admiralty, 3 May 1949. Report by Madden to the Commander-in-Chief, Far East Station, 7 July 1949.
11. Reports in the *South China Morning Post*, 23 January 1949 and *The Age* (Melbourne) 31 January 1949.
12. Despatch from Officer to the Minister of State for External Affairs, 15 February 1949.
13. Report by Madden to the Admiralty, 3 May 1949.
14. Comments to naval researcher Captain Hugh Stevenson and the author, 27 March 2012.
15. Report on the 'Yangtze River Incident' by Tapp for Australia's Department of the Navy, 1 May 1949.
16. Stuart's memoirs, *Fifty Years in China*, Chapter 11.
17. Imperial War Museum interview, 9 March 2000.

18. Report by Madden to the Commander-in-Chief, Far East Station, 7 July 1949.
19. James Tuck-Hong Tang, *Britain's Encounter with Revolutionary China, 1949–54*, Chapter 2, and report by Madden to the Commander-in-Chief, Far East Station, 7 July 1949.
20. Message from Hall to Attlee, 21 April 1949.
21. Foreign Office telegram No 394, 20 April 1949.
22. Telegram No 454 from Stevenson to the Foreign Office, 21 April 1949.
23. Report of operations in the Yangtze River – 20 April to 23 April 1949 by Madden for the Commander-in-Chief, Far East Station.

Chapter 3
1. HMS *Amethyst*'s final report of the Yangtze Incident, Phase 1, Kerans, 30 November 1949, report by Lieutenant Weston, 8 October 1949, and report by Lieutenant Berger, undated.
2. Imperial War Museum interview, 6 June 1990.
3. Report by Lieutenant Berger, undated.
4. Imperial War Museum interview, 9 March 2000.
5. HMS *Amethyst*'s final report of the Yangtze Incident, Phase 1, Kerans, 30 November 1949, and report by Lieutenant Weston, 8 October 1949.
6. Imperial War Museum interview, 6 March 2000.
7. Papers of Captain Richard Hare, Liddell Hart archives, King's College London.

Chapter 4
1. Report on *Consort*'s actions by Commander Ian Robertson, 26 April 1949.
2. Report by Madden to the Commander-in-Chief, Far East Station, 7 July 1949.
3. Report on *Consort*'s actions by Commander Robertson, 26 April 1949, initial report on *Consort*'s actions, unattributed and undated, and written comments of Sub Lieutenant William Robson, 1991.
4. Imperial War Museum interview, 10 April 1997.
5. Report on *Consort*'s actions by Commander Robertson, 26 April 1949, initial report on *Consort*'s actions, unattributed and undated.
6. Written comments of Sub-Lieutenant William Robson, 1991.
7. Report on *Consort*'s actions by Commander Robertson, 26 April 1949.
8. Imperial War Museum interview, 10 April 1997.
9. HMS *Consort* Association, *Loyal and Steadfast, The Story of HMS Consort*, Chapter 4.
10. Booklet 'Commemorating the 60th Anniversary of the Yangtze Incident', privately published by former crew of HMS *Consort* and HMS *Black Swan*.
11. Private papers.

Chapter 5
1. HMS *Amethyst*'s final report of the Yangtze Incident, Phase 1, Kerans, 30 November 1949, and report by Lieutenant Berger, undated.
2. Report by Madden to the Commander-in-Chief, Far East Station, 7 July 1949.
3. Booklet 'Commemorating The 60th Anniversary Of The Yangtze Incident', privately published by former crew of HMS *Consort* and HMS *Black Swan*.
4. London auctioneers Dix Noonan Webb. Sudbury was awarded the MBE (civil) for his actions in HMS *London*, and his medal with documentation was sold at auction in September 2006.
5. Report of HMS *London*'s actions, written by Commander John Hodges in the first person on behalf of the wounded Captain Peter Cazalet, 28 April 1949, and report by Madden to the Commander-in-Chief, Far East Station, 7 July 1949.
6. Parker-Jervis quoted in Iain Ballantyne, HMS *London*, Chapter 16.
7. Papers of Captain Richard Hare, Liddell Hart archives, King's College London.
8. Parker quoted in Iain Ballantyne, HMS *London*, Chapter 16.
9. Account by Harwood published in *Warship World*, January 2003.
10. Catlow quoted in Iain Ballantyne, HMS *London*, Chapter 16.
11. Account by Harwood published in *Warship World*, January 2003.
12. Report by Madden to the Commander-in-Chief, Far East Station, 7 July 1949.

13. Foreign Office memo from Burgess, 22 April 1949, on press statements released by the British embassy, Nanking.

Chapter 6
1. HMS *Amethyst*'s final report of the Yangtze Incident, Phase 1, Kerans, 30 November 1949.
2. Report by Lieutenant Weston, 8 October 1949.
3. Imperial War Museum interview, 8 May 1996.
4. Report of Sunderland's missions, Group Captain John Jefferson, 29 April 1949.
5. Papers of Wing Commander Peter Howard-Williams, 1991.
6. Imperial War Museum interview, 8 May 1996.
7. Papers of Gerard Devany, 1994.
8. Lawrence Earl, *Yangtse Incident*, Chapter 15, and report by Lieutenant Weston, 8 October 1949.
9. Imperial War Museum interview, 8 May 1996.
10. Report of Sunderland's missions, Group Captain John Jefferson, 29 April 1949.
11. Papers of Gerard Devany, 1994.
12. Report of Sunderland's missions, Group Captain John Jefferson, 29 April 1949, and written memoirs of Gerard Devany, 1994.

Chapter 7
1. Papers of Rear Admiral Sir David Scott, The *Amethyst* Incident, and Malcolm Murfett, *Hostage on the Yangtze*, Chapter 6, reference note on Kerans.
2. Nigel Farndale, *Last Action Hero of the British Empire*, Royal Navy Officers 1939–1945 website, and Worcestershire Regiment website.
3. Alan Tyler, *Cheerful and Contented*, Chapter 7.
4. Nigel Farndale, *Last Action Hero of the British Empire*, and Lieutenant Commander Geoffrey Mason, 'Service Histories of Royal Navy Warships in World War 2', http://www.naval-history.net/xGM-aContents.htm.
5. HMS *Amethyst*'s final report of the Yangtze Incident, Phase 1, Kerans, 30 November 1949, report by Lieutenant Colonel Dewar-Durie, 30 April 1949, 'The Army and the *Amethyst*', unpublished article by Dewar-Durie, 1959, obituary of Dewar-Durie, *The Independent*, 21 April 1999, and article by Jan Herman, historian of the US Navy Medical Department, undated.
6. Information removed from HMS *Amethyst*'s final report of the Yangtze Incident, Kerans, 30 November 1949, and originally not due to be made public until 2025 (ADM 116/5740B, The National Archives, Kew, London).
7. 'The Army and the *Amethyst*', unpublished article by Lieutenant Colonel Dewar-Durie, 1959.
8. HMS *Amethyst*'s final report of the Yangtze Incident, Phase 1, Kerans, 30 November 1949, and report by Lieutenant Weston, 8 October 1949.
9. Report by Lieutenant Colonel Dewar-Durie, 30 April 1949, and 'The Army and the *Amethyst*', unpublished article by Dewar-Durie, 1959.
10. HMS *Amethyst*'s final report of the Yangtze Incident, Phase 1, Kerans, 30 November 1949.

Chapter 8
1. Telegram from Stevenson to the Foreign Office, 20 April 1949, and telegram from Stevenson to the consul in Peking, 21 April 1949.
2. Telegram from the consul in Peking to Stevenson, 22 April 1949.
3. Telegram from Stevenson to the Foreign Office, 22 April 1949.
4. Report by Youde on his 'attempt to secure a safe-conduct pass for HMS *Amethyst* after she had been crippled by Communist gunfire', undated.
5. Report by Youde, undated, and telegram from Stevenson to the Foreign Office, 24 April 1949.
6. Report by Youde, undated.
7. Telegram from Stevenson to the Foreign Office, 24 April 1949.

Chapter 9
1. HMS *Amethyst*'s final report of the Yangtze Incident, Phase 2, Kerans, 30 November 1949.
2. Report by Madden to the Commander-in-Chief, Far East Station, 7 July 1949.
3. HMS *Amethyst*'s final report of the Yangtze Incident, Phase 2, Kerans, 30 November 1949.
4. Report by Madden to the Commander-in-Chief, Far East Station, 7 July 1949.
5. Imperial War Museum interview, 8 August 2000.
6. HMS *Amethyst*'s final report of the Yangtze Incident, Phase 2, Kerans, 30 November 1949.
7. Diary of Leslie Frank and Imperial War Museum interview with Gordon Wright, 6 June 1990.
8. Imperial War Museum interview, 25 October 1990.

Chapter 10
1. Official note of First Sea Lord's press conference at Exercise Trident, 20 April 1949.
2. Letter to Lady Brind, written at the United Services Club, London, 21 April 1949.
3. *The Times*, 23 April 1949.
4. *The Daily Telegraph*, 23 April 1949.
5. *Daily Express*, 22 April 1949.
6. Foreign Office briefing paper, author unknown, 21 April 1949.
7. Telegrams from the British embassy, Washington, to the Foreign Office on US press reports, 26 and 29 April 1949.
8. Translation of New China News Agency report sent from the British embassy, Nanking, to the Foreign Office, 24 April 1949.
9. *Daily Express* and *The Daily Telegraph*, 23 April 1949.
10. *Daily Express*, 25 April 1949.
11. *Sydney Morning Herald*, 28 April 1949.
12. *The Age*, 23 April 1949.

Chapter 11
1. *Daily Express* and *The Times*, 27 April 1949.
2. HMS *Amethyst*'s final report of the Yangtze Incident, Phase 3, Kerans, 30 November 1949.

Chapter 12
1. Notes by the First Sea Lord on specific points arising from questions in Parliament after the prime minister's statement on 26 April.
2. Telegrams from Stevenson to the Foreign Office, 23 and 25 April 1949, and Chester Ronning, *A Memoir of China in Revolution*.
3. Stuart's memoirs, *Fifty Years in China*, Chapter 12.
4. Odd Arne Westad, *Decisive Encounters, The Chinese Civil War 1946–1950*, Chapter 7.
5. Report on the 'Yangtze River Incident' by Tapp for Australia's Department of the Navy, 1 May 1949.
6. *Shoalhaven*'s monthly report, April 1949, Tapp.
7. Report of the Committee of Inquiry into Defence Awards (Australia 1994) headed by General Peter Gration. The report said: 'The committee . . . does not believe that either HMAS *Warramunga* or HMAS *Shoalhaven* were involved in action of sufficient moment or involved such hazards that made it clearly more demanding than normal peacetime service. The committee does not recommend any awards.'
8. Report by Madden to the Commander-in-Chief, Far East Station, 7 July 1949.
9. Question asked by Archie Cameron in the House of Representatives, 1 June 1949.
10. Report by Madden to the Commander-in-Chief, Far East Station, 7 July 1949.
11. *Daily Express*, 2 May 1949.
12. Message to the Admiralty, 2 May 1949.
13. *The Economist*, Notes of the Week, 30 April 1949.
14. Letter dated 18 May 1949.

15. Far Eastern Department minute, 10 June 1949.
16. Christopher Lew, *The Third Chinese Revolutionary Civil War, 1945–49*, Chapter 5, quoting Deng Xiaoping, *Selected Works*.

Chapter 13
1. HMS *Amethyst*'s final report of the Yangtze Incident, Phase 3, Kerans, 30 November 1949.
2. Ibid and information removed from HMS *Amethyst*'s final report of the Yangtze Incident and originally not due to be made public until 2025 (ADM 116/5740B, The National Archives, Kew, London).
3. HMS *Amethyst*'s final report of the Yangtze Incident, Phase 3, Kerans, 30 November 1949.
4. Telegram to Stevenson with copy to the Admiralty, 20 May 1949.
5. Personal message to Brind from Fraser, 20 May 1949.
6. HMS *Amethyst*'s final report of the Yangtze Incident, Phase 3, Kerans, 30 November 1949.
7. Letter written on board *London*, 29 May 1949.
8. HMS *Amethyst*'s final report of the Yangtze Incident, Phase 3, Kerans, 30 November 1949.
9. Imperial War Museum interview, 21 July 1996.
10. George Hickinbottom, *The Seven Glorious Amethysts* and Patrick Roberts, *Famous Felines*. http://www.purr-n-fur.org.uk/famous/.
11. Imperial War Museum interview, 23 May 1990.
12. Patrick Roberts, *Famous Felines*.

Chapter 14
1. Odd Arne Westad, *Decisive Encounters, The Chinese Civil War 1946–1950*, Chapter 7.
2. Ibid.
3. Minutes of the Cabinet's China and Southeast Asia Committee, 10 Downing Street, 13 May 1949.
4. Comments to a meeting of the British Residents' Association, date unknown.
5. Private papers of Howard-Williams, 1991.
6. Australian Associated Press/Reuters report 14 July 1949 based on Peking radio broadcast, and Stuart's memoirs, *Fifty Years in China*, Chapter 12.
7. Telegram to the Secretary of State for the Colonies, Arthur Creech Jones, 30 April 1949.
8. Briefing document 'Appreciation of the situation in China', marked top secret, 28 April 1949, but unattributed.
9. Minutes of meeting of the Chiefs of Staff Committee, 25 April 1949.
10. Report by the Joint Planning Staff, Ministry of Defence, 29 April 1949.
11. Message from the Secretary of State for the Colonies Arthur Creech Jones to Hong Kong Governor Sir Alexander Grantham, 28 May 1949.
12. Report of the Defence Co-ordination Committee, Far East and the Joint Intelligence Committee, Far East, 2 June 1949.

Chapter 15
1. HMS *Amethyst*'s final report of the Yangtze Incident, Phase 3, Kerans, 30 November 1949.
2. Letter to Haley, 9 June 1949.
3. Letter to Fraser, 15 June 1949.
4. Message to the Admiralty, 9 June 1949.
5. Message to Stevenson from Urquhart, 11 June 1949, and message to Stevenson from Brind, 12 June 1949.
6. HMS *Amethyst*'s final report of the Yangtze Incident, Phase 3, Kerans, 30 November 1949.
7. Message to Stevenson, 17 June 1949.
8. HMS *Amethyst*'s final report of the Yangtze Incident, Phase 3, Kerans, 30 November 1949.

9. Cabinet briefing paper, 22 June 1949.
10. HMS *Amethyst*'s final report of the Yangtze Incident, Phase 3, Kerans, 30 November 1949.
11. Message to the Admiralty, 23 June 1949.
12. Cabinet document, 23 June 1949.
13. Message to *Amethyst*, 25 June 1949, and message to Donaldson, 2 July 1949.
14. Message to Donaldson, 30 June 1949.
15. Message to *Amethyst*, 2 July 1949.

Chapter 16

1. HMS *Amethyst*'s final report of the Yangtze Incident, Phase 3, Kerans, 30 November 1949.
2. Imperial War Museum interview, 6 March 2000.
3. Diary of Coxswain Leslie Frank, entry for 10 July 1949.
4. Article by Kerans in *The Naval Review*, February 1950.
5. HMS *Amethyst*'s final report of the Yangtze Incident, Phase 3, Kerans, 30 November 1949.
6. Telegram, 6 July 1949.
7. Report titled 'Appreciation of the situation arising from the enforced presence of HMS *Amethyst* in the Yangtze River', 5 July 1949. The report may have been compiled by Commander Peter Dickens, Admiral Brind's staff officer operations.
8. Imperial War Museum interview, 23 May 1990.
9. Diary of Coxswain Leslie Frank, entry for 11 July 1949.
10. Report by Madden to the Commander-in-Chief, Far East Station, 7 July 1949.
11. HMS *Amethyst*'s final report of the Yangtze Incident, Phase 3, Kerans, 30 November 1949.

Chapter 17

1. HMS *Amethyst*'s final report of the Yangtze Incident, Phase 3, Kerans, 30 November 1949.
2. Memoirs of Rear Admiral Sir David Scott, unpublished.
3. HMS *Amethyst*'s final report of the Yangtze Incident, Phase 3, Kerans, 30 November 1949.
4. Message sent to *Amethyst* but circulated throughout fleet, dated 14 July 1949.
5. Diary of coxswain Leslie Frank, entry for 17 July 1949.
6. It is not clear when Brind sent his message but Madden replied on 16 July 1949.
7. Memoirs of Rear Admiral Sir David Scott, unpublished. A full explanation of how the code worked is contained in an appendix to the memoirs.

Chapter 18

1. HMS *Amethyst*'s final report of the Yangtze Incident, Phase 3, Kerans, 30 November 1949. Memoirs of Rear Admiral Sir David Scott, unpublished.
2. Diary of Coxswain Leslie Frank, entry for 26 July 1949.
3. Telegram from Stevenson to Brind, 26 July 1949.
4. Telegram from Stevenson to the Foreign Office, 28 July 1949.
5. Message received by Brind on 30 July 1949.
6. HMS *Amethyst*'s final report of the Yangtze Incident, Phase 3, Kerans, 30 November 1949.
7. Diary of coxswain Leslie Frank, entry for 30 July 1949.

Chapter 19

1. HMS *Amethyst*'s final report of the Yangtze Incident, Phase 4, Kerans, 30 November 1949.
2. Imperial War Museum interview, 21 September 1990.
3. Diary of Coxswain Leslie Frank, entry for 30 July 1949.
4. HMS *Amethyst*'s final report of the Yangtze Incident, Phase 4, Kerans, 30 November 1949. Material from the report originally closed until 2025. Article by Kerans in *The Naval Review*, February 1950.
5. Ibid.

6. Material originally closed until 2025 from HMS *Amethyst*'s final report of the Yangtze Incident, Phase 4, Kerans, 30 November 1949.
7. Memoirs of Rear Admiral Sir David Scott, unpublished.
8. Message from Brind to Admiralty, 29 July 1949.
9. Memoirs of Rear Admiral Sir David Scott, unpublished.
10. Imperial War Museum interview, 8 August 2000, *Navy News*, September 2009.
11. HMS *Amethyst*'s final report of the Yangtze Incident, Phase 4, Kerans, 30 November 1949.
12. Imperial War Museum interview, 21 September 1990.
13. Messages from Fraser and Brind, 30 July 1949. Imperial War Museum interview with Hett, 23 May 1990.
14. HMS *Amethyst*'s final report of the Yangtze Incident, Phase 4, Kerans, 30 November 1949. Article by Kerans in *The Naval Review*, February 1950.
15. Imperial War Museum interview with Hett, 23 May 1990.

Chapter 20
1. *The Life and Times of HMS Concord*, published by the HMS *Concord* Association in January 2012.
2. HMS *Amethyst*'s final report of the Yangtze Incident, Phase 5, Kerans, 30 November 1949.
3. Brind asked the Commodore Hong Kong to distribute the press release.
4. Imperial War Museum interview with *Daily Express* reporter Frank Goldsworthy, 4 April 1990.
5. Hett's comment on navigating – information supplied to the author by Hett and Michael Pocock of MaritimeQuest. Articles in the *Daily Express*, *The Daily Telegraph*, *The Times* and the *Daily Mirror*, all 1 August 1949.
6. *Daily Express*, 3 August 1949.
7. Imperial War Museum interview, 4 April 1990.
8. HMS *Amethyst*'s final report of the Yangtze Incident, Phase 5, Kerans, 30 November 1949.
9. Imperial War Museum interview, 8 August 2000.
10. Imperial War Museum interview, 6 June 2001.
11. Letter to the Under Secretary, 15 July 1949.
12. Letter from D R Spendlove, news editor, Press Association, 2 August 1949.
13. Reply to Brind's letter dated 2 September 1949.
14. Transcript of radio broadcast sent from Singapore to the Foreign Office on 8 August 1949.
15. Telegram to Stevenson, 10 August 1949.
16. Statement by General Yuan and comment by New China News Agency, both 31 July 1949.
17. Telegram from the consul to the Foreign Office, 4 August 1949.
18. Telegram from the Shanghai consul to the Foreign Office, 6 August 1949.
19. *The Times*, 6 August 1949.
20. Telegram to the Foreign Office, 6 August 1949.
21. Telegram to the Foreign Office, 2 August 1949.

Chapter 21
1. Message dated 31 July 1949.
2. Eric Grove, *Vanguard to Trident*, Chapter 4.
3. Minutes by Coates and Tomlinson, 9 August 1949, and telegram from MacDonald, 7 August 1949.
4. Press release from the HMS *Concord* Association, 10 February 2009, and article by Anthony Lonsdale in *Warship World* magazine, November/December 2010.
5. Ministry memorandum, 16 August 1949.
6. Message to the Foreign Office, 23 August 1949.
7. Press release from the HMS *Concord* Association, 10 February 2009.
8. Material from HMS *Amethyst*'s final report of the Yangtze Incident, Kerans, 30 November 1949, originally closed until 2025.
9. Maritime Quest website, 22 October 2010.

10. Letter dated 29 November 2010.
11. Letter to Devine, 18 November 2007.
12. Military Medals Review, Sir John Holmes, July 2012.
13. Letter from Peter Lee-Hale, chairman of the HMS *Concord* Association, to Sir John Holmes, 5 June 2012, letter from Holmes to Lee-Hale, 16 January 2013, author's conversations with Lee-Hale and Derek Hodgson, May/June 2013.
14. Message from Brind to the Admiralty, 17 August 1950, and telegrams from Hutchison to the Foreign Office, 18 and 21 August 1950.
    Note: many naval signals relating to *Amethyst* were in Admiralty files originally closed until 2025. ADM 116/5697, ADM 116/5708.

Chapter 22

1. Statement made by Lieutenant Weston, 8 October 1949, letter sent by Weston from the University Hospital, Nanking, to his parents, 5 May 1949, letter sent by Weston from the British embassy, Nanking, to his mother, 26 June 1949.
2. HMS *Amethyst*'s final report of the Yangtze Incident, Phase 3, Kerans, 30 November 1949.
3. Statement made by Weston, 8 October 1949.
4. HMS *Amethyst*'s final report of the Yangtze Incident, Phase 3, Kerans, 30 November 1949.
5. Statement made by Weston, 8 October 1949.
6. Private papers of Peter Howard-Williams, 1991.
7. *South China Morning Post*, 31 July 1949.
8. Weston detailed his escape from Shanghai in an appendix to HMS *Amethyst*'s final report of the Yangtze Incident, Kerans, 30 November 1949. The appendix was originally closed until 2025.
9. Ibid.
10. Ibid.
11. Ibid.
12. Letter from Naval Intelligence Division, 3 September 1949.

Chapter 23

1. Letter from the Colonial Office to Grantham, 30 September 1949.
2. Cabinet minutes, 26 May 1949.
3. Message from Chifley to Attlee, 15 June 1949.
4. Report by the Joint Intelligence Committee, 14 July 1949, and originally closed until 2030.
5. Report by the Joint Intelligence Committee, 10 August 1949. Cabinet documents, 9 November 1949, in files originally closed until 2030 and now heavily redacted. CO 537/4998, CO 537/4999, CO 537/5000.
6. Report by Urquhart, 1 July 1949.
7. *South China Morning Post*, 1 September 1949.
8. *South China Morning Post*, 14 August 1949.
9. *Sunday Pictorial* and *News of the World*, 16 October 1949.
10. *News of the World*, 16 October 1949.
11. William Louis, *Ends of British Imperialism: The Scramble for Empire, Suez, and Decolonization*, Chapter 12.

Chapter 24

1. *South China Morning Post*, 5 August 1949.
2. Letter undated but received 3 August 1949.
3. Letter from Commodore Hans Henriksen, naval attaché, Norwegian embassy, London, to Sir John Lang, Secretary of the Admiralty, 2 August 1949.
4. Letter from Chifley, 3 August 1949.
5. Letter from Williams, 14 August 1949.
6. Report on Tapp covering period 15 January 1948 to 8 August 1949.
7. Report on Tapp covering period 18 August 1949 to 15 March 1950.
8. Report on Tapp covering period 1 December 1950 to 23 October 1952.
9. Report on Tapp covering period 7 January 1958 to 15 November 1958, Rear

Admiral Wilfred Harrington.
10. William Stenhouse Hamilton, *Notes from Old Nanking 1947–1949*, Chapter 28.
11. Letter to the Naval Secretary, 24 August 1949.
12. Memo from the head of M Branch, 30 August 1949.
13. *Evening Standard*, 25 August 1949.
14. *News Chronicle*, 26 August 1949.
15. Bowhill's letter 1 September 1949, Fraser's reply 5 September 1949.

Chapter 25

1. *Daily Express*, 1 November 1949, *Singapore Free Press*, 16 November 1949.
2. Far Eastern Department minutes, 25 and 26 October 1949, *Radio Times*, 14 October 1949.
3. Message from the head of M Branch, 29 October 1949.
4. *The Daily Telegraph*, *The Times*, 2 November 1949.
5. *Daily Express*, 2 November 1949.
6. *The Daily Telegraph*, *The Times*, 17 November 1949.
7. Papers of Gerard Devany, 1994.
8. *The Times*, 18 November 1949.
9. First Sea Lord's minutes, 9 November 1949.
10. Patrick Roberts, *Famous Felines*, http://www.purr-n-fur.org.uk/famous/.
11. Imperial War Museum interview, 21 September 1990.
12. *The Sunday Times*, 18 September 1949.
13. Letter from the Chief of Naval Information to the secretary to the First Sea Lord, 21 November 1949.
14. Letter from the First Sea Lord, 22 November 1949.
15. Letter from the Chief of Naval Information to the Fifth Sea Lord, 3 August 1949, and letter from the Chief of Naval Information to the private secretary of the First Lord, 23 August 1949.
16. *Navy News*, September 2009.

Chapter 26

1. Letter from Maberly Dening, head of the Far Eastern Division, to P Synnott.
2. Letter from P Synnott to Maberly Dening.
3. Statement, 7 September 1949.
4. Statement undated.
5. Statement undated.
6. Statement, 12 September 1949.
7. Statement, 1 September 1949.
8. Report titled *Amethyst* Case, undated.
9. Admiralty memo by Cly Cardo for M Branch.
10. Letter from Cly Cardo, M Branch, to P Scarlett, Foreign Office, 27 October 1949.
11. Letter from P Scarlett to Cly Cardo, 9 November 1949.
12. Briefing document by A Franklin, 20 March 1951.
13. Qiang Zhai, *The Dragon, The Lion, and the Eagle, Chinese-British-American Relations, 1949–1958*, Chapter 1.

Chapter 27

1. *The Daily Telegraph*, 23 April 1949, *Sunday Pictorial*, 24 April 1949.
2. *Sunday Tribune* (Far East), date unknown.
3. Jung Chang and Jon Halliday, *Mao, The Unknown Story*, Chapter 33.
4. Odd Arne Westad, *Decisive Encounters, The Chinese Civil War 1946–1950*, Chapter 7.
5. John Stuart, *Fifty Years in China*, Chapter 11.
6. Statement to committees on foreign affairs and foreign relations, US Congress, 20 February 1948.
7. Estimate by General George Marshall. Odd Arne Westad, *Decisive Encounters, The Chinese Civil War 1946–1950*, Chapter 5.
8. Letter dated 2 October 1944.
9. Letter from Eden to Alexander, 21 March 1945.

10. Report by M Branch, 19 April 1948.
11. Message from Bevin to Stevenson, 18 May 1948.
12. Memorandum by the First Lord of the Admiralty, 12 June 1948.
13. Bruce Swanson, *Eighth Voyage of the Dragon, A History of China's Quest for Sea Power*, Chapter 13. Material based on US Navy intelligence reports.
14. Report dated 8 May 1948.
15. Bruce Swanson, *Eighth Voyage of the Dragon, A History of China's Quest for Sea Power*, Chapter 15.

Chapter 28
1. HMS *Amethyst*'s final report of the Yangtze Incident, Phase 4, Kerans, 30 November 1949. Material from the report originally closed until 2025.
2. Message from the naval attaché, Nanking, to the Admiralty and Foreign Office, 23 August 1949. Letter from the British embassy, Peking, to the Foreign Office explaining background, 10 November 1954.
3. Foreign Office minutes by Burgess, 8 September 1949.
4. M Branch Admiralty, 28 June 1950.
5. Foreign Office minute dated 17 July 1950.
6. British embassy letter dated 10 November 1954.
7. Minutes of the Far Eastern Department, Foreign Office, various dates in December 1954 and January 1955.
8. Foreign Office letter to the Admiralty, 18 January 1955.
9. Letter from M Branch to C E Branch, 21 January 1955.
10. C E Branch records, February, June, July 1955.
11. Letter to C E Branch, 31 August 1955.
   Note: most of the documents relating to Sam Leo were in an Admiralty file originally closed until 2031. ADM 1/25885.

Chapter 29
1. *The Naval Review*, February 1950.

Chapter 30
1. Nigel Farndale, *Last Action Hero of the British Empire*.
2. Ibid.
3. Ibid.
4. Obituary of Kerans, *The Times*, 13 September 1985, death notice in *The Times*, 16 September 1985.
5. Anthony Paul, *Time* magazine, 24 September 2001.
6. Obituary of Berger, *The Daily Telegraph*, 23 October 2003.
7. Information supplied by the Army Legal Services Association, obituary of Weston, *The Times*, 22 May 1993.
8. Imperial War Museum interview, 21 September 1990, obituary, *The Times*, 22 January 2007.
9. *The Times*, 10 October 1963.
10. Obituary of Madden, *The Times*, 22 September 1964.
11. Obituary *The Daily Telegraph*.
12. Tom Driberg, *Guy Burgess, A Portrait with Background*, Chapter 5.
13. Patrick Wright, *Passport to Peking*, Chapter 16.

Bibliography

Arthur, Max, *The Navy 1939 to the Present Day* (Hodder & Stoughton, 1997).

Attlee, Clement, *As It Happened* (Heinemann, 1954).

Ballantyne, Iain, HMS *London* (Leo Cooper, 2003).

Boardman, Robert, *Britain and The People's Republic of China 1949–1974* (The Macmillan Press, 1976).

Bullock, Alan, *Ernest Bevin, Foreign Secretary* (Heinemann, 1983).

Chang, Iris, *The Rape of Nanking* (Basic Books, 1997).

Chang, Jung, and Halliday, Jon, *Mao, The Unknown Story* (Jonathan Cape, 2005).

Colledge, J J, and Warlow, Ben, *Ships of the Royal Navy* (Chatham Publishing, 2006).

Cotterell, Arthur, *Western Power in Asia, Its Slow Rise and Swift Fall 1415–1999* (Wiley, 2010).

Driberg, Tom, *Guy Burgess, A Portrait with Background* (Weidenfeld and Nicolson, 1956).

Earl, Lawrence, *Yangtse Incident* (Harrap, 1950).

Farndale, Nigel, *Last Action Hero of the British Empire* (Short Books, 2001).

Fenby, Jonathan, *The Penguin History of Modern China, The Fall and Rise of a Great Power, 1850–2009* (Penguin Books, 2009).

Frank, Leslie, *Yangtse River Incident 1949, The Diary of Coxswain Leslie Frank* (reprinted by The Naval & Military Press, undated).

Goncharov, Sergei, Lewis, John, and Litai, Xue, *Uncertain Partners, Stalin, Mao and The Korean War* (Stanford University Press, 1993).

Grove, Eric, *Vanguard to Trident, British Naval Policy Since World War II* (The Bodley Head, 1987).

Hamilton, William Stenhouse, *Notes from Old Nanking 1947–1949* (Pandanus Books, 2004).

Hayward, John, Birch, Diana, and Bishop, Richard, *British Battles and Medals*, seventh edition (Spink, 2006).

Hickinbottom, George, *The Seven Glorious HMS Amethysts 1793–1956* (published by the author, 1994).

HMS *Concord* Association, *The Life and Times of HMS Concord* (published by the association, 2012).

HMS *Consort* Association, *Loyal and Steadfast, The Story of HMS Consort* (published by the association, 2008).

Holzman, Michael, *Guy Burgess, Revolutionary in an Old School Tie* (Chelmsford Press, 2012).

Humble, Richard, *Fraser of North Cape* (Routledge & Kegan Paul, 1983).

Hutcheon, Robin, *China-Yellow* (The Chinese University Press of Hong Kong, 1996).

Konstam, Angus, *Yangtze River Gunboats 1900–49* (Osprey, 2011).

Lew, Christopher, *The Third Chinese Revolutionary Civil War, 1945–49* (Routledge, 2009).

Louis, William Roger, *Ends of British Imperialism: The Scramble for Empire, Suez, and Decolonization* (I B Tauris, 2006).

Lucas Phillips, C E, *Escape of the Amethyst* (Heinemann, 1957).

Lynch, Michael, *The Chinese Civil War 1945–49* (Osprey, 2010).

Melson, P J (ed), *White Ensign – Red Dragon, The History of the Royal Navy in Hong Kong 1841–1997* (Edinburgh Financial Publishing, 1997).

Murfett, Malcolm, *Hostage on the Yangtze* (Naval Institute Press, 1991).

Perrett, Bryan, *Gunboat! Small Ships at War* (Cassell, 2000).

Porter, Brian, *Britain and the Rise of Communist China* (Oxford University Press, 1967).

Ronning, Chester, *A Memoir of China in Revolution: From the Boxer Rebellion to the People's Republic* (Pantheon Books, 1974).

Shaw, Yu-ming, *An American Missionary in China* (Harvard University, 1992).

Stuart, John, *Fifty Years in China* (Random House, 1954).

Swanson, Bruce, *Eighth Voyage of the Dragon, A History of China's Quest for Sea Power* (Naval Institute Press, 1982).

The Navy League, *The Glorious Story of HMS Amethyst* (sponsored by *The Daily Telegraph*, undated).

Tolley, Kemp, *Yangtze Patrol, The US Navy in China* (Naval Institute Press, 1971).

Tuck-Hong Tang, James, *Britain's Encounter with Revolutionary China, 1949–54* (The Macmillan Press, 1992).

Tyler, Alan, *Cheerful and Contented* (The Book Guild, 2000).

Welsh, Frank, *A History of Hong Kong* (HarperCollins, 1997).

Westad, Odd Arne, *Decisive Encounters, The Chinese Civil War, 1946–1950* (Stanford University Press, 2003).

Westad, Odd Arne (ed), *Brothers in Arms, The Rise and Fall of the Sino-Soviet Alliance 1945–1963* (The Woodrow Wilson Center Press, 1998).

Winchester, Simon, *The River at the Centre of the World* (Viking, 1997).

Wright, Patrick, *Passport to Peking, A Very British Mission to Mao's China* (Oxford University Press, 2010).

Zhai, Qiang, *The Dragon, The Lion and the Eagle, Chinese-British-American Relations, 1949–1958* (The Kent State University Press, 1994).

Acknowledgements

I am most grateful for interviews given by members of the ship's company who were on board HMS *Amethyst* when she was attacked on 20 April 1949: Raymond Calcott, Jack French, Charles Hawkins, Lieutenant Commander Stewart Hett, Eric Monaghan, Ernest Munson, Donald Redman, Ronald Richards, William Smith, Robert Stone, Thomas Townsend and Gordon Wright.

The reports of Lieutenant Commander John Kerans were, of course, invaluable – as were those of Lieutenant Peter Berger, Captain Peter Cazalet (HMS *London*), Lieutenant Colonel Raymond Dewar-Durie, Commander Ian Robertson (HMS *Consort*), Lieutenant Geoffrey Weston and Edward Youde.

My thanks also for material and guidance from the Australian War Memorial, Ian Bailey, curator, Adjutant General's Corps Museum, Professor Robert Bickers of the University of Bristol, the British Library Newspapers, London, the Churchill Archives Centre, Cambridge, Gerard Devany (Royal Air Force), Thomas Flanagan (*Consort*), the Foreign & Commonwealth Office (Information Management Group), the Foyle Special Collections Library at King's College London, Frank Goldsworthy (*Daily Express*), Captain Richard Hare, Fred Harwood (*London*), George Hickinbottom (*Amethyst*), Derek Hodgson (*Concord*),Wing Commander Peter Howard-Williams, Peter Lee-Hale, chairman of the HMS *Concord* Association, the Imperial War Museum picture archive, London, the Imperial War Museum research centre, London, William Leitch (*Consort*), Gordon Leith, curator, Department of Research, Royal Air Force Museum, London, the Liddell Hart Centre for Military Archives at King's College London, Dr Chi-kwan Mark of the Royal Holloway, University of London, the Ministry of Defence Medal Office, The National Archives, London, the National Archives of Australia, the National Museum of the Royal Navy, Portsmouth, Michael Pocock of MaritimeQuest, William Robson (*Consort*), Major General Anthony Rogers, chairman of the Army

Acknowledgements

Legal Services Association, John Smith, senior researcher of the Naval Historical Society of Australia, and Captain Hugh Stevenson, Royal Australian Navy.

Guidance given by Duncan McAra and Seaforth's Robert Gardiner, Julian Mannering and Stephen Chumbley has been much appreciated.

Brian Izzard

2014

Index